3/03

david robson

geoffrey bawa

the complete works

with over 500 illustrations, 250 in color

Thames & Hudson

p.1 The approach to Lunuganga, pp.2–3. The western terrace at Lunuganga, Geoffrey Bawa in 1992. pp.4–5 Geoffrey Bawa in his office, 1984. p.6 Steps leading up to the southern terrace at Lunuganga. p.7 A courtyard at Lunuganga. pp.8–9 The northern terrace at Lunuganga. p.10 View from the guest room towards the eastern terrace at Lunuganga. p.11 View from the the northern terrace down to the water meadow at Lunuganga

thanks

Many people have helped me in researching and writing this book. Firstly, I must thank Channa Daswatte and Anjalendran, Geoffrey Bawa's friends and associates, for their support over a long period. Ismeth and Delini Raheem acted as my hosts in Colombo and shared many memories with me. Christoph Bon, a dear friend who died in 1999, encouraged me from the outset and later gave me his archive of pictures. I have received enormous help from people associated with Bawa's office: his former partner Dr K. Poologasundram and de facto partner Ulrik Plesner, his office secretary Janet Kanageswaran, and his former colleagues Nihal Bodhinayake, Amila de Mel, Dilshan Ferdinando, Waruna Gomis, Sumangala Jayatilleke, Milroy Perera, Stanley Perera, Senake Pieris, Anura Ratnavibushana, Laki Senanayake, and Turner Wickramasinghe. Geoffrey Bawa's trustees, Sunethra Bandaranaike, Ward Beling, Michael Mack and Suhanya Raffel, have always been supportive. Among Geoffrey Bawa's friends I should mention: Ena de Silva, S. M. A. Hameed, Kerry Hill, Guy Strutt, Edward Williams and the late Aimée Williams. Among his clients: Bashir and Najma Currimjee, Druvi and Charmini de Saram, Chloé de Soysa, Martin and Margaret Henry, Rohan and Dulanjalee Jayakody and Peter White. Others who offered help and advice include Michael Brawne and Christopher Beaver. Finally, I must thank my wife Ursula and my daughters Isabel and Julia for their patience and encouragement.

acknowledgments

Much of the illustrative material used in this book has been drawn from the Geoffrey Bawa Archive, which exists in embryo form in Brighton and Colombo. Photographs are by the author unless otherwise indicated. Other photographs are by Hélène Binet, Christopher Beaver, Christoph Bon, Channa Daswatte, Nihal Fernando, Waruna Gomis, Milroy Perera, Ulrik Plesner, Christian Richters, Isabel Robson, Dominic Sansoni, Jürgen Schreiber and Harry Sowden. Maps and diagrams have been prepared by David Adams.

First published in hardcover in the United States of America in 2002 by Thames & Hudson Inc., 500 Fifth Avenue, New York, New York 10110
thamesandhudsonusa.com

Library of Congress Catalog Card Number 2001099692
ISBN 0-500-34187-7

Printed and bound in Hong Kong by C&C Offset

contents

I

II

III

I

Consult the Genius of the Place in all;
That tells the Waters or to rise, or fall;
'Of the Use of Riches', Alexander Pope (Pope 1985)

Geoffrey Bawa has come to be regarded as one of the most important Asian architects of the twentieth century. The Malaysian architect Ken Yeang has said: 'For many of us…Geoffrey will always have a special place in our hearts and in our minds. He is our first hero and guru' (Keniger 1996). And yet Bawa 'the man' remains something of an enigma and the true identity of Bawa 'the architect' has been obscured because he has been typecast as a romantic vernacularist. This book aims to shed more light on Bawa's complex personality and to look behind the labels that have misrepresented his work.

I first met Geoffrey Bawa in 1969 when I was teaching in the new School of Architecture in Colombo and he took part in a review of student work. Although immensely tall and quite intimidating, he treated the students with great patience and understanding. He was then in his fiftieth year and I was exactly half his age. My friends at the time, Ismeth Raheem, Anura Ratnavibushana, Pherooze Choksy and Vasantha Jacobsen, were all assistants in his office and, like them, I treated Bawa with due deference. His practice was only eleven years old but he had already completed a clutch of innovative buildings including the Ena de Silva House and the Bentota Beach Hotel. Anura Ratnavibushana recalls the atmosphere in the office at that time: 'We would work late into the night, consuming coffee and lovely sandwiches served up by Ulrik's "Man Friday", and GB would inhale deeply on his Peacock cigarettes and smile divinely as some vital detail was discussed, resolved and drawn up with infinite pleasure.'

Early in 1970 Geoffrey invited my wife and me to his garden at Lunuganga for Poya lunch. 'I'll be chopping trees down, so do be prepared to take me as you find me,' he warned. As we drove to Bentota we tried to imagine our host in a loud check shirt, dripping with sweat, attacking tree trunks with a huge axe. When we arrived we were ushered up the steps to the south terrace and through the house to find our lumberjack host, immaculately dressed, seated on the north lawn with a gin and tonic at his side, a cigarette in one hand and a megaphone in the other, while an army of gardeners with machetes carved the trees to his command. Geoffrey was not a man of action: he simply caused things to be done. He was the conductor of an orchestra, the director of a play, an architect of enormous talent with few practical skills.

I returned to Sri Lanka in 1980 as an advisor on the government's 'Hundred Thousand Houses' programme. Geoffrey was up to his eyes in work on the National Parliament, Ruhunu University and the Triton Hotel. My friends had all left his office to start out on their own, with the exception of Vasantha Jacobsen, who was now his principal architect. Geoffrey felt ill at ease with the scale and administrative complexity of these large projects and clearly missed the family atmosphere of the early 1970s. We would meet occasionally for a drink at his home in 33rd Lane to chew over the problems of the day and exchange titbits of gossip – he loved to hear my stories about the exploits of Prime Minister Ranasinghe Premadasa – the bête noire of the middle classes – whom he greatly respected. Invariably we would move through to his improvised 'home office' next to the garage to pore over the model of Ruhunu or look at the latest sketches of the Parliament's copper roof. I had been a great admirer of the Bentota Beach Hotel, and I can remember once

expressing some disappointment when the Triton Hotel first came out of the ground. He became quite angry and accused me of trying to make him a prisoner of his own past. Later I came to realize that Geoffrey was continually reinventing himself and that the Triton represented an important transitional move in his development away from his 'neo-vernacular' phase.

In 1995 Geoffrey was on his way to Brazil for the opening of an exhibition of his work when he stopped off in London for what would be his last visit to Britain, in order to buy a new wheelchair from Bell and Croydon of Wimpole Street. Not for the first time he asked me to give him a tour of what was new in town. We went to see Norman Foster's ITN Building and Sackler Galleries at the Royal Academy, both of which he loved; Julyan Wickham's housing scheme beside Tower Bridge, which bored him; and Robert Venturi's extension to the National Gallery, which he absolutely loathed. That evening we had dinner at South Edwardes Square with his friends Christoph Bon and Jean Chamberlin. During the meal I suggested that the 'White Book' (Taylor 1995) – a survey of Geoffrey's architecture that had just been republished some nine years after its first appearance – no longer did justice to his work. I argued that there was now a need for something more comprehensive and more critical. Christoph agreed and suggested that I collaborate with Geoffrey to produce a new monograph. Geoffrey seemed to be intrigued by the idea and said that he would give it some thought. He later wrote to me from Sri Lanka: 'It would be nice to see you here again and if writing a book would get you here then perhaps that would be a reason…although I do rather shy away from the purpose of the book. But with you doing it, perhaps one is less terrified. So I say "Yes, why not?" and it's very good of you to want to.'

I flew out to Colombo in August 1997 and found that Geoffrey still seemed to be in two minds. He remained as mistrustful as ever of theorizing but conceded that, if a book were to be written, I might be the least unacceptable author to hand. In the meantime *AA Files*, the journal of the Architectural Association in London, wanted a piece on his work and he asked me if I would write it. I spent the next fortnight revisiting Geoffrey's buildings and talking to his former associates and clients.

On 17 August I went down to stay with Geoffrey at Lunuganga and accompanied him on a site visit to Mirissa, where the Jayewardene House was nearing completion. Geoffrey roamed the site in his battery-driven wheelchair and, with the help of his partner Channa Daswatte, his old friend C. Anjalendran and his client Pradeep Jayewardene, set out the line of the driveway and finalized the landscaping plan. It was clear that, for all his physical frailty at this time, his mind was as sharp as ever and he knew exactly what needed to be done to give the project its last 'ten per cent'.

The following day I persuaded him to accompany me on a visit to Dr A. S. H. de Silva's house, which he had designed in 1959 for a steeply sloping site on the outskirts of Galle. Dr de Silva had been dead for some time but the house now belonged to his son and was still very much in its original state. A copy of the plan drawn by his colleague, Laki Senanayake, was hanging next to the entrance. It was the first time Bawa had seen the house for many years and, as he leaned against a wall and looked across the main living room towards the garden, tears began to well up in his eyes. The two houses we had visited were separated by forty years, but for Bawa they were simply two points on a single journey of exploration.

That evening we stopped off for a drink with his friends Dick Dumas and Charles Hulse in Galle. 'So what brings you to Sri Lanka?' I was asked. Channa answered for me: 'David wants to write a book about Geoffrey, but Geoffrey won't agree to it.' 'Of course I've agreed to it!' said Geoffrey impatiently, as if it were already signed and sealed. So that was that!

I was due to fly back to England in a few days and there wasn't time to advance things further. It was agreed that I would return in 1998 having mapped out a structure for the book and talked to publishers. Geoffrey, in the meantime, would sort out his papers and sit down with Channa to record a few memories and observations.

In October, Geoffrey formally severed his ties with his old practice and bought out his former partner's share in the office in Alfred House Road. He then presided over a massive clear-out of drawings and papers so that the buildings could be converted into a restaurant. The office records had never been properly maintained and, over the years, had been ravaged by white ants and humidity. Now they were systematically decimated, and the few pieces of paper that survived the onslaught were unceremoniously dumped in the garage in 33rd Lane. It was as if Geoffrey were trying to make my task as difficult as possible.

In February of 1998, soon after receiving a visit from Prince Charles at Lunuganga, Geoffrey suffered a stroke that tragically left him paralysed and unable to speak. His incapacity ruled out any possibility of our working together on a book that would serve as his final testament and by general consent the project was put on hold. Confounding expectations, he has clung tenaciously to life, and his health has slowly improved, though he has never regained the power of speech or the ability to communicate effectively. In 2001 it was agreed by the members of the Geoffrey Bawa Trust that the book should go ahead, not as a testament, but as a tribute to the man and his work. Channa Daswatte and Anjalendran offered their help and have since tried valiantly to represent Geoffrey's point of view.

This book attempts to put Geoffrey Bawa's work into perspective, describing it in relation to his life and times and the evolving context of Sri Lanka. The opening chapters set the scene, telling the story of his early life and offering a brief history of Sri Lankan architecture. The central chapters then go on to describe the main phases of his work, corresponding as they do to the key periods of political and economic development in post-independence Sri Lanka. The first of these chapters begins in 1957 with Bawa's return to Sri Lanka as a newly qualified architect at the age of thirty-eight, and charts his rapid evolution from Tropical Modernist to regionalist; the second begins in 1970 with the election of a socialist government and Bawa's ensuing reinvention as an architect of the state; the third begins in 1977 with the return of a nationalist government and his elevation to 'grand designer'; the fourth begins in 1988 when, as Sri Lanka descended into anarchy and civil war, Bawa withdrew from his practice to work from home with a fresh team of young assistants. The final chapters describe the two projects that have always remained closest to his heart – his labyrinthine courtyard house in Colombo's 33rd Lane, and his garden landscape at Lunuganga on Sri Lanka's south-west coast – and assess the importance of Bawa's work.

Above all else, however, this book is intended to stand as a tribute to a man who saw architecture as a means to give pleasure to all the senses and to create a unique sense of place.

terms
The name 'Ceylon' was replaced in 1972 by 'Sri Lanka', though Geoffrey Bawa stubbornly continued to use the old name. This book uses the name 'Sri Lanka' in the context of events that occurred after 1972.

The words 'Ceylonese' and 'Sri Lankan' refer to all citizens, while the words 'Sinhalese' and 'Tamil' refer to particular ethnic groups. The term 'Muslim' is commonly used today to describe people of mixed Arab descent, even though they may not be followers of Islam. Although Sri Lanka has officially adopted the decimal system, old imperial measures persist in many areas. In particular land is still measured in 'perches'. A linear perch is one quarter of a chain (which is the length of a cricket pitch) and is 16.5 feet (5 metres). The square perch, known simply as the perch in Sri Lanka, is 272.25 square feet or approximately 25 square metres. There are 160 perches to an acre, 400 to a hectare.

Serendipity: the faculty of making happy chance finds. A word inspired by Horace Walpole's tale *The Three Princes of Serendip*, whose heroes 'were always making discoveries, by accidents and sagacity, of things they were not in quest of'.
Chamber's Twentieth-Century Dictionary, 1972

Geoffrey Bawa seems to have devoted almost half a lifetime to aimless travel and self-discovery before finally stumbling, as if by chance, upon his true vocation. He was born in 1919 in the British Crown Colony of Ceylon and reached the age of thirty-eight before he finally qualified as an architect in 1957. Once aroused, however, his passion for architecture was so total, so consuming, that it became hard to imagine a time when it was not with him, if only in embryo. Although his childhood and schooldays seem to be remote from his later career, the circumstances of his family and early years hold the key to an understanding of his astonishing metamorphosis from rootless dilettante and reluctant lawyer to architect extraordinary.

While Geoffrey was always a very private person and preferred to draw a veil over his early life, his elder brother, Bevis, was much less reticent. He was famous as a raconteur and would happily recount elaborate stories about himself and his family to anyone who would listen, whether in the officers' mess, in planters' clubs or at Colombo tables, guided always by a belief that 'a well-told lie is worth a hundred truths'. Later he wrote down his stories and they appeared in a series of newspaper articles and as an anthology entitled *Briefly by Bevis*.

The two brothers were born into a mixed and yet highly stratified society where position and status were determined almost wholly by nuances of family background. The union of their own parents represented a fusion of so many strands of Ceylon's ethnic weave that it was impossible for them to be identified by a single word. Eurasian? Burgher? Moor?…perhaps the only label that accurately described them, and the one that Geoffrey himself came to prefer in later years, was 'Ceylonese'.

Geoffrey grew up on the fringes of the cultured but slightly dislocated world of the Colombo Burghers, a world vividly described by Michael Ondaatje in his book *Running in the Family* (Ondaatje 1982). The word Burgher came to be applied loosely to almost anyone of mixed European and Ceylonese blood, but in its strictest sense it signified a person of mixed race who could claim unbroken paternal descent from a European employee of the original Dutch East India Company. The Burghers have been described as 'the people in-between': although they prospered and found favour during the British period, the British never fully accepted them into their exclusive and essentially expatriate society, while the Sinhalese viewed them with mistrust. Their community flourished between the world wars, however, and produced a brilliant generation of lawyers and doctors, artists and writers, including the painter George Keyt and the photographer Lionel Wendt. After independence the Burghers viewed the rise of Sinhalese nationalism with growing alarm and many emigrated to Australia and Canada. Although of mixed race, the Burghers were very conscious of their genealogies and discriminated punctiliously between degrees of Burgher authenticity. Perhaps it was for this reason that Bevis and Geoffrey Bawa took such pleasure in embroidering the details of their various ancestors.

In his anthology Bevis Bawa wove an elaborate fantasy of how their grandparents first met. A Mrs Ablette and her daughter Henrietta were sailing out to visit their cousins in Australia. When their boat put into Galle for watering, the young Henrietta slipped ashore by herself in a 'jolly boat' intending to explore the town:

Geoffrey in his toy car, *c.*1927

Top: Geoffrey's father,
Benjamin Bawa
Middle: Geoffrey's mother,
Bertha Bawa

She was at the hotel sipping a cup of coffee and being swindled by one of those 'fleece and vanish' chaps one comes across even today. A handsome young Muslim chap, Ahamadu Bawa by name, who had dropped in for lunch, saw what was happening and saved her in the nick of time. He apologized for barging in but only did so as he hated to see a charming woman done in the eye. (Bevis Bawa 1985, p.37)

Henrietta and the young Bawa fell in love instantly and were married the same afternoon by special licence.

A more plausible account of the meeting of the Bawa grandparents is given by Alfred Bawa, Geoffrey's uncle, in Arnold Wright's *Twentieth Century Impressions of Ceylon* (1907). This records that Ahamadu Bawa was a Muslim proctor from the ancient Arab port of Beruwela, who went to London in 1863 to complete his law studies. There he met and married a Miss Georgina Matilda Ablett, the daughter of J. T. Ablett of Colbrooke Row in Islington, a descendant of French Huguenot immigrants. The couple returned to Ceylon and Ahamadu Bawa practised law in Galle, Kandy and Colombo. They had six children, the eldest, Benjamin William, born in 1865.

When Ahamadu Bawa died, much of his property was mortgaged and his widow and children were left penniless. Benjamin had been expected to follow in his father's footsteps and become a lawyer but there was no money to pay for his studies. However, he won a scholarship to Royal College, Colombo's elite boys' school, where he became a model student and, in 1883, took the coveted Turnour Prize. On leaving school he embarked on his law studies and was articled to James Van Langenberg, a famous Dutch Burgher lawyer. In 1887 he was called to the Colombo Bar and soon began to make his name in the Appeal Court. Later he went to London to complete his studies and in 1904 was called to the Bar at the Middle Temple.

Benjamin Bawa was a skilled advocate with a charismatic personality, said to have been one of the most handsome men of his generation. He was a keen tennis player and accomplished horseman and became a prominent member of Colombo society. In 1893 he was commissioned as a lieutenant in the Ceylon Light Infantry, a sort of non-European 'Dads' Army', and was later promoted to captain, serving as aide-de-camp to Sir William Manning, governor of Ceylon from 1918 to 1925.

In 1906 Bawa bought Chapman House, a former residence of the bishop of Colombo, which lay at the southern end of Darley Road. Colombo was still a pleasant small-scale town of leafy avenues and large colonial bungalows and the affairs of business and government were conducted within the area known as the Fort and around the harbour. Darley Road ran south along the east of the Beira Lake and connected the Fort to the new suburb of Cinnamon Gardens. It was dotted with stately houses and clubs and was considered to be one of the best addresses in town. The house was one of a group of large nineteenth-century villas in the Italianate style occupying a block of land opposite Hyde Park on the east side of Darley Road. Today the junction of Union Place and Darley Road forms the hub of a commercial and business district, and the small fragment of Chapman House that survives is hemmed in by factories and warehouses and overlooked by office buildings, including, ironically, Geoffrey Bawa's own Mahaweli Tower.

In 1908, at the age of forty-three, Benjamin Bawa married Bertha Marion Campbell Schrader. Born in 1876, Bertha was the eldest of the five children of Frederick Justus Schrader, a Dutch Burgher, and Elizabeth Harriet Campbell, who was of mixed Scottish and Sinhalese parentage. The Dutch Burgher Union, an exclusive club of Dutch Burghers, maintained a record of the genealogies of what were regarded as the bona fide Burgher families and counted the Schraders amongst their number. The Schraders claimed descent from a German mercenary called Julius Schrader, born in Brunswick in 1683, who came to Ceylon with the Dutch East India Company at the beginning of the eighteenth century and is recorded as having married a Dutch woman called Christina Roellofz in Jaffna in 1716. They owned estates at Kimbulapitiya and Wester Seaton near Negombo and had a town house on one of Colombo's last cinnamon plantations in what is now Ward Place. Frederick Schrader's daughters all married lawyers, while his son, Fred, took over the running of the estates.

Chapman House was a solid two-storey 'bungalow' set well back from the road within a large garden. Soon after her marriage Mrs Bawa used some of her considerable fortune to buy the single-storey annexe that abutted the main house, doubling the size of the property. The annexe was linked to the side of the house by a *porte cochère*, and its flat roof served as an elevated terrace. There were extensive stables, garages and servants' quarters to the rear. On the lower floor of the house rendered arches were set within columnated bays, while on the upper floor a continuous open balcony ran behind a colonnade. The family also owned a house in Nuwara Eliya, which they occupied for a month each year during the 'season'.

The Bawas had two sons: Bevis Bawa, born in 1909 and Geoffrey Manning Bawa, born ten years later on 23 July 1919. Geoffrey took his middle name from his godfather, Governor Manning, whom Benjamin Bawa served.

In 1922 Benjamin Bawa was diagnosed as having Bright's Disease. Accompanied by his wife and two sons he set sail for England to seek treatment, but the London doctors could do nothing for him and he died early in the following year while convalescing in Harrogate. Mrs Bawa was devastated and returned to Colombo with her two sons at the end of 1923 to take up the life of a widow. Although still wealthy, she turned her back on society and became something of a recluse. It is said that one of her main pastimes was keeping birds; after spoiling them for a time, she would release them in the hope that they would one day fly back to her. She shared her household with her husband's two sisters, Rose and Violet, and the three women devoted themselves to the welfare of the boys.

Violet ran a photographic studio and was considered 'artistic'. She had a reputation as a caricaturist and published a book of sketches, dedicated to Bevis. Her talent for sketching was passed on to Bevis, who later illustrated his newspaper articles with caricatures. There is no evidence, however, to suggest that Geoffrey showed any aptitude for drawing.

Geoffrey grew up at the centre of an extended family of servants. He was brought up by an *ayah* (nurse) called Ensa, who remained with him until her death in the 1980s. Ensa's daughter, Leela, later became the housekeeper at the estate at Lunuganga and her husband became head gardener. Geoffrey also had a personal manservant called Miguel, who came from a district in Travancore where many Burgher families recruited their servants. Miguel remained with Geoffrey until the former's death from cancer in 1982.

Geoffrey was tall and fair with wavy blond hair and a European countenance. Bevis was even taller but much darker and was often taken to be a Moor or 'Thambi'. Bevis was later to tell how, during a tour of the island in 1949 when he drove up to the Queen's Hotel in Kandy in his Rolls-Royce Phantom with Geoffrey, the porter exclaimed 'Aiyo *Thambi*, in those days you used to come here with your mother in your own car: now you're the white man's chauffeur!'

Bevis Bawa had been very close to his father and early photographs often show him astride a horse or dressed in military uniform. While Geoffrey looked up to his dashing elder brother, Bevis was jealous of the attention that his

younger brother received from their mother, particularly after the early death of their father. The ten-year gap in their ages meant their lives were often out of phase: Bevis left school and quit home at the age of seventeen when Geoffrey was only seven. He was sent to work as an apprentice estate manager, first with his Uncle Fred at Kimbulapitiya and later with his father's brother, Alfred, at Eladua, before his mother set him up as manager of his own rubber estate at Brief near Bentota. In 1928, following in his father's footsteps, he obtained a part-time commission in the Ceylon Light Infantry and later served as aide-de-camp to a series of four British governors.

Geoffrey spent much of his childhood with his mother's relations in Colombo and on the family's estates near Negombo. The larger estate at Kimbulapitiya was managed by his mother's brother, Fred Schrader. Its bungalow dated back to the mid-nineteenth century and sat on a small hill within a mixed plantation of coconut and rubber. Visitors arriving at the estate caught a first glimpse of the house above them through the trees before the road swung round and made its final ascent to a *porte cochère*. This led to a wide front verandah, connecting to a long, high central hall flanked on either side by a pair of bedrooms. Beyond the main hall a rear verandah ran round an enclosed courtyard or *meda midula* connecting to the bathrooms, kitchens and servants' quarters. In plan the house was not unlike a traditional Sinhalese manor house or *walaawe*, though it was 'Anglo–Dutch' in style.

The Wester Seaton estate bungalow, belonging to a cousin called Ronald Schrader, was typical of mid-nineteenth-century coconut estate bungalows, comprising a large central hall flanked by pairs of bedrooms under a single hipped roof of half-round tiles. A continuous deep verandah supported by chunky Tuscan 'milk-bottle' columns ran round the main house and connected it to a separate service wing at the side.

The Schrader clan houses exhibited many of the key characteristics of Ceylonese–Dutch domestic architecture, clearly exerting a strong influence on Bawa's perceptions: 'At Kimbulapitiya it was marvellous sitting on the long verandah after lunch having endless conversations of limited interest… when somebody gave the latest gossip about Aunt Harriet… and somebody else said 'what a shame'…and everybody nodded in agreement' (in conversation with Channa Daswatte, 1997). Both estate bungalows still exist. Kimbulapitiya is now a guest house of dubious repute and goes under the name of 'Golden Heaven'. It contains much of the original Schrader

Top: Mr and Mrs Bawa in front of the Chapman House annexe, around 1910
Middle: Kimbulupitiya, Fred Schrader's Chevrolet
Bottom: The rear verandah at Wester Seaton

family furniture and Uncle Fred's 1927 Chevrolet still stands in perfect running order under the *porte cochère*. Wester Seaton, by contrast, is a home for children with learning disabilities.

Motor cars became something of an obsession with the Bawas, probably prized more as symbols of status and modernity than as objects of convenience. Benjamin Bawa's first car, a Sunbeam tourer, was bought in 1915. At the time there were few motorable roads outside Colombo and no network of filling stations. The Bawas' chauffeur, Rahim, had to be a fully qualified mechanic, and long journeys required careful planning, with spare tyres and cans of petrol being sent ahead to strategic staging posts. In 1928 Mrs Bawa returned from England with a bright yellow sleeve-valved Daimler tourer. A huge wooden crate accompanied her from the port to Chapman House and was opened to reveal the new car in all its glory, ready for the road. Bevis became the proud owner of the old Sunbeam until 1930, when his mother gave him a new six-cylinder Humber as a twenty-first birthday present.

Both brothers became automobile enthusiasts and both, over the years, owned a succession of exotic cars. Geoffrey's interest in cars was encouraged by his brother and by Rahim, and he developed considerable mechanical skills under their tutelage. His first car, however, was a pedal-operated toy that he rode around the garden as a child, but his favourite toy was a massive Hornby railway set, for which he built an elaborate track running from his bedroom out along the verandah and back via the corridor. This railway layout was preserved by his mother and remained in place throughout the eight years of his later stay in London.

During the 1920s the southward shift of Colombo's centre of gravity was marked by the construction of a vast new town hall on the north-east corner of Victoria Park. This gleaming pile of classical white confectionery was designed by S. J. Edwards, the founder of the practice Geoffrey would later make his own. The new building lay just round the corner from Chapman House and Geoffrey passed the construction site every day on his way to school.

Mrs Bawa was a keen traveller and made several trips to Europe. In those days the sea voyage via the Suez Canal took about three weeks and was accompanied by much pomp and ritual. Departing passengers would be given a big send-off in Colombo by their friends and relatives and the journey was punctuated by a highly formalized round of social events. In 1934 Bevis Bawa was diagnosed as having tuberculosis and was

advised to take a long sea voyage. This was used as an excuse for the whole family to embark on a ten-week round trip to China with the Blue Funnel Line. Geoffrey was fifteen at the time and the journey made an enormous impression on him. Indeed it was the first of many voyages of discovery that were to punctuate his life and that filled his encyclopaedic mind with a vast storehouse of images. The boat sailed to Penang, Singapore, Hong Kong and Shanghai before the Bawas left it at Tsin Sintau, travelling overland to Peking and rejoining it at Port Arthur. The return voyage took in Yokohama and Kobe. Bawa later recalled:

> I remember going to China. I remember, vaguely, walking through dusty Chinese squares, yellow walls, big doors. I don't think at the time that one assessed these as walls or doors or colours…but it all gave me a feeling of pleasure, because one enjoyed the whole journey. I remember the Summer Palace and that great marble boat, pretending to be afloat…and lots of long corridors, galleries of red lacquer.
> (In conversation with Channa Daswatte, 1997)

In 1937, when Geoffrey was eighteen, Mrs Bawa received repayment of a long-outstanding debt and decided to invest it in property. For Bevis, to whom she had already gifted the estate at Brief, she bought a house in Deal Place; for Geoffrey she built a new house on a plot in a development to the south of the racecourse between Torrington Avenue and Buller's Lane. The plans were drawn up by Oliver Weerasinghe, one of a trio of Ceylonese who had trained as architects at the University of Liverpool in the 1920s.

Bevis and Geoffrey had grown up with Arthur Van Langenberg, grandson of their father's mentor, James Van Langenberg. Arthur, who was later to become an important figure in the Ceylonese theatre, had already started to move in artistic circles and was a subscriber to the London journal *The Studio*. He persuaded Geoffrey to take an interest in the planning of the house and, much to the irritation of the architect, the two of them tried to influence the design of the interiors. As a consequence of their interventions the staircase was built with open concrete treads and flowing tubular steel handrails. The result was a fairly conventional colonial villa with Art Deco pretensions, given the name 'Cluny'. Geoffrey never lived in it: upon its completion in 1938 it was rented to an expatriate family and in 1946 he sold it to Ian Pieris for 100,000 rupees.

Opposite
Top: Geoffrey in military
uniform, around 1924
Middle: Geoffrey and Bevis,
around 1927
Bottom: Geoffrey with his
Meccano set, around 1932

This page
Left: Geoffrey and Bevis, around
1930

While Bevis Bawa identified himself as Ceylonese without hesitation, during much of his early life Geoffrey preferred to play down his Asian origins. English was the family's main language and the brothers knew only basic 'kitchen' Sinhalese. Geoffrey was a pupil at Royal College between 1924 and 1936 and rubbed shoulders with sons of the Colombo elite, though it is said that throughout his schooldays he remained shy and aloof. At the beginning of the school year, when each boy had to call out his name and identify his race and religion, Geoffrey announced himself as a 'Moorish Christian Burgher' and was duly punished for flippancy.

He was a studious boy and it was assumed that he would follow his father and study law. In 1937 he entered University College, Colombo, but was later advised to seek a university place in Britain. In the autumn of 1938 he applied to the University of Cambridge, where he was offered a place for the following October to read English at St Catherine's College. To act as his guardian his mother had appointed her London banker, Mr Richardson, who looked after Geoffrey's affairs and kept a watchful eye on him throughout his stay in Britain.

Early in 1939 Geoffrey went to Paris, where he stayed with his cousin, Georgette Camille, granddaughter of a sister of Georgina Ablett, Geoffrey's grandmother. She was a well-known figure in literary and artistic circles and through her Geoffrey was able to meet Braque and Léger. Although his mother had written imploring Georgette to 'look after my sweet child', it was through his cousin that Geoffrey went to a number of avant-garde parties and caught his first tantalizing glimpses of what he later described as 'alternative possibilities'.

Oblivious to the threat of impending war, Geoffrey set out on a tour of Italy in the summer of 1939. When the full gravity of the unfolding political situation was finally brought home to him in Venice he hurriedly left Italy on a train that took him via Trieste to Budapest. At this point Mr Richardson intervened and ordered him to return immediately to London, having arranged a safe passage for him through Switzerland and France. Geoffrey scraped home on one of the last trains to cross France before it was invaded.

His debut in Cambridge coincided with the outbreak of war and many of his contemporaries gave up their studies to enlist. By nature a gentle person who avoided conflict, he seems to have been strangely untouched by the war, demonstrating a capacity for detachment that would later serve him well during the political storms and civil disturbances that afflicted Ceylon.

Cambridge offered a number of alternative role models: there were hearties, who rowed, played rugger and downed beers in the bar; there were the studious types; and there were the aesthetes. He later recalled: 'St Catherine's was a very dull college, full of people who rowed and wanted me to row because I was the right size, but I couldn't row and I escaped. It seemed mad to me to get up early on winter mornings to run about in the snow' (in conversation with Channa Daswatte, 1997). So Geoffrey joined the aesthetes and entered something resembling the world of Evelyn Waugh's *Brideshead Revisited*. He moved out of college and took rooms in King's Parade. He had not yet developed any specific interest in architecture but he already had a keen sense of how a room should be arranged and decorated. He devoted much time, effort and money to

furnishing his King's Parade flat and gained a reputation as a designer and man of taste. As a consequence friends often sought his advice when furnishing their own apartments.

Handsome and exceptionally tall, Geoffrey would stride around town in a long black cloak with a gold-handled cane. He had always felt something of an outsider in Colombo, but his eccentricities were welcomed in Cambridge, where he soon found a niche for himself. He moved within a wide circle of friends and developed a reputation for entertaining conversation and cutting wit. For the first time in his life he felt accepted and he was happy:

> I liked Cambridge very much. It was a fantasy…I fantasized
> a great deal and pictured all sorts of approaches to life…
> and lived a few of the fantasies. One was as free as a bird.
> I never had a problem. I was financially comfortable… I can
> say this without shame because I never had too much…just
> enough. (In conversation with Channa Daswatte, 1997)

It was in Cambridge that he was able to explore his own inner feelings and come to terms with his sexuality. But he remained ambiguous about his origins and always encouraged people to think that he was a Ceylon-born European. Many of his friends were members of the minor aristocracy and he was often invited to their country estates for weekends. One of these friends, Guy Strutt, was the son of Lord Rayleigh, whose family owned Terling Place in Essex and Beaufront Castle near Hexham in Northumberland. He told Channa Daswatte in 1997: 'It was during my time in Cambridge that I grew to love the English country house and its landscaped park. A number of my friends had rather nice country houses and I would visit them during the vacations…and they all had their very nice eccentricities.'

Another friend, Edward Williams, took Geoffrey to his home in Kew and introduced him to his family. Edward was the son of Iolo Williams, an expert in nineteenth-century watercolours and a correspondent for the *Times*. At the end of 1941 Edward interrupted his studies to join the navy and, by some happy coincidence, was posted to Ceylon, where he visited Geoffrey's mother and became a close friend of Bevis. During the absence of their own son the Williams family adopted Geoffrey, who became very attached to both Edward's mother, Eleanor, and his sisters, Jane and Elizabeth, and was encouraged to treat the house in Kew very much as his home from home.

During this period Geoffrey renewed a friendship with Aimée Jonklaas, a childhood playmate from Ceylon who was two years his junior. The daughter of a Burgher lawyer from Gampola, Aimée had been sent to school in Switzerland at the age of fourteen. Initially trapped by the war she managed to reach England in 1940 and joined the Women's Air Corp, where she worked for a time in intelligence before becoming one of a very small band of women pilots. Geoffrey invited Aimée to be his partner at the 1941 May balls. She remembers him as being strikingly handsome and gallant: he met her at Cambridge station with a bunch of flowers and insisted on buying her separate bouquets to match each of her dresses. Throughout their close friendship Geoffrey demonstrated a curious trait that was to become more pronounced in later life: he kept his different friends in separate compartments. Aimée met none of his close Cambridge friends and they remained unaware of her existence. Geoffrey and Aimée would often meet for dinner at the Café Royal, but never in the company of others. Geoffrey used these dinners as an excuse to winkle extra money out of Mr Richardson, giving rise to speculation back in Colombo that Aimée and Geoffrey were about to marry. Later it became a Jonklaas family joke that Aimée had been responsible in Mrs Bawa's eyes for leading Geoffrey astray and draining the family coffers. Aimée Jonklaas went on to outlive four husbands, but she and Geoffrey remained the best of friends.

Top left: Cartoon of Geoffrey at Cambridge
Middle left: Miniature portrait of Geoffrey at Cambridge
Top right and opposite: Geoffrey in his rooms in Cambridge

Studying English meant that 'one could read all the things one wanted to read anyway and still pass one's exams', and at the end of three years Geoffrey successfully obtained his degree. In 1943 he moved to London to study for the Bar and entered the chambers of William Fordham at 6 Pump Court in the Middle Temple. He lived first at Queen's Gate and then shared a house in William Mews, Belgravia, with Guy Strutt. Their housekeeper was a fierce Austrian woman called Mrs Leopoldina, who was famous for her cakes. In 1944 he passed his final law exams and was called to the Bar.

It was at this time that Geoffrey bought his first Rolls-Royce: a Phantom One tourer with an enormously long bonnet and a maximum speed of 150 kilometres, or 95 miles, per hour. He had inherited the family fascination with cars and surprised his friends with his mechanical skills. During the autumn of 1945 he accompanied his friend Guy Strutt on a visit to Italy. A sister of Guy's brother-in-law had married the Duca de la Grazie before the war and they were invited to stay in her villa at Cola-di-Lazise near the south-east tip of Lake Garda. Cola-di-Lazise is close to Verona and offers an excellent base from which to visit the Veneto. An architect friend of the Duchese called Benjolini was quite an expert on Italian Renaissance gardens and he accompanied Geoffrey on many excursions and seems to have awakened his interest in the subject. Together they visited a number of Palladio's villas and stayed for a few days in the Villa Foscari.

Geoffrey's mother suffered from diabetes, an affliction that was later inherited by both of her sons, and during his stay in London her health slowly deteriorated. Finally, in late 1945, she suffered a stroke and was admitted to the Wycherly Nursing Home in Buller's Road, Colombo. It was the best nursing home on the island and she was well looked after. However, Mrs Bawa's long illness and Geoffrey's even longer absence had both stretched the family's finances and Bevis Bawa simply didn't have enough money to pay the bill. The Bawas still owned considerable property, but the market was depressed and it was not possible to raise any capital. After several weeks Bevis was told that his mother would have to leave if the account was not settled.

Mrs Bawa's condition was deteriorating and Bevis urged Geoffrey to return quickly to Ceylon in order to spend some time with her. As aide-de-camp to the governor, Bevis was able to pull strings to get his brother a seat on an RAF transport plane. The flight from London to Ceylon went via Malta and

Cairo and took four days. Geoffrey arrived at Ratmalana on 26 January 1946, ending an exile of over seven years. He recalled:

When I got back Mama was still in the nursing home and Bevis was away on duty. I walked into Chapman House after seven years to find that nothing had changed, except that there was no car, no petrol, and half the house had been requisitioned by the government. Old John, who had been there for a hundred years, just asked if I wanted scrambled eggs for breakfast as if I'd never been away. I discovered that I'd forgotten my Sinhalese completely. (In conversation with Channa Daswatte, 1997)

Geoffrey and Bevis managed to raise sufficient money from the family lawyers to cover the bills and Mrs Bawa was moved back to Chapman House. Her health continued to deteriorate, however, and she died in April 1946. Her death came as a severe blow to Geoffrey, particularly as he had seen so little of her during the last years of her life. He and Bevis each inherited half of Chapman House in addition to various coconut and rubber estates but they were saddled with substantial death duties as well as a number of outstanding debts.

Soon after returning to Colombo, Geoffrey had joined the law firm of Noel Gratiaen and embarked on his career as a lawyer. The Rolls-Royce Phantom had been shipped out from Britain, and he derived enormous pleasure from driving it down Darley Road and through Maradana to Hultsdorf in full lawyer's rig. He would later say he was not temperamentally suited to the law and feared that his incompetence would result in innocent men being punished. On one occasion, when he appeared in the Appeal Court, having taken copious notes throughout the proceedings he infuriated the judge by refusing to plead, saying that he bowed to the experience of the bench and would accept any decision that was handed down.

Bevis Bawa was a well-known figure in Colombo society and managed to move effortlessly between a number of seemingly disconnected worlds. As well as being a planter, part-soldier and aide-de-camp to the governor, he was also a peripheral member of the '43 Group', a clique of avant-garde artists that included the painters Justin Deraniyagala, Ivan Pieris and George Keyt and the photographer Lionel Wendt. He was also a friend of the young architect Andrew Boyd, who had built the first Modern Movement houses in Ceylon at the beginning of the war. Back in London, Boyd was now a member of the editorial board of *MARG*, a Bombay-based journal on the arts, and had written a number of articles on

the traditional architecture of Ceylon (Boyd 1939, 1947a and 1947b). Geoffrey, however, seems to have remained aloof from this world of artists and architects. He felt constrained by Colombo and missed the cosmopolitan life of Cambridge and London.

Although Ceylon emerged almost unscathed from World War II, Colombo had changed almost beyond recognition during the seven years of Geoffrey's exile. The business district expanded ever further from the Fort, and the stately villas around Chapman House to the south were being replaced by office buildings and factories. Car ownership had ceased to be the exclusive prerogative of the very wealthy and Darley Road had become a main traffic artery. The banks of the Beira Lake were lined with slums and the lake itself was now badly polluted.

In the autumn of 1946 Geoffrey decided to quit Ceylon and set out on a grand tour. He sold his house in Torrington Avenue, using it to pay off his share of the death duties and to finance his travels. Bevis had already sold his half of Chapman House and Geoffrey invited him to live in the other half while he was away. Bevis also bought Geoffrey's precious Rolls-Royce Phantom. Finally, in November, he quit Gratiaen's office and boarded a Norwegian schooner bound for San Francisco via Penang, Indonesia and the Philippines, on the first leg of what was to be an eighteen-month tour of the Far East, the United States and Europe.

In San Francisco Geoffrey met up with a young film actor called Victor Chapin, who was planning to drive cross-country to New York to deliver some paintings for a friend, and invited Geoffrey along for the ride. The two drove slowly across the

United States in Chapin's Dodge, arriving in New York in July 1947. Geoffrey was exhilarated by the United States and stayed there for a total of ten months. After visiting Florida for a while, he and Chapin sailed across the Atlantic at the end of 1947 and briefly passed through London before moving on to Italy. In Italy he rented a villa near Cola-di-Lazise overlooking Lake Garda and spent a few happy months exploring the gardens of Tuscany. He still showed no specific interest in architecture and preferred sitting in cafés, gossiping with friends and watching the world go by, to looking at buildings.

Geoffrey was now twenty-eight. He had spent almost a third of his life outside Ceylon and seemed to feel more at home in Europe and more at ease in the company of Europeans. His mother was dead and there was little to tie him to Ceylon. He now found himself facing the dilemma he had been avoiding for years – that of 'the people in-between': was he a European with Ceylonese connections, or a Ceylonese who happened to have some European blood in his veins?

Finally, in the spring of 1948, just as Ceylon was moving towards independence, he decided to sever his connections with his home and settle in Italy for good. His solicitors in Colombo were instructed to sell his half of Chapman House as well as his remaining estates in Kurunagala so that he could buy the villa he had been renting. The purchase progressed very slowly, however, and he felt frustrated at every stage by the machinations of his Italian lawyers. Suddenly, in July, he abandoned the whole project. Perhaps he realized his money did not count for as much as he had imagined in post-war Europe and that he would be better able to afford the sort of life of which he dreamed in Ceylon. Or it may be that he came to the conclusion that he was more Asian than European. Whatever the reason, he decided to return to Colombo.

Geoffrey was now homeless and readily accepted an invitation from Bevis to stay on the estate at Brief. Bevis was still acting as aide-de-camp to the governor and divided his time between Brief and the Queen's House in Colombo. While he continued to manage his Brief estate as a commercial rubber plantation, he had transformed the area immediately around the house into a beautiful landscaped garden. This attracted large numbers of admiring visitors and, as its fame spread, he began to receive commissions to design gardens for other people.

Bevis urged Geoffrey to forget about villas in Italy: he should buy an estate in Ceylon and settle down. The idea appealed to Geoffrey and he decided to search for a piece of land next to a lake or river, where he could build his own version of an English country house set within an Italian garden. The two brothers began immediately to comb the south-western corner of the island to find the perfect site. At last, after a fortnight of fruitless search, with Geoffrey threatening to pack his bags and return to Europe, they met one evening a local Excise Inspector on the verandah of the Bentota Rest House. Hearing of their quest the inspector told them of a bungalow on an old rubber estate only a couple of miles inland from Bentota that an old lady from Beruwela was trying to sell. The estate had an area of about ten hectares and occupied a strip of land across a promontory that jutted out into the Dedduwa Lake.

When Geoffrey visited the property the next morning he found that it was exactly what he had been looking for. A substantial bungalow occupied the crown of a low hill in the middle of a dense forest of rubber trees. Although the site was hemmed in by trees, its position held out the promise of stunning views across the lagoon in two directions. Geoffrey contacted the owner and engaged Corbet Jayewardene, the brother of J. R. Jayewardene, Sri Lanka's future president, to act as his agent. Although the principal owner was willing to sell and a price was agreed, it soon transpired that there were a total of forty-eight other sub-owners, mostly relatives of the main owner, who would have to be included in the deal. All forty-nine were brought together in the Bentota Rest House by Jayewardene, who set about negotiating an agreement. At one point the sale nearly fell through when one of them refused to sell, but Jayewardene incited the others to persuade the objector to join them.

Bawa rechristened the estate 'Lunuganga' or 'salt river' and threw himself into the project of creating a landscaped garden, abandoning all plans of returning to Europe. While the act of buying Lunuganga might be construed as a subconscious acknowledgment of his Ceylonese roots and a commitment to his newly independent homeland, it certainly marked the beginning of his interest in building and garden-making and the start of a new chapter in his life.

Although much of his time was devoted to the Lunuganga project, he continued to work sporadically as a lawyer and needed a *pied-à-terre* in Colombo. In 1949 he bought a flat in Galle Face Court, an elegant block opposite the Galle Face Hotel built in Indian Art Deco style by Edwards, Reid and Begg. He also needed a suitable car: having previously sold his Rolls-Royce Phantom to Bevis, he now bought Bevis's second Rolls-Royce, a blue open tourer.

Lunuganga offered enormous potential. Geoffrey's first step was to remodel the house, converting the old porch entrance on the west elevation into a half-enclosed terrace and remodelling the whole approach so that visitors arrived at the house from the south. In 1949 he received his first visitors from Europe, among them his cousin Georgette and his friend Victor Chapin, now working as a film actor in Italy. They arrived in Colombo by boat, though Georgette was held up at customs because she refused to pay duty on an enormous glass chandelier that was in her baggage, protesting that she always travelled with her chandelier. Finally she got her way, and the chandelier still hangs in the sitting room at Lunuganga. Georgette found Geoffrey in a slightly subdued mood. Although he was brimming over with ideas he had recently discovered that he lacked the technical knowledge to put them into effect. She was clear in her advice that he should stop spending his own money on building terraces and shifting hills for himself and become an architect so that he could do what he liked doing best for other people with their money. He was obviously good at it.

If there ever was a single moment when it could be said that Bawa took the decision to become an architect this was it. He now acknowledged his growing fascination with landscape design and dreamt for the first time of designing houses and gardens for other people. For this to happen, however, he knew that he would need to acquire the professional skills that he so obviously lacked. He consulted his friend Neville Wynne-Jones, who had been chief architect of the Public Works Department before independence. Wynne-Jones advised him to return to

Middle: Georgette Camille at
Lunuganga, 1949
Bottom: Early visitors to
Lunuganga, Eleanor Williams and
her daughter Elizabeth, 1949

Opposite
Middle: Geoffrey in Italy,
around 1956
Bottom: Geoffrey's student
design for housing in Holloway
Road (published in *AD* October
1956)

England to study in a school of architecture, but suggested that he ought first to try working in a local practice for a short period to see if it suited him.

Early in 1951 Geoffrey persuaded H. H. Reid, the sole surviving partner of Edwards, Reid and Begg, to take him on as a part-time assistant. Reid was still held in high esteem by the expatriate community and attracted clients from the business and planting communities. During 1951 he was involved in the planning of the Colombo Plan Exhibition, an event that marked the signing of the British Commonwealth Colombo Plan agreement, a mutual economic aid treaty. Geoffrey worked as an assistant on the project and helped to design various temporary pavilions in Viharamahadevi Park, as well as a house on Charles Circus for the Illangakoon family.

In the same year Geoffrey received his first independent commission (p.62). Paul Deraniyagala, a Cambridge-educated zoologist and director of the Colombo Museum, was the son of Sir Paul Pieris, Parliament's first Ceylonese Speaker, and brother of Justin Deraniyagala, the foremost painter of the day. His wife, Preeni, came from the Mollamure family, which owned vast lands near Ratnapura and acted as guardians to the famous Saman Devale temple. The Deraniyagalas were part of a powerful clique of patrician families steeped in tradition, but they were also progressive, cultured and highly educated. In later years many of Bawa's clients would come from this same extended family network.

Paul Deraniyagala's grandmother, Mrs Obeyesekera, owned a house called Maligawa, which occupied a large garden between Guildford Crescent and the racecourse. In 1948 she divided part of her garden into plots to give to each of her many grandchildren along with money to build houses. By the end of 1951 the Deraniyagalas had still not started to build and Mrs Obeyesekera called them to task. When they explained that they did not like the type of houses then being built in Colombo, Mrs Obeyesekera suggested that they should try 'some young lawyer chap called Bawa who wants to become an architect' (Arjun Deraniyagala in conversation with the author). Preeni Deraniyagala contacted Geoffrey and invited him to a meeting. Her son, Arjun, remembers coming home from school to find a blue Rolls-Royce parked in the drive and a tall young man in lawyer's robes talking with his mother.

Geoffrey found that he and Mrs Deraniyagala had many ideas in common: she wanted to build a house that would be modern and progressive but that would also embody some

of the best features of traditional Ceylonese architecture. She persuaded Geoffrey to visit a number of buildings associated with her family and appointed her son, Siran, to act as guide and chauffeur. Together they visited the beautifully preserved Mollamure family *walaawe* at Eknelligoda, the Saman Devale temple at Ratnapura, Justin Deraniyagala's home at Nuge Dole near Pasyala, and the Obeyesekeras' hilltop villa at Dikkande, designed in the late 1920s by Edwards, Reid and Begg.

Geoffrey struggled to produce a satisfactory design for the Deraniyagalas, finding that he lacked the necessary technical skills. He knew what he didn't like, but was unable to articulate an alternative. When H. H. Reid died suddenly in March 1952 after suffering a heart attack during a site visit, Geoffrey decided to return to Britain in order to study architecture. When he told Mrs Deraniyagala of his decision and advised her to look for another architect she assured him that she liked his ideas and would wait until he qualified. And wait she did!

Bawa returned to Cambridge in the autumn of 1952, renting rooms in Thompson's Lane and hiring a private tutor to teach him civil engineering and structural design. This was a dislocated year in which he renewed contact with old friends, travelled around Britain looking at country houses and gardens, and made the occasional trip to Italy. Finally, he decided to apply for a place at the Architectural Association School (AA) in London's Bedford Square. Stuart Lewis, who was to become a friend and student colleague, remembers him arriving at the school office for an interview in September 1953. Distinguished, tall and full of confidence, he persuaded the secretary to fill in his application for him. He also persuaded the head of the school, Michael Patrick, to take into account his work experience and his private studies in Cambridge and to offer him a place in the third year of the five-year course, starting in September 1954. He later recalled:

> The decision to go to the AA didn't really come as a
> surprise…one didn't feel frightened…one knew instinctively
> that what one wanted to do was a possibility which wasn't
> wrong…one had the confidence at that stage: an amateur
> confidence, not an intellectual one…this removes the fear
> of creativity. (In conversation with Channa Daswatte, 1997)

Geoffrey spent the winter of 1953 in Ceylon working at Lunuganga. Then in June 1954, having arranged for Neville Wynne-Jones and his wife to keep an eye on the garden, he set sail once again for Britain to begin his architectural studies.

For a while Geoffrey lived at Kew with the Williams, but later he rented a flat in Berkeley Street off Piccadilly. As soon as he was established he bought himself, from 'a lady in Brighton', a Rolls-Royce, the car that still sits in the porch of his Colombo home.

This was an interesting time to be a student at the Architectural Association. The teaching staff included John Killick, Peter Ahrends, Peter Smithson, Arthur Korn, Edward Cullinan and the architectural historian John Summerson. The school had embraced International Modernism and was divided between Miesians, who followed Mies van der Rohe's cubic functionalism, and Corbusians, who favoured the sculptural plasticity of Le Corbusier. Bawa remembered: 'I went to lectures on the Modern Movement, on Le Corbusier. I thought it was marvellous, though I didn't find Corb any more interesting than Alberti or Vignola or Palladio' (in conversation with Channa Daswatte, 1997).

Geoffrey stood out as being the tallest, oldest and one of the wealthiest students of his day. He remained detached from the polemics of the various Modernist factions and drew on his skills as a lawyer and the vast first-hand knowledge of architecture he had accumulated during his travels to argue with tutors and fellow students against the reductionist aspects of Modernism. He also studiously avoided other Sri Lankan students who were his contemporaries, including Valentine Gunasekera, who was later to become his partner in Edwards, Reid and Begg.

During his penultimate year he joined John Killick's unit and took part in a detailed study of the housing needs of the London Borough of Islington. As part of this study he teamed up with Stuart Lewis and Tony Mathes to produce detailed designs for a housing development on Holloway Road. The trio's proposal for a high-rise slab block with split-level flats served by horizontal access decks was clearly inspired by Le Corbusier's Unité d'Habitation at Marseilles, which Geoffrey had visited during the previous summer. Their drawings were published in *Architectural Design* (Killick 1956) with an accompanying text, which stated that: 'The buildings are faced with rough pre-cast concrete cladding. In contrast to this a chiaroscuro pattern is provided by the changing planes of the different dwelling types, with incidental textural variations supplied by cast-iron balcony fronts…[into which]…two-inch-thick coloured glass is set…to obtain maximum effect at night.' Bawa avoided taking sides in the debates that raged across the

school and in his later work would acknowledge the influences of both Mies and Corb. His friend Roman Halter remembers that his preferred modern architect had always been Frank Lloyd Wright, though he rejected what he regarded as Wright's later megalomania. Halter remembers that Bawa's student projects seemed to have been designed mainly with a view to challenging prevailing orthodoxies and provoking arguments with tutors. Of his time at the Architectural Association, he later told Channa Daswatte: 'The AA gave me a discipline, though it didn't push me in any particular direction, which is why it is so good. I mean people who were bad were left bad, and people who were good were not interfered with' (in conversation with Channa Daswatte, 1997). In a similar vein, he told Jimmy Lim in 1990:

> The AA was splendid and it left you on your own entirely and it did not teach you anything! The School gave you the opportunity to meet intelligent people, all doing different intelligent things. I don't think architecture can be taught: you have to learn it. At the AA they leave you alone. Occasionally they praise you or sneer at what you have done, but they don't give you a theorem.' (Interview with Jimmy Lim; Lim 1990)

After studying for two years with students much younger than himself, Geoffrey seems to have tired of London. He opted to spend much of his final year in Italy, where he shared an apartment in Rome with his old Cambridge friend Guy Strutt, driving occasionally back to London at breakneck speed in his Rolls-Royce when his presence was required at a tutorial or a project review. During this time he started to look more systematically at the buildings and gardens of the Renaissance and developed a taste for Mannerism and the Baroque, and particularly for the work of Michelangelo, Vignola and Guilio Romano. Among his favourite places were the gardens at the Villa Lante at Bagnaia, the Villa Farnese at Caprarola and Count Orsini's 'Sacra Bosco' at Bomarzo. His final dissertation paper was a study of the German Baroque architect, Balthasar Neumann.

His long absences from the Architectural Association do not seem to have worried his tutors and in June 1957 he passed his final examinations and was elected an associate member of the Royal Institute of British Architects (RIBA). A few weeks later he boarded ship in Southampton and set sail for Colombo. At the age of thirty-eight Geoffrey Bawa's career as an architect was finally about to begin.

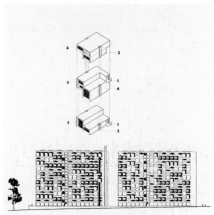

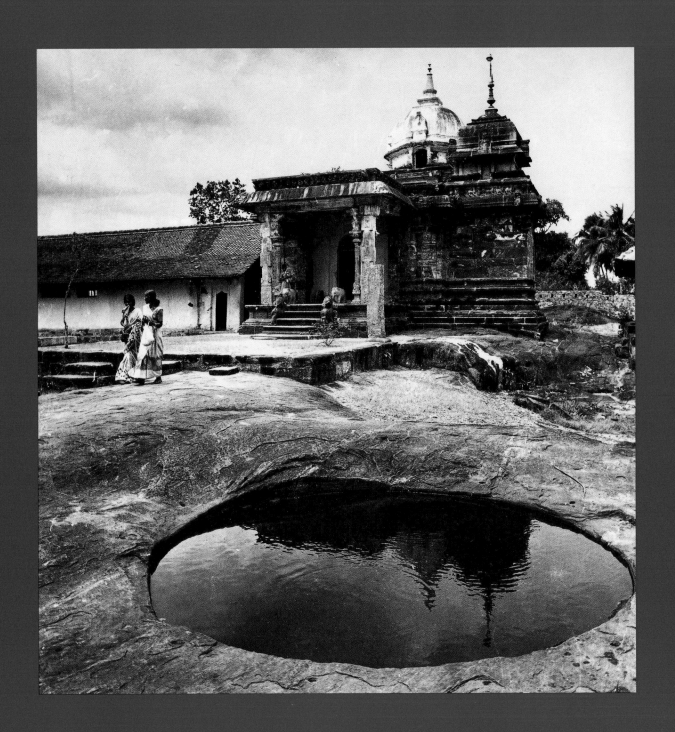

The Temples of their Gods are so many that I cannot number
them. Many of them are of Rare and Exquisite work, built of
Hewn Stone, engraven with Images and Figures.

Robert Knox: An Historical Relation of Ceylon (Knox 1681)

Introduction

Although Geoffrey Bawa would sometimes feign ignorance
of Sri Lanka's architectural history, he had visited most of the
island's archaeological sites and was well acquainted with its
ancient buildings and architectural traditions. As his career
developed, he continued to draw on his knowledge of European
architecture, but he responded more and more to the context
of Sri Lanka – to its climate, its physical resources, its social
conditions, its culture and its ways of building. For this reason
he should be regarded first and foremost as a Sri Lankan
architect, and his work should be viewed in the context of
the geography, people, history and traditions of Sri Lanka.

The island

Sri Lanka has been known down the centuries by a bewildering
assortment of names, which have reflected the complexities of
its history and the diversity of its contacts with the rest of the
world. The British called it 'Ceylon', a name that evolved from
the Portuguese 'Ceilão', derived originally from the Sanskrit
'Simhaladvipa' – the island of the Lion People; in early Sanskrit
literature the island was referred to as 'Ratnadvipa' or 'Island
of Gems'; the Indian chroniclers of the *Ramayana* called it
'Lankadvipa'; the Greeks knew it as 'Taprobane', a name derived
from an ancient port called Tambapanni; to the Arabs it was
'Serendib'; and in Tamil epics it was known as 'Elankai'. Only
in 1972 was it rechristened 'Sri Lanka' or 'resplendent land'.

Sri Lanka lies at the centre of the Indian Ocean, a few
degrees north of the Equator. Although it is separated from
the south-eastern tip of India by the shallow Palk Strait, the
two are tenuously linked by a thin necklace of islands known
as Adam's Bridge. Measuring over 400 kilometres from north
to south, the island covers an area of 65,000 square kilometres.
Its main mountain massif rises steeply from the west coast to
peaks of over 2,500 metres, and interacts with the monsoons
to produce two distinctive regions: the Dry Zone of the north
and east, which covers about two-thirds of the island, and the
hot and humid Wet Zone of the south-west.

On a map of the world Sri Lanka appears to be a marginal
place, cut off from centres of power and influence, far from the
great cities and the main overland trade routes. Throughout its
history, however, it has been influenced by its proximity to India
and its position between the Arabian Sea and the Bay of Bengal.
India was the source of Sri Lanka's early settlers and of its two
main religions, Buddhism and Hinduism, while the ocean
brought seafarers from the four corners of the earth.

The population of Sri Lanka increased almost sixfold
during the twentieth century and today stands at about twenty
million. The Sinhalese account for nearly three-quarters of the
total and are mainly Buddhist, descended from mixed groups
of migrants from the north and west of India who moved down
India's western seaboard and crossed Adam's Bridge during the
sixth and fifth centuries BC to settle in the Dry Zone. About a
fifth of the population are Tamils, who are mainly Hindu by
religion: of these about half are descended from early migrants
from South India who settled on the Jaffna peninsula and along
the north-east coast, and half are estate Tamils descended from
indented labourers brought from India by the British at the end
of the nineteenth century to work in the tea plantations. The
balance is made up mainly of the mixed descendants of Arab

Bawa's own photograph of the
Gadaladeniya temple

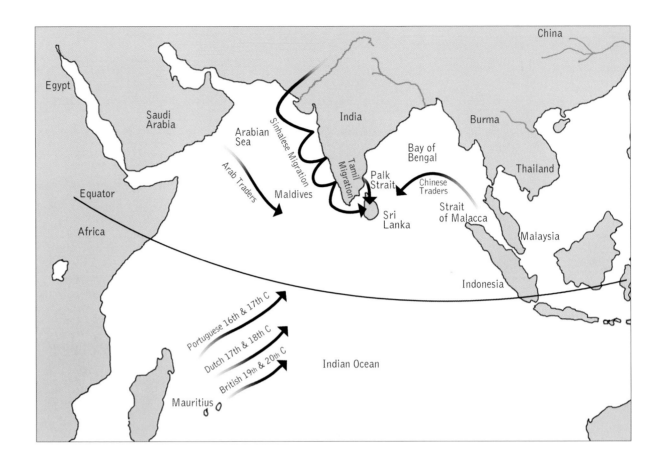

seafarers, known as Moors or Muslims, and smaller groups of Malays, Chetties, Dutch Burghers and Eurasians.

The first settlements

The first Sinhalese colonists settled in the northern Dry Zone and depended on seasonal rain and sparse rivers for their agriculture. They threw simple dams across river valleys to create small reservoirs or tanks that would hold monsoon waters in reserve for the dry season, and planted terraces of rice on the valley floors, reserving the higher ground for grazing and growing vegetables. Their villages were built above the fields and probably consisted of relatively dense clusters of houses, sheds and storage bins arranged around protected pockets of communal space. The houses themselves would have been constructed from wattle and daub (*wareechchi*) or rammed earth (*thaappa*), with overhanging roofs of straw thatch, and would have incorporated covered verandahs and enclosed courtyards.

The early settlers lived in a loose network of separate clans; a unifying structure developed only during the fourth century BC with the emergence of the northern kingdom of Rajarata, centred on the town of Anuradhapura. Lying about 80 kilometres from the sea, Anuradhapura was well protected from the threat of sudden invasion from either coast or from the often unreliable southern province of Ruhunu.

The Sinhalese developed ever more sophisticated ways to conserve and move water and by the beginning of the first century AD they were able to build huge tanks that covered hundreds of hectares and held millions of cubic metres of water. These were fed by long canals, often built to very low gradients, which connected separate river basins and moved water from one area of rainfall to another. The setting out and construction of this system required surveying and engineering skills of the highest order, while its operation and management demanded complex social structures to ration and control the distribution of the precious water. This vast hydraulic network

became one of the crowning achievements of Sinhalese civilization. Although the system fell into disuse after the twelfth century, remaining lost and forgotten under the jungle for hundreds of years, large parts of it have been restored and today there are an estimated eighteen thousand tanks in use across the island.

Water has played a central part in the lives of the Sinhalese people not only as the means to cultivate crops, but also as a source of physical and aesthetic pleasure. During the classical period, tank-building skills were used to create bathing ponds in monasteries and complex water gardens in royal palaces. To this day, rural people gather each evening at their village tank to enjoy the sheer sensual delight of plunging into water.

Early Buddhist architecture

At first the Sinhalese followed the Hindu religion of their forefathers, but when Buddhism permeated India during the third century BC it soon spread to Sri Lanka and took a firm hold. Early Buddhist monasteries and temples were often sited in caves or beneath overhanging cliffs, and rocks became an important element of Sinhalese architecture. During the classical period, religious precincts were usually planned orthogonally, often within a rectangular compound, but axes would be shifted and symmetries broken out of deference to rocky outcrops or streams.

A typical monastery would include cells for the monks, a prayer hall, an image house containing one or more figures of

the Buddha, a bo tree platform and a *dagoba*. The *dagoba* was a Sinhalese development of the Indian *stupa*, a solid masonry hemisphere built around a small relic chamber, but the *dagoba* in Sri Lanka followed a separate line of evolution to become a unique indigenous architectural icon. Builders abandoned the early hemispherical form of the first *stupas* at Sanchi in favour of such shapes as the 'bell', the 'water droplet' and the 'pile of rice'. Although early *dagobas* were of modest size and located on simple platforms, later developments included concentric walled enclosures, roofed canopies and ever more massive structures.

Anuradhapura

The development of Buddhism and the consolidation of a unified state laid the foundations for more than a thousand years of progress. Although there were dynastic struggles, civil wars, brief periods of Tamil hegemony and occasional invasions from South India, the lasting impression of the period from 250 BC to AD 900 is one of peace and prosperity: the irrigation system was extended, agricultural output increased and, as the shipping lanes of the Indian Ocean opened, trade between East and West Asia expanded. At the same time monasteries became centres of learning as well as points of spiritual and political power, and the arts, not least architecture, flourished.

At the hub of this remarkable civilization was Anuradhapura, at its zenith one of the most magnificent cities of the world. It had grown up on a ridge of high ground on the west bank of the Malwattu Oya River and was surrounded by a necklace of tanks that served to irrigate the surrounding farmland and supply the city. By the sixth century AD it measured about 25 square kilometres in area and accommodated a considerable population, including an estimated fifty thousand monks.

The core of the city comprised a rectangular walled citadel covering an area of about 80 hectares with gates at each of the cardinal points. Within were residential quarters, as well as a royal place and a temple in which the famous tooth relic of the Buddha was kept. According to Fa-Hsien, a Chinese monk who visited Sri Lanka at the beginning of the fifth century AD, 'The dwellings of the merchants are very grand…the streets are level and well kept…at all points where four roads meet are chapels for preaching the faith' (Hulugalle 1965). *The Mahavamsa*, an ancient historical chronicle compiled during the sixth century, records that residential suburbs grew up beside each of the main gateways and that the town was serviced with running water and drainage (Geiger 1950). The king appointed a

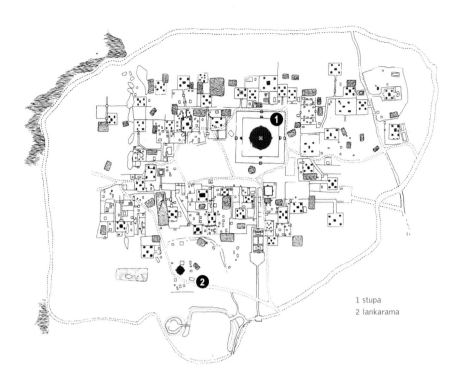

1 stupa
2 lankarama

mayor who ran the civil guard and organized street cleaning and refuse collection. There were markets, hospitals, cemeteries and prisons. Very little is known about the domestic architecture of the period, although a group of courtyard houses of uncertain date was excavated within the citadel by the Archaeological Survey at the beginning of the twentieth century (Hocart 1924).

The citadel was separated from the outer cordon of tanks by a belt of parkland in which were located seventeen separate monastic foundations as well as various public buildings and palaces. The sacred bo tree, grown originally from a sapling of the original mahabodhi tree under which the Buddha achieved enlightenment in Bodh Gaya, still flourishes within a stepped enclosure to the south of the citadel and is one of the most venerated objects in Sri Lanka.

Smaller monasteries consisted typically of an inner sacred precinct in which were located the *dagoba*, the preaching hall, the image house and the bo tree enclosure, and an outer cordon of residential pavilions, all contained by a moat and a massive masonry wall. Larger monasteries served as centres for separate chapters of monks and functioned as small independent satellite towns. An outer labyrinth of cell clusters, some housing their own prayer halls, libraries and *dagobas* would define a protected central area, within which were located the main prayer halls, the image houses and the principal *dagoba*.

The Abhayagiri Monastery, founded during the first century BC, covered at its peak an area of 200 hectares and housed a total of five thousand monks. The main *dagoba*, built during the second century AD, rose to a height of 110 metres and was surrounded by thirty separate cell clusters, each within a walled enclosure and planned as a *pancavasa* or quincunx, with four residential pavilions set around a central teaching hall. Pavilions stood on raised brick plinths with a lower storey supported on limestone columns and a timber upper storey under a clay-tiled roof. The main *dagoba* of the Jetavana Monastery was constructed during the third century AD and was at the time the tallest structure in Asia, towering 120 metres above its square platform and containing an estimated hundred million bricks.

One further group, known as the Western Monasteries, was built outside the cordon of tanks between the sixth and ninth centuries. These forest hermitages housed an ascetic order known as the *pamsukulikas* or 'rag-robed' monks, who repudiated the excessive luxury of the main orders. Their monasteries were built without *dagobas* or image houses and consisted of groups of rectangular pavilions built on raised plinths within walled enclosures. Surviving evidence would suggest that these buildings were plain and austere, without ornament or embellishment. Natural features were treated with reverence: for example, outcrops of rock were invariably incorporated into the composition. The Western Monasteries were the subject of a special study by the archaeologist Senake Bandaranayake (Bandaranayake 1974), which had a profound effect on Bawa's designs for the Seema Malaka temple and the Kotte Parliament.

Left: Plan of the Abhayagiri Monastery showing the arrangement of quincunx clusters of cells around the main *dagoba*
Right: Aerial view of Anuradhapura with the Thuperama and the Ruvanvelisaya Dagoba

Opposite
Left: The ruins of Kasyapa's palace on the summit of Sigiriya
Centre: Plan of Sigiriya
Right: The water gardens at Sigiriya

Sigiriya

In 477 AD the great tank-builder king, Dhatusena, was murdered by his son, Kasyapa. Fearing retribution, Kasyapa shifted the capital to the relative safety of Sigiriya Rock, about 60 kilometres to the south-east of Anuradhapura, and built a palace for himself on its lofty summit. Although the site had been occupied since the middle of the first millennium BC, much of what has survived is now thought to be the work of Kasyapa's builders and succinctly illustrates many important characteristics of classical Sinhalese art and architecture.

The rock's oval summit covers an area of about 1.5 hectares and sits about 200 metres above the surrounding plain. The palace was planned on an orthogonal grid aligning with the main north–south axis of the summit, but the ordering of its plan and section responded organically to the profile of the rock. The buildings step down from the private rooms of the inner palace at the north-west end of the rock towards the more public terraces and the palace gardens in the south, connected by a pavement spine.

The west face of the rock was covered in frescoes, a small group of which has survived in a hollow to bear witness to the vibrant school of Sinhalese painting that existed during the fifth century. The base of the rock was encircled by an inner citadel occupying an area of scree and rock formerly used as a monastery and transformed by Kasyapa into a 'boulder garden'.

This acted as a buffer between the royal water gardens to the west and the inner and outer precincts of the formally planned town that lay to the east. The whole complex was contained by an outer rectangle of double moats and ramparts.

The royal water gardens were laid out according to a formal plan that was distorted to accommodate the changing terrain. A principal west–east avenue passed first through a large formal garden with symmetrical arrangements of brick-lined pools contained within a rectangular walled enclosure, then crossed four moated islands that appeared like rocky outcrops rising out of natural lakes, and finally entered an area of smaller formal ponds and pavilions insinuated into the terrain at the base of the rock and acting as the prelude to the boulder garden.

The Sigiriya complex embodies remarkable achievements in the arts of town planning, architecture, painting, garden design, and sculpture. The gardens in particular demonstrate a sophistication of design and execution that seems quite out of place in the fifth century. The Sinhalese were able to put their practical mastery of hydraulics to use in creating a unique work of garden art, but they also used their love of picturesque planning to create an exquisite juxtaposition of formal and informal elements, contrasting the man-made and the natural. In this they anticipated the great gardens of Mogul India and Renaissance Italy and later inspired Bawa the garden-maker.

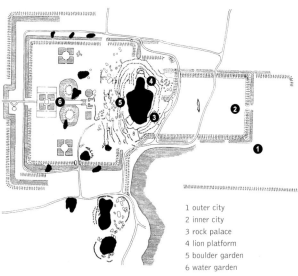

1 outer city
2 inner city
3 rock palace
4 lion platform
5 boulder garden
6 water garden

Left: Parakramabahu's
Palace, Polonnaruwa
Centre: Aerial view of the
Polonnaruwa Quadrant
Right: The Polonnaruwa
vatadage

Polonnaruwa

During the fifth and sixth centuries three rival Hindu powers – the Pandyas, the Pallavas and the Cholas – embarked on a long struggle for control of Southern India. This turmoil was to have profound implications for Sri Lanka and led to a marked increase in South Indian influence. The Sinhalese, however, managed to stave off major disaster by allying themselves at different times with one or other of the foreign powers. Finally, in the early part of the eleventh century, the Cholas invaded Sri Lanka and annexed the Sinhalese kingdom, instigating sixty years of foreign rule and effectively ending the Anuradhapura millennium.

The new rulers shifted the capital about 75 kilometres to the south-east from Anuradhapura to Polonnaruwa, which was more accessible and better placed to control the wayward southern province of Ruhunu. They persecuted Buddhism, dismantling many monasteries and building new Hindu shrines in their place, but during the mid-eleventh century the Sinhalese king Vijayabahu succeeded in driving them back to India. Anuradhapura now lay in ruins and he established his capital in Polonnaruwa, using it as a base from which to reunite the kingdom and restore the primacy of Buddhism.

The city of Polonnaruwa – never more than a third of the size of Anuradhapura, stretching 5 kilometres from north to south at its height – had developed on a ridge of high ground overlooking a series of irrigation tanks fed by the Amban Ganga. During the reign of Parakramabahu I (1153–86) these smaller tanks were joined to create the Sea of Parakramabahu which, with a surface area of 25 square kilometres, became the largest of Sri Lanka's reservoirs. The ancient *Culavamsa Chronicle* records that 'The monarch now had a high chain of walls built, which on all sides enclosed the fortified town, which…gleamed with its coating of lime bright as autumn clouds' (Geiger 1953, 73.53). The town walls enclosed a dense network of streets and buildings laid out more or less on an orthogonal grid aligning north–south. Within the town a smaller inner citadel enclosed the massive palace of Parakramabahu, where, according to the *Culavamsa*: '[The King] erected a second inner wreath of walls and built thereon a palace seven storeys high, furnished with a thousand chambers and adorned with many pillars painted in diverse hues' (Geiger 1953, 73.60). Parakramabahu's council chamber lay opposite the palace and consisted of an open-sided columnated hall raised high on a stone plinth formed by three separate stepped ledges, each decorated with friezes. The main entrance was reached by a noble staircase decorated with moonstones, guardstones and lions. This building became a prototype for later council buildings such as the Audience Hall in Kandy and served as a precedent for Bawa's debating chamber in the Kotte Parliament.

Polonnaruwa's principal monasteries are located to the north of the walled town and away from the tank. Perhaps the most impressive is the huge monastic complex known as the Alahana

Parivena, stepping up the sides of a hill in a series of rectangular terraces formed by brick retaining walls towards upper platforms crowned by the Kiri *dagoba*, the Lankatilaka image house and the monastery's main chapter house. The terraces, connected by broad alleyways and staircases, were dotted with small *stupas*, bathing ponds, and columnated pavilions but the spaces between were almost as important as the buildings themselves, offering an ever-changing scenographic experience to any visitor. The whole complex was ordered on a regular north–south grid, though the various elements were sited according to the topography in a way that undermined any obvious symmetries. It demonstrates clearly many of the principles that Bawa later adopted when planning complex projects such as the Ruhunu University.

The ruins of three great twelfth-century Buddha image houses or *patimagharas* – the Thuparama in the Quadrangle, the Lankatilaka in the Alahana Parivena and the Tivanka in the Northern Monastery – illustrate both the extent and limits of Indian influence during the Polonnaruwa period. While earlier image houses had been built with tiled roofs supported on a framework of timber and stone, these structures were conceived as massive vaulted basilicas of solid brick masonry, attempting to match the corbelled stone vaults used in the Hindu temples of the Cholas.

The Thuparama is the oldest and best preserved of the three. Its narrow nave led to a rectangular cella that housed a massive standing Buddha of plastered brickwork. The walls were built of brick set in lime mortar to a thickness of more than 2 metres and tapered inwards to reduce the span of the corbelled vaults. The roof of the cella supported a square tower of masonry topped by a solid dome and spire, echoing the *sikhara* of a Chola temple. The Thuparama's elevations were decorated with brick reliefs finished in lime plaster, achieving a simplicity and serenity usually absent from South Indian architecture. Its deep plinth featured a single

frieze of lions, while the main wall surface was divided into panels by flat pilasters, each topped by a capital and bracket that recalled the eaves detail of earlier timber roofs. The panels themselves carried images of temple buildings that served as niches for sculpted deities and now offer some clue as to how the Thuparama itself might have appeared.

The great builder kings of Polonnaruwa – Vijayabahu, Parakramabahu and Nissankamalla – enjoyed between them only about seventy years of peace. Periods of progress and prosperity were interspersed with debilitating interludes of internecine squabbling when rival factions jockeyed for power and even enlisted aid from India to promote their causes. After the brief nine-year rule of Nissankamalla, ending in 1196, the country slid into confusion, and successive waves of Pandyan and Cholan marauders pillaged the land.

Top left: Aerial view of the
Alahana Parivena, Polonnaruwa
Top centre: The Lankatilaka and
the Kiri Dagoba, Polonnaruwa
Top right: The Thuperama,
Polonnaruwa
Bottom right: Side entrance to
the Lankatilaka, Polonnaruwa

Characteristics of Sinhalese classical architecture

The term 'Sinhalese classical architecture' is generally used to describe architecture of the middle and late Anuradhapura and Polonnaruwa periods, from about AD 100 to about AD 1200. While many features of Sinhalese architecture can be viewed as having developed from Indian archetypes, the extent of Indian influence should not be overstated. Time and again Sri Lankan artists and craftsmen, responding to their particular set of circumstances, developed unique designs that were wholly Sri Lankan in spirit. This ability to absorb and transform external influences became an enduring characteristic of Sinhalese architecture during later periods of European hegemony and also proved to be a distinguishing characteristic of Geoffrey Bawa's own working method.

From earliest times Sinhalese builders demonstrated a unique approach towards topology and water, deliberately choosing sites within dramatic rocky landscapes and developing a geomorphic approach that celebrated naturalistic compositions of buildings, boulders, winding staircases, caves and narrow passageways. In the same way they sought to incorporate water both in naturally occurring pools and streams and as formally planned ponds and channels.

The courtyard and the verandah are also persistent elements of Sinhalese architecture that occur in everything from simple dwellings to large public buildings. The use of both elements in conjunction with conventional rooms creates an interesting dialogue between inside and outside space and increases the possibilities for natural ventilation.

The architects of the classical period based their designs on systems of mathematics and proportion developed from ideas about the cosmos. Their larger public buildings and layouts for towns were based on rectangular grids, usually aligned to the points of the compass. More complex buildings were often axial in plan and incorporated subtle hierarchies of main and subsidiary axes. While such compositions often proceeded from a symmetrical *parti*, deliberate asymmetries were introduced to add surprise and interest.

Although Sri Lanka could boast a long tradition of building with stone, the use of this material was never as widespread as it was in India. During the second half of the first millennium, Sinhalese craftsmen graduated from working in limestone and sandstone to working in harder and more durable granites as the quality of their tools improved, but they seldom matched the achievements of their Indian counterparts. Most buildings were built mainly of brick, often finished with a hard white plaster, and covered by a roof of flat clay tile on timber, the use of stone being limited to dressings, columns, capitals and sculptural adornments.

Many of these characteristics are features equally of Geoffrey Bawa's architecture: the incorporation of natural features; the breaking down of barriers between interior and exterior space; the inclusion of courtyards and verandahs; the preference for axial orthogonal compositions tempered by deliberate asymmetries to animate the whole; and the use of brick, timber, clay tile and plaster as inexpensive but appropriate construction materials.

Decline and dispersal

The decline of Polonnaruwa during the early part of the thirteenth century prompted the Sinhalese to abandon the Dry Zone and move *en masse* to the central highlands and western coastal plains of the Wet Zone. Many reasons have been advanced for their sudden retreat from their homeland of nearly two thousand years – the debilitating effects of successive invasions from South India, internal political instability, the growing power of the Tamil kingdom in the north, the progressive collapse of the irrigation system, the arrival of the malaria mosquito – and it may be that all of these contributed in some way to the inexplicable migration. Slowly the lands of the ancient Sinhalese kingdom reverted to jungle: tank bunds were breached, canals disappeared, cities were invaded by wild animals, palaces collapsed and temples crumbled. Soon even the memory of the lost civilization was erased from the minds of the people who had created it.

During the ensuing centuries the Sinhalese established a succession of short-lived kingdoms centred on temporary capitals at Dambadeniya, Yapahuva, Kurunegala, Gampola, Kotte, Sitavaka and finally at Kandy. Often two and sometimes even three separate kingdoms existed simultaneously, vying for supremacy while, across an expanding buffer of jungle, a series of Tamil kingdoms flourished in the north.

The main centre of power shifted to hill country during the latter half of the fourteenth century and the capital was established at Gampola. This period is remembered for a brief architectural renaissance manifested in a group of temples that show the transformation of the classical style into a more localized vernacular that responded to the climate and vegetation of the hill country.

Bottom: Map showing the shifting centres of power in Sri Lanka

Opposite
Top, middle and bottom left: Sectional elevation, plan, and exterior view of the Lankatilaka Temple, near Kandy
Middle and bottom centre: The exterior of the Gadaladeniya Temple, near Kandy, and view of the pseudo-stupas
Bottom right: The drumming hall of the Embekke Devale

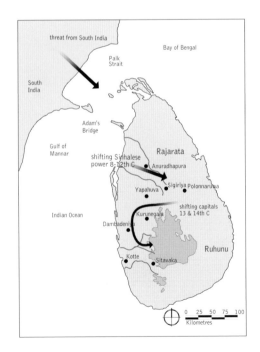

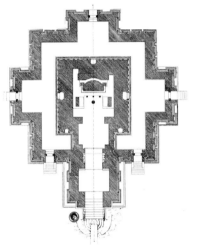

The Lankatilaka temple combines the functions of Buddhist temple and Hindu *devale*. The main temple was originally built in the manner of the Polonnaruwa image houses, with thick walls of brick supporting brick vaults, topped by a solid brick *sikhara*. The whole structure was later covered by a stepped roof of flat clay tiles, signifying a retreat from the massive masonry construction of the late Polonnaruwa period towards the lighter tile-roofed pavilions of earlier centuries. The primacy of such pitched roofs as an element of Sinhalese architecture was challenged by Bawa during the early part of his career, when he struggled to develop modern forms based on solid concrete construction, but eventually he too came to recognize the need for an 'umbrella'. A few kilometres further north, the temple complex at Gadaladeniya offers another interesting example

of transitional design. Here the main Buddha image house, built of stone, shows strong Pandyan influence, though its dome is more like a *dagoba* than a conventional *sikhara*. Nearby, five shrines arranged in a small cluster and capped by domes in the form of pseudo *dagobas* are protected by a canopy of much later date, consisting of a double-pitched 'Kandyan roof' made of flat tiles and supported on four Tuscan columns of Portuguese descent. Gadaladeniya offers a tantalizing glimpse of how architects of the period responded to new circumstances and how they incorporated stylistic elements of widely differing origin. At Embekke the whole village is laid out on either side of a grand processional avenue that runs from an elephant-mounting platform to a temple precinct, where all attempts to ape classical stone detailing have been abandoned and the full sophistication of a new medieval style of timber construction is in evidence.

The end of the fourteenth century was marked by periods of fierce rivalry between competing Sinhalese kingdoms and conflict with the Tamil kingdom in the north. One breakaway group, led by a Sinhalized South Indian called Alakesvara, founded a new capital at Kotte, a few miles inland from the modern city of Colombo, and it was from this base that Parakramabahu VI managed to unify the whole island during the early part of the fifteenth century. This period of unity was short-lived, however, and by the end of the fifteenth century the kingdom had split three ways between Kotte, Jaffna and a new capital at Kandy in the hills, setting the stage for the arrival of the Portuguese.

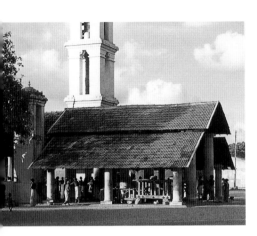

The Arabs and the Chinese

Long before the Portuguese invaded Sri Lanka, Arab and Chinese traders were regular visitors. From the middle of the first millennium Arab sailors dominated the sea lanes of the Indian Ocean and effectively controlled a string of ports around the rim of the Arabian Sea. Arab merchants had come to the shores of fabled Serendib from earliest times to trade for 'apes, ivory and gemstones', while Chinese and Malay sailors had sailed from the east through the Straits of Malacca to gain access to the emporia of South India. The shallow Palk Strait offered a passage for boats of low draught between the Arabian Sea and the Bay of Bengal and the Sri Lankan port of Mantai became an important entrepôt, attracting merchants from as far afield as Greece and Rome in the west and China in the east.

Although the Sinhalese doubtless profited from this trade and may have exercised some control over it, they never became a maritime nation. Their major towns were all located away from the coast while their ancient ports were never substantial and were cosmopolitan in character. Arab and Malabar traders are thought to have founded the modern ports of Colombo and Galle and it is their descendants who later constituted Sri Lanka's Muslim community, including amongst their number Geoffrey Bawa's grandfather Ahamadu Bawa.

The Portuguese

The Portuguese first arrived off the coast of Sri Lanka in 1505 and during the following decades established a chain of forts and trading posts along the west coast of the island. Their main aim was not to seize territory, but rather to challenge Arab domination of the Indian Ocean, wresting control of the lucrative spice trade, and to promote the Catholic religion. By the end of the sixteenth century the Portuguese had toppled the Tamil kingdom of Jaffna and brought most of Sri Lanka's coastline under their sovereignty.

For over a century the Portuguese were a dominant force in the affairs of Sri Lanka. They established their main trading post at Colombo, which lay conveniently close to the Sinhalese citadel at Kotte and offered one of the safest havens on the west coast of the island, the harbour being protected from the monsoons by a rocky headland and from land attack by a ring of lagoons. There they built a massive fort with walls of granite set in lime mortar, enclosing both the main town and the native quarter to its east (the Pettah), which were connected by the Rio Directo, the forerunner of today's Main Street. The Portuguese

writer Ribiero reported that there were nine hundred 'noble families' and a further fifteen hundred 'Porto–Sinhalese families' living within the fort at the beginning of the seventeenth century (Brohier 1984).

The invaders remained in a state of almost perpetual conflict with the Sinhalese, and are remembered for their cruelty and wanton destruction of countless 'pagan pagodas'. Perhaps surprisingly, their attempts to introduce Catholicism by fire and sword met with some success and many Sinhalese converted and adopted Portuguese names. In spite of their unpopularity they also influenced many aspects of Sinhalese life. Sadly none of their buildings has survived in its original form and all that remains are a few vestiges that have been incorporated into later structures. Although Barbara Sansoni was able to record the remains of several churches on the Jaffna peninsula during the 1970s (Lewcock et al. 1998), most of these are now thought to have been destroyed in the civil war. The building techniques and architectural elements that the Portuguese introduced were, however, assimilated into the mainstream vernacular tradition; for example, the timber shutter and the use of large windows in domestic dwellings. They also bequeathed a vocabulary of simplified Western classical elements, such as the squat Tuscan column and the round-arched wall opening, and the half-round clay tile known as the *sinhala-ulu* is sometimes referred to as the 'Portuguese tile', though it may originally have been introduced by the Arabs.

The Dutch

The Dutch East India Company established its main base in Batavia, in modern Jakarta, at the end of the sixteenth century and sought to gain a foothold on the Indian subcontinent in order to share in its lucrative spice trade. The Kandyan king, Rajasinghe II, wishing to rid himself of the Portuguese, formed an alliance with the Dutch, who quickly overran Portugal's outposts in the south of Sri Lanka and finally captured Colombo after a long siege in 1656. Much to Rajasinghe's dismay, however, the Dutch soon made it clear that they had no plans to leave. Like the Portuguese, the Dutch failed to conquer the whole island but they eventually governed most of the coastline and managed the prized cinnamon trade, leaving the Kandyan Sinhalese in control of the hill country.

One fascinating account of life in the Kandyan kingdom at the beginning of the Dutch period was furnished by Robert Knox, a sailor in the British East India Company who was captured by Kandyans in 1660 and held prisoner for almost twenty years:

> Their houses are small, low, thatched cottages, built with sticks, daubed with clay, the walls made very smooth…They employ no carpenters or house builders…but each one buildeth his own dwelling. The great people have handsome and commodious houses…commonly two buildings, one opposite each other, joined on each side by a wall, which makes a square courtyard in the middle…against the walls are banks of clay to sit on…Their furniture is but small…a few earthen pots that hang up in slings…a stool or two without backs. (Knox 1958, p.162)

More organized and pragmatic than their predecessors, the Dutch saw Ceylon as simply another department in a much larger commercial organization with its headquarters in Batavia. They were puritanical Calvinists and, though they tolerated the Buddhists and Hindus, they persecuted Catholicism and Islam. They rebuilt and strengthened the Portuguese forts at Colombo, Galle, Matara and Jaffna, and added new forts along both the west and east coasts, built with massive outer walls, tessellated in accordance with the latest theories of defence and surrounded by sculpted glacis. Within their larger forts they created townships laid out on strict rectangular grids, the streets lined with large shade trees and the buildings fronted by deep verandahs with overhangs supported on slender wooden columns.

Dutch houses were built to accommodate the various offices of life in a colonial family and were conceived very much with a view to comfort and domesticity. Unlike the Portuguese, whose houses were usually planned on two or three storeys as defensible keeps, they were predominantly of one storey and consisted of enfiladed rooms connecting to open verandahs, grouped around internal courtyards (Lewcock et al. 1998). Often a wide verandah known as the *stoep* ran along the street frontage, linked to a main reception room, separated from the more private quarters by a first inner courtyard. Kitchens and service rooms were then disposed around a second rear service court, linked in turn to a rear garden. The building industry was dominated by the Porto–Sinhalese, who continued the practices of earlier periods. As a result, although the architectural elements – door frames, gables, fanlights – used by the Dutch reflected changing tastes in eighteenth-century Holland, the spatial qualities of their houses seem to have been developed from Asian models: the town houses of the Moors of Ceylon and the Malabar Coast, the manor houses of the Kandyan Sinhalese, and the traditional houses of Batavia. As surviving churches in Galle, Matara and Colombo show, Dutch public buildings were built in a plain and sombre Baroque style with undulating walls and small windows.

The Dutch East India Company recruited employees from all over northern Europe and encouraged them to bring their families. But life was not easy and the gravestones in the churches bear witness to the high mortality rates they experienced. The Dutch wife of Geoffrey Bawa's maternal ancestor, Julius Schrader, himself a company employee, bore ten children in as many years and only four survived to adulthood.

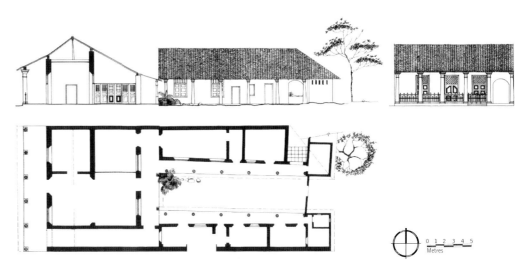

The British

The British ousted the Dutch from Ceylon in 1796 after a brief military campaign. Having secured the coastal regions, they began to extend their influence into the interior and in 1815 became the first foreign power to occupy Kandy and control the whole island.

Unlike the Dutch, the British were not satisfied simply to trade: they established a plantation system that eventually transformed the entire landscape of Sri Lanka. The western foothills were planted with cinnamon and coconut and later with rubber, the mountain forests were cleared to make way for coffee and tea, and over time even the ancient irrigation systems of the eastern Dry Zone were revived to support new settlements. All of this endeavour necessitated huge infrastructural developments and during the nineteenth century the British built up an extensive civil administration in a network of towns linked by a comprehensive road and railway system. This work was handled by military engineers until 1867 when a civil Public Works Department (PWD) was established.

During the first half of the nineteenth century most smaller-scaled public buildings were designed or built much as they had been under the Dutch: work was either entrusted to local contractors, many of them Porto–Sinhalese or Muslims, or carried out using 'direct labour' based on the old feudal *rajakariya* system, encouraging a persistence of traditional forms. Thus the government salt store at Nilaveli, commissioned by a British governor in 1810, combines a vari-pitched Kandyan roof with a supporting structure of heavy Portuguese bottle columns and could have been built any time after 1600.

When they came to build major public buildings, the British broke with Portuguese–Dutch traditions and adopted a ponderous neoclassical style to express their imperial gravitas. In 1811, for example, the new central wing of the Hultsdorf Law Courts was built in heavy, lumbering Doric, a far cry from the delicacy of the Slave Island Hospital the Dutch had built only twenty years earlier. Where the British architects and engineers excelled, however, was in ordinary, everyday buildings: simple, utilitarian and often beautiful rest houses, railway stations, staff quarters, circuit bungalows, pumping stations, *kachcheris* (provincial administrative offices) and the like.

In terms of domestic architecture, the British did not take to the sprawling courtyard houses bequeathed to them by the Dutch, and preferred to live in compact bungalows set within generous gardens. In their houses, as in their mode of dress, they were less concerned with comfort than with a desire to express their aloofness. A typical bungalow plan consisted of two wings of enfiladed rooms ranged on either side of a central hall, which ran from a front *porte cochère* to a rear verandah. Later 'bungalows' were built with a second storey of bedrooms arranged on either side of a landing and set behind recessed balconies. Kitchens and servants' rooms would be located in separate outhouses. Early designs incorporated Dutch–Sinhalese details, but these were later displaced by Italianate elements, which became common currency throughout the British colonies of the Far East. Geoffrey Bawa's childhood home was a two-storeyed bungalow in the Italianate style built in the 1870s.

While the British moved mountains and felled forests, the Sinhalese continued to build very much as they had done during the previous three or four centuries. Few domestic buildings built before 1800 have survived, however, and most of what now passes for Sinhalese vernacular architecture was probably built during the British period. Ananda Coomaraswamy's descriptions of Kandyan domestic architecture differ little from those written

Left: The salt store at Nilaveli
Centre: Railway worker's house at Kurunegala
Right: A late nineteenth-century bungalow in Cinnamon Gardens, Colombo

Opposite
Bottom left: Plan of the Eknelligoda Walaawe
Top right: Front verandah of the Eknelligoda Walaawe
Middle right: View of the main hall of the Eknelligoda Walaawe
Bottom right: Bawa's own photograph of the Gintota Walaawe (demolished)

by Knox some two centuries earlier, though he provides interesting evidence of the written and oral traditions of the master builders. He quotes from the *Mayamataya*, a text for builders and architects translated from Sanskrit into Sinhala at the beginning of the nineteenth century:

> O master builders, this is an incomparable book, written in the common tongue, which if any regard with the eye of wisdom, 'twere for the bettering of work in this world…How to build houses aright, what site and month are meet, how beams should be cut, to explain I shall unfold the virtues of Mayamataya. (Coomaraswamy 1908, p.125)

Even today villagers consult their local *gurunansa* or soothsayer, who draws on a body of wisdom passed down from generation to generation, and offers advice that is a mixture of superstition and good common sense – where to build, how many doors and windows to use, what materials to employ, when to start building.

The process of recording examples of vernacular buildings was begun in 1960 by Bawa's partner, Ulrik Plesner, and then continued by his friend Barbara Sansoni. This led eventually to the publication of an anthology (Lewcock et al. 1998) that includes, as well as a few examples of Dutch and British domestic buildings, a rich sample of the houses and village

temples of the Sinhalese, the Tamils and the Moors. What emerges is a picture of a continuous tradition that retains echoes of the past while incorporating influences from other cultures.

For example, the manor houses or *walaawe* owned by the aristocracy contained the same elements as the homes of their more humble cousins, but were more elaborate and included architectural elements of European origin. Thus the famous *walaawe* at Eknelligoda, seat of the Mollamures, dates in its present form from the mid-nineteenth century and could be described as a Sinhalese house of the British period built on a Dutch–Palladian plan with Sinhalese–Portuguese details. Temple architecture was also influenced by the colonial presence. The Saman Devale temple at Ratnapura, a Buddhist–Hindu shrine dating from the late eighteenth century, incorporates Portuguese, Dutch and Keralan elements within a Sinhalese *parti*.

The new Ceylonese middle classes chose to live in smaller and often more eclectic versions of the houses of their colonial masters. One interesting stylistic variation known locally as the *mal-laali* or 'floral panel' style appeared during the early years of the twentieth century as the local manifestation of an ornate verandahed bungalow typology that emerged simultaneously in many different corners of the Tropics. Similar styles were adopted by the estate-owning class, whose houses are illustrated

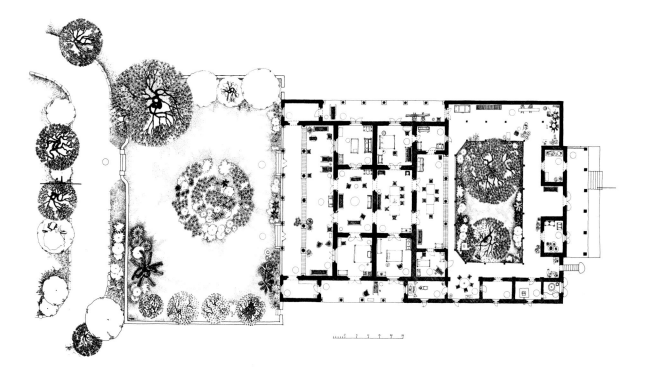

in Arnold Wright's fascinating directory of leading Ceylonese families, *Twentieth-Century Images of Ceylon* (Wright 1907). The estate bungalows of Bawa's grandfather Schrader at Kimbulapitiya and Wester Seaton near Negombo date from the mid-nineteenth century and were built in typical Anglo–Dutch style.

The transformation of Sri Lanka during the nineteenth century was accompanied by an accelerating wave of urbanization: country villages became market towns, established towns became regional centres and Colombo began to spread far beyond the confines of the Dutch fort and the Pettah. In the towns Ceylonese shopkeepers and merchants built narrow-fronted 'shop-houses' based on earlier Muslim and Dutch models, while the urban poor were housed in company lines or left to fend for themselves in spontaneous shanties.

By the end of the nineteenth century the walls of Colombo's Dutch fort had been almost completely demolished to allow the central business district to expand. Within the Fort itself the Dutch street pattern remained, though one by one the old bungalows were replaced by a first wave of public and commercial buildings built of solid masonry to a height of two or three storeys. Most public buildings were still designed by the architects of the PWD, though a handful of private architects served the commercial and private sectors. After 1910 the use of steel-frame construction was pioneered by the architects Walker and Adams, later Adams and Small, who built a second wave of taller buildings such as the Prince Building of 1911 and the Hongkong and Shanghai Bank of 1921.

Between 1900 and 1948 Ceylon's population more than doubled from three million to seven million and Colombo spread beyond its municipal limits like half an octopus, extending along the main roads to the north, east and south. A first British suburb had grown up around the hill of Mutwal to the north of the port but the arrival of coal-fired steamships precipitated a mass migration of the middle classes southwards to Cinnamon Gardens, where a new Garden City suburb with broad, tree-lined avenues, a park and a racecourse was established. Ceylon remained largely unaffected by the architectural fashions sweeping the West after World War I. During the 1920s a Renaissance classical style continued to be employed for important buildings such as the Parliament and the new Colombo Town Hall, though a more utilitarian, stripped-down neoclassicism was used for lesser public buildings. At the same time a growing interest in the ancient architecture of Sri Lanka led to the use of pseudo-Sinhalese motifs as decorative elements within a classical *parti*. Modernism of a sort finally arrived after 1930 when the influence of Hollywood movies and US magazines spawned a tropical version of Art Deco for houses and commercial buildings.

Top left: The Saman Devale
at Ratnapura
Middle left: A bungalow in
the 'Mal-Laali' style
Top right: Bawa's own photograph
of lattice screens on a house at
Negombo
Middle right: A Muslim house in
Messenger Street, Colombo

The first examples of true International Modern architecture did not appear in Ceylon until the late 1930s. In 1939 a young British tea-taster-turned-architect called Andrew Boyd designed three remarkable houses, two of them in Colombo and a third in Kandy, all in a clear, white, abstract, cubist style. Two years later the Swiss architects Egender and Muller, assisted by the famous bridge engineer Robert Maillart, built a revolutionary block of flats and offices for the Swiss import company of A. Baur & Co in the area of Colombo known by then as the Fort. However, these buildings had little impact on popular taste or the work of other architects.

Ceylon had little direct part in World War II, though after the fall of Singapore the British established their South-East Asia command in Kandy and the island was threatened with invasion from Japan. But the war was a watershed for the British Empire and it soon became apparent that the days of British colonial rule were numbered. In 1948 Ceylon finally regained its independence after four centuries of foreign rule.

The extent to which the people of Ceylon benefited from 150 years of British rule can be debated, though few would disagree with historian K. M. de Silva's view that:

> The civic and public architecture of this period was decidedly less successful…[and] was totally occidental in concept. Indeed the British architectural legacy in Sri Lanka is extraordinarily uninspiring, without a single building or monument that could stand comparison with those of the past for originality of design or aesthetic appeal.' (de Silva 1981)

Bawa's view of history

Bawa used history and tradition in a subliminal way: memories of the family homes of his childhood and the buildings and places he visited in his youth were stored to be tapped into at

the right moment. His background reflected the complexities of Sri Lankan society and his life spanned the colonial and post-colonial period, making him uniquely qualified to act as a link between Western and local ways of thinking and doing. His attitude to history was perhaps best expressed in one rare article in the *Times of Ceylon Annual* (Bawa 1968):

> In my personal search I have always looked to the past for the help that previous answers can give…By the past I mean all the past, from Anuradhapura to the latest finished buildings in Colombo, from Polonnaruwa to the present – the whole range of effort, peaks of beauty and simplicity and deep valleys of pretension. I prefer to consider all past good architecture in Ceylon as just that – as good Ceylon architecture, for that is what it is, not Dutch or Portuguese or Indian, or early Sinhalese or Kandyan or British colonial, for all examples of these periods have taken Ceylon into first account.

Top left: The Galle Face Hotel, Colombo, (1894)
Middle left: The Gaffoor Building in Colombo Fort
Top centre: Cargill's Department Store (1902) with the Hong Kong & Shanghai Bank (1921) and the Prince Building (1919), Colombo Fort
Top right: Colombo's changing skyline
Bottom right: A house in Kandy by Andrew Boyd (1939)

Geoffrey Bawa gained his first taste of working in an architect's office in 1951, when he joined Edwards, Reid and Begg as an apprentice and worked intermittently for about a year with H. H. Reid, the sole survivor of the eponymous trio. Six years later, when he returned, fully qualified, from London, Reid was dead and the firm was being run by a local architect, Jimmy Nilgiria. Bawa became a junior partner but, one by one, he ousted his rivals and by 1967 had become the firm's principal partner. He continued to practise under the title of his predecessors until 1988, though increasingly the firm was known by the acronym 'E. R. & B.' or 'Ee-ar-and-bee'. Thus the names Edwards, Reid and Begg came to be used long after their owners' deaths and were associated with Sri Lanka's most successful and prolific architectural practice for almost three-quarters of a century.

In 1923 the Colombo Municipality staged an open competition to design a town hall on the north-east corner of the Viharamahadevi Park in the new suburb of Cinnamon Gardens. The decision to hold a competition was probably influenced by the fact that the architects of the Public Works Department (PWD) were fully engaged with the design of a new Parliament. Two entries were received from practices in Allahabad and one from Singapore, but, because the architectural profession was still in its infancy in Ceylon, there were no local entries. The competition was judged by Austin Woodeson, the chief architect of the PWD, and the eventual winners were S. J. Edwards and R. Booty of Singapore.

Edwards' design adopted a pompous, 'Wrenaissance', classical style rendered in white painted stucco, and was not far removed in spirit from Woodeson's design for the Parliament. A giant, double-height, Doric order created a continuous loggia around the building's perimeter, while a 'double-square' plan created two pleasant courtyards on either side of a central council chamber, which was placed below a tall false dome. The

foundation stone was laid in 1924 and the building was completed by Gammon & Co in 1928.

The commission required Edwards to open an office in Colombo and for a time he practised under the style 'Booty and Edwards'. However, Edwards soon severed his ties with Booty and, in 1927, invited H. H. Reid and R. G. Booth to join him as partners under the name 'Edwards, Reid and Booth'. Reid had studied in Aberdeen at the Grey School of Art and worked for a time in Bolton with Bradshaw, Gas and Hope, before joining the Ceylon PWD in 1923. He had worked on the design for the new Parliament and been involved in a number of archaeological surveys. R. G. Booth was a graduate of the Architectural Association in London and was a highly skilled draughtsman.

Over the next ten years Edwards, Reid and Booth became the most successful architects in Colombo, attracting work from the government, the commercial sector and private clients. The practice was run along similar lines to practices in India and other parts of Britain's Eastern Empire: the partners were all British, while the assistants and secretarial staff were Ceylonese. Some senior assistants had studied architecture in India while the draughtsmen and technicians were encouraged to attend night classes at the Maradana Technical College. The partners enjoyed prominent positions in Colombo society and lived in large bungalows in Colombo's southern suburbs, working a three-year tour of duty followed by six months of fully paid leave in Britain.

E. R. & B. had a reputation for good planning, competent detailing and solid professionalism. Typically, their buildings employed heavy masonry construction with deep window reveals, generous ventilation openings and sunscreens, and achieved reasonable levels of comfort in the tropical climate. Their architecture was fairly eclectic, embracing 'colonial

R. G. Booth, S. J. Edwards and
H. H. Reid

classical', Art Deco and Moderne styles, often embellished with decorative devices culled from traditional and classical Sri Lankan architecture. Many of their buildings have survived to this day and become familiar monuments.

In the Colombo Fort area they rebuilt the Grand Oriental Hotel and designed the Gaffoor Building, the Times Building and the Chartered Bank. Outside the central district they built the chapel of St. Joseph's College, the flats at Galle Face Court, the Colombo Art Gallery, a chapel and classroom blocks for Ladies' College, the main grandstand of the Colombo racecourse, the Regal Theatre and the Mount Lavinia Hotel. They also built cinemas, filling stations, factories, showrooms, and offices. Their private houses included a sombre mansion at Nugedolle near Pasyala for the Deraniyagala family, the Obeyesekeras' rocky hideout at Dikkande near Nittambuwe, and the Villa Venezia in Colombo's Queen's Road.

Colombo's racecourse has long since disappeared under a mess of piecemeal development, but the massive grandstand still stands as a neoclassical memorial to British colonialism. The Art Gallery on Sir Ananda Coomaraswamy Mawatha was designed as a plain neoclassical composition with Sinhalese trimmings. The main gallery is illuminated and ventilated from hidden clerestory windows, which line the perimeter walls and produce a beautiful even light on the paintings.

The period between the wars was the 'Indian Summer' of the plantation industry and Edwards, Reid and Booth built at least twenty tea-estate bungalows, as well as the famous Hill Club at Nuwara Eliya. The bungalows were invariably situated in commanding positions with stunning views of mountain scenery, designed in an Arts and Crafts style, with low hipped roofs clad with timber shingles. An exception was the imposing stone villa at Adesham, built for Sir Thomas Villiers.

Edwards used his link with Booty to secure commissions from abroad and designed new university buildings in Madras, the Racing Club in Karachi, a hotel in Penang and Raffels College in Singapore. His first commission, the Colombo Town Hall, remained his most prestigious and, though today it still offers a monumental presence, it speaks unequivocally of empire and appears very much as a 'foreign body'.

Reid retained an interest in the ancient architecture of Ceylon and was responsible for remodelling the Kelaniya temple on the outskirts of Colombo and for adding new buildings to the Temple of the Tooth in Kandy, creating a courtyard around the central shrine as well as the platforms and staircases now used by pilgrims. The supervision of the rebuilding of the Kelaniya Temple was one of the practice's most important commissions. It was seen as a project of great national and cultural significance in the years leading up to independence. The *dagoba*, dating from the third century, is believed to mark the spot where the Buddha once set foot on the island of Lanka and the destruction of the whole complex by the Portuguese in 1575 is remembered as an act of colonial barbarity. The impetus to rebuild the temple was born out of the Buddhist renaissance of the early years of the twentieth century and the revival of the annual Kelaniya *Perahera* (a Buddhist procession held on the night of a full moon). The programme was largely funded by the Wijewardene family, owners of Associated Newspapers.

Reid was appointed architect for the reconstruction of the main image house or *patimaghara* in 1927 and acted as an adviser on the remodelling of the whole temple precinct, working closely with Buddhist scholars and the monks of the temple until final completion in 1946. His designs took their inspiration from the fourteenth-century shrines of Lankatilaka and Gadaladeniya and sparked off a new interest in classical

Top: Colombo Town Hall
Centre: Prince Building, Prince Street, Colombo Fort
Right: St. Joseph's College Chapel, Darley Road, Colombo

Opposite
Bottom left: Galle Face Court, Galle Road, Colombo
Top right: Kelaniya Temple
Centre right: The Hill Club, Nuwara Eliya
Bottom right: Colombo Art Gallery

architecture and traditional craftsmanship. Running friezes of carved swans, imps and elephants decorate the plinth, copied from the Tivanka image house at Polonnaruwa, and the main façade is punctuated by free-standing and engaged Kandyan columns, which support a projecting cornice. The interiors were decorated with murals and painted ceilings by the artist Solis Mendis, signalling the emergence of what was to become a new but short-lived school of modern temple painting.

Reid's work at Kelaniya and Kandy is accepted today as part of the 'inheritance of the past' and few are aware that these important national monuments were designed during the 1930s by a Christian Scot from Aberdeen. The Kelaniya temple was highly influential and inspired a number of misguided attempts to re-create a Sinhalese 'national style' based on random bor-rowings from historical sources. These included the Peradeniya University Campus (1942–52), designed by Shirley de Alwis as a lumbering collection of pavilions embellished with pseudo-Sinhalese motifs, and the Independence Memorial in Colombo (1953), designed by Neville Wynne-Jones as a scaled-up model of the Kandy Audience Hall in reinforced concrete. Both are remarkable only for their lack of authenticity and inappropriate fusion of old forms with new methods of construction.

In 1932 Edwards, Reid and Booth moved to new premises in the Prince Building in Prince Street. Booth quit in 1935, to be replaced by K. G. Begg, a shadowy figure who stayed for only four years but gave his name to the practice. Edwards retired in 1936 and Begg resigned in 1939 to enlist for war service.

During the war years, work was at a low ebb and Reid acted as head of Colombo's Civil Emergency Services, keeping Edwards, Reid and Begg ticking over with a skeleton staff. After the war he had to rebuild the practice virtually from scratch and, as independence approached, he took in Jimmy Nilgiria

as his 'local partner'. Nilgiria was a Colombo Parsee who had trained at the 'JJ' School in Bombay. He was a popular figure and a keen Rotarian but an incompetent architect. They were joined after 1948 by an Englishman called Morris Russell. The workload increased after independence and Reid was able to pay himself what was then a princely salary of £9,000 per year.

In 1951 the practice was responsible for planning the Colombo Plan Exhibition in collaboration with the British designer Misha Black. It was during this period that Reid agreed to allow Geoffrey Bawa to work with him for a trial period, helping to plan a number of temporary buildings for the exhibition and to design a private house.

Reid suffered a heart attack during a site visit and died in March 1952 at the age of fifty-five. He had intended to pass the practice on to his son, who had recently qualified as an architect, but Nilgiria exercised his rights under their partnership agree-ment and bought Reid's share from his widow. Reid's son came out to Colombo and tried to establish a foothold in the practice but was frustrated by Nilgiria and returned to Britain in 1955.

Following Reid's death, the practice went into a decline. Nilgiria acted as general manager while Russell ran the design office. Between 1953 and 1957 they built the Savoy and the Liberty cinemas, the Rowlands car showroom and a string of undistinguished houses. It was said that Nilgiria showed little interest in design and would set his draughtsmen to copy plans from American magazines. Russell quit the practice in 1957 and returned to Britain, leaving Nilgiria as sole partner. Nilgiria was a good networker but recognized his own short-comings as an architect: he needed qualified assistants to keep the office alive. When Geoffrey Bawa and Valentine Gunasekera, both former employees, returned to Colombo with AA diplomas in 1957 he offered them jobs as '10 per cent partners'.

When Geoffrey Bawa returned to Colombo in 1957 at the age of thirty-eight almost ten years had slipped by since Ceylon had shaken off the shackles of empire, ten years since Bawa, abandoning his dreams of a sybaritic life on an Italian hillside, had bought his beloved estate at Lunuganga. Through these years he had dreamed of becoming an architect and had stumbled, sometimes aimlessly, towards his chosen profession. Now the dreaming could stop and he could start building.

Political and social change

Bawa's return coincided with the end of a decade of stability and political consensus in Ceylon, and the beginning of a new period of pluralism and uncertainty. The early years of his professional career would be set against a background of economic constraint, social upheaval and increased communal tension.

Ceylon's transition in 1948 from British colony to independent dominion within the British Commonwealth had been both smooth and peaceful. The elections of 1947 had brought victory to D. S. Senanayake's United National Party (UNP), a centre party that included Tamils, Muslims and Christians as well as Sinhalese Buddhists. In foreign affairs Senanayake pursued a policy of non-alignment, while on the home front he maintained a separation of state and religion. The economy was

relatively strong, thanks to high world commodity prices, and the government was in a position to pursue welfare policies that supported free education and health and provided subsidized rice rations for the poor. However, communal tensions were never far from the surface and there was growing restlessness among the large number of Tamil estate workers of Indian origin who had been denied citizenship.

The first cracks in the consensus emerged in 1951 when S. W. R. D. Bandaranaike quit the UNP to form the Sri Lanka Freedom Party (SLFP) under a broadly Sinhalese Nationalist programme. In the 1956 elections the SLFP joined other small parties to form the People's United Front (MEP) and swept into power on a largely Buddhist Nationalist vote. Bandaranaike launched a programme of state control with the nationalization of public transport. Although he favoured a federal solution to the ethnic problem, he was increasingly boxed into a corner by the more extreme elements in his coalition. Tragically and ironically, in September 1959 he was assassinated by a Buddhist monk.

Bandaranaike's death threw the country into turmoil but after two elections the SLFP was re-elected in 1960 under the leadership of Bandaranaike's widow, Sirimavo, who became the world's first woman prime minister. Mrs Bandaranaike introduced land reforms to help the

landless peasants of the Kandyan region and, following her husband's commitment to nationalization, took over the oil industry, while Catholic and Muslim schools were also brought under state control. In 1965, however, the UNP was re-elected under Dudley Senanayake, who succeeded in improving food production but failed to stimulate the economy.

The period from 1948 to 1970 also witnessed massive social and economic change. The population grew from seven million in 1948 to thirteen million in 1970, provoking problems of landlessness and unemployment in the countryside and triggering rapid expansion of the urban population, particularly in and around Colombo. Once a small, verdant town, Colombo had sprawled to accommodate the ranks of the urban poor and the new middle classes. Increasing densities and growing urban unemployment exacerbated already fragile intercommunal tensions and successive governments struggled with sporadic outbreaks of ethnic violence. For the first time housing was recognized by the government as a problem and half-hearted attempts were made to improve the decaying slums of the central districts and discourage the growth of shanty settlements on the marshes to the east. The middle classes, meanwhile, were building houses in the gardens of their grandparents on ever-decreasing plots.

Steel Corporation Offices, Oruwela

Top: Chatham Street, Colombo
Fort in the early 1960s
Middle: The Independence
Memorial, Colombo, 1951
Bottom: Peradeniya University,
Kandy, 1949

The architectural profession

In 1957 the architectural profession in Ceylon was still in its infancy and the total number of qualified architects in Colombo was probably less than twenty. This included a handful of European architects such as Bawa's friend Neville Wynne-Jones who had 'stayed on' after independence, and the few Ceylonese architects who had studied abroad. There was no institute of architects and no school of architecture, though courses in building construction were offered at Maradana Technical College. Major public buildings were still designed and built by the Public Works Department, which employed a few architects but was staffed mainly by engineers and locally trained draughtsmen. A small number of private practices were in operation but, with the exception of E. R. & B., the expatriate architecture offices that had flourished before independence had disappeared. In the towns run-of-the-mill buildings were put up by local contractors, often Muslim, to designs by moonlighting PWD draughts-men, while in the villages buildings were still either self-built or built by the local *baas* (craftsmen).

The architecture of the period after independence was largely uninspired. In deference to the spirit of independence public buildings were expected to make overt reference to Kandyan and classical Sinhalese motifs. Thus the new university campus at Peradeniya was designed in 1949 by Shirley de Alwis as a picturesque composition of heavyweight pavilions decked out with Kandyan roofs and pseudo-Kandyan decorations, while the Independence Memorial in Colombo was designed by Wynne-Jones in 1951 as a grotesque, double-sized, reinforced-concrete replica of the timber Audience Hall of the kings of Kandy. A few commercial buildings appeared in

a clean modern style, influenced by the 1951 Festival of Britain, while private houses were built in a variety of post-colonial and post-Hollywood styles.

However, the year 1957 did see a small group of architects come together to form the Ceylon Institute of Architects. Modelled very much along the lines of the Royal Institute of British Architects, in 1960 the new body was granted 'Allied Society' status by its parent institute.

Ee-are-and-bee

Valentine Gunasekera, Bawa's former colleague at E. R. & B. and fellow AA graduate, was a talented architect as well as a devoted Catholic with a puritanical streak who took his work very seriously. He and Bawa had avoided each other during their time at the AA: Gunasekera disliked Bawa's flamboyant lifestyle, while Bawa was irritated by Gunasekera's zeal. Jimmy Nilgiria persuaded them both to rejoin Edwards, Reid and Begg, partly because he needed their talents and partly to ensure that they did not join a rival firm. Bawa, no doubt using his legal training, drew up a partnership agreement that gave the junior partners the option to buy out Nilgiria at the end of three years.

The office at this time was located in the Prince Building in the Fort. Among the existing staff were Stanley Perera, Nihal Amarasinghe and Turner Wickramasinghe. Perera was an experienced technician who had studied at Maradana Technical College. He was a cousin of the LSSP politician N. M. Perera and through his political connections was to prove a useful asset both in attracting government work and in obtaining statutory consents. Amarasinghe and Wickramasinghe were employed as trainee draughtsmen but both later went to London, where Amarasinghe studied at the AA and Wickramasinghe at the Regent Street Polytechnic.

Although Bawa had almost no experience of working in an architectural practice, he was now expected to take charge of a busy office. Jimmy Nilgiria preferred to spend his time at the Rotary Club looking for new commissions and was happy to leave matters of design and office management to his new partners. Almost immediately Bawa found himself dealing with clients, supervising design teams and managing work on site.

His first task was to complete the design of a house for the Deraniyagala family, which had started back in 1951 before he left for England (p.62). Although he was less than satisfied with the final outcome, the Deraniyagalas were well connected and this commission soon led to others. The practice had acted as architects for most of Colombo's major private schools and Bawa also took charge of two school projects as well as being given responsibility for a number of the commercial jobs.

Ulrik Plesner

In 1958 Bawa was introduced to a young Danish architect called Ulrik Plesner at the Queen's Hotel in Kandy. Plesner had arrived in Ceylon at the end of 1957 to work in the office of Minette de Silva, who had studied architecture in Bombay and at the AA in London, becoming the first Asian woman member of the RIBA in 1948. In 1950 she set up an office in Kandy and during the following decade built a series of innovative houses in Kandy and Colombo. Her sister Anil was one of the founders of the Bombay-based journal *MARG*, which in 1953 carried de Silva's account of her Kurunaratne House and a brief exposition of her ideas for a 'modern regional architecture in the Tropics' (de Silva 1953). Her buildings and writings inspired a whole generation of young Sri Lankan architects and, though she and Bawa were not the best of friends,

Left: Minette de Silva on site
at Watapiluwa, Kandy in 1957
Centre: Ulrik Plesner
Right: Plesner and Bawa at
Lunuganga

there can be little doubt that de Silva's early designs were an important influence for him.

Plesner was becoming increasingly exasperated with the eccentric ways of his employer and was bored by provincial life. De Silva was an inspired architect but she had an overbearing manner and was forever falling out with clients and contractors. As a result she often failed to collect fees and was unable to pay him a regular salary. Bawa was up in Kandy for a weekend party at a tea estate and invited Plesner to accompany him. The other guests included Benjamin Britten and Peter Pears as well as a cross-section of Colombo society, and the weekend gave Plesner a peep of what life in Colombo might offer. When Bawa invited him to come and work with Edwards, Reid and Begg, Plesner accepted immediately.

At first Nilgiria would employ Plesner only as a freelance, though he recognized that a European assistant would impress the expatriate commercial companies that supplied the practice with the bulk of its fee-earning work. Plesner worked initially

on new favtory buildings for Lever Brothers and Baur & Co (1959; p.70) and an industrial estate at Ekala (1959; p.70). He soon began to work more and more with Bawa, however, and came to be regarded as his *de facto* partner.

Between 1959 and 1965 Plesner and Bawa were almost inseparable: during the week they worked long into the night together, dined together, talked architecture together; at weekends they went on trips around Sri Lanka to look at old buildings, or they retired to Lunuganga to work on the garden. Each had his own projects, though they regularly conferred and shared advice. As partners each could supply what the other lacked: Plesner offered technical skills and professional know-how and he was also an inventive designer with strong ideas of his own; Bawa had good taste, a sure eye and a depth of knowledge and experience gained from years of travel.

They first worked together on a number of school and industrial projects. Bawa was still very much influenced by his memories of the AA in London and the battles that

raged between supporters of Mies and Corb. Plesner had grown up with the Scandinavian Modernism of the early 1950s, which valued simple abstract functionalism and honest use of natural materials. Their early projects adopted the Tropical Modernist mode that had been promoted by the AA's Tropical School and was associated with such architects as Maxwell Fry and Jane Drew. The classroom extensions for St. Thomas's Preparatory School (1957; p.66) and for Bishop's College (1960; p.67), and the industrial estate at Ekala were designed as white cubic architecture with sharp-edged prismatic forms and elegant *brise-soleil* façades. These buildings looked superb in strong sunlight but were not really suited to the humid monsoon conditions that usually prevailed in Ceylon.

Although pitched roofs were anathema to International Modernists, logic suggested that buildings in the Tropics needed to be protected from the sun and the beating rain by generous roofs with overhanging eaves. Bawa and Plesner came to realize that the use of such traditional roof forms

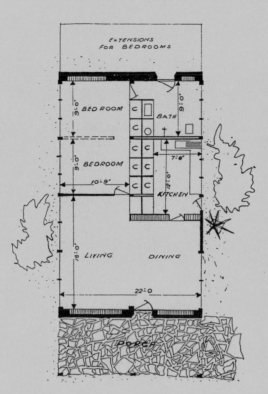

would enable them to achieve other Modernist goals such as open room planning and the free flow of space between inside and outside. At the same time Bawa also came to accept that, instead of trying to achieve crisp whiteness, the architect working in a hot and humid climate should accept the inevitability of decay and exploit the patinas that inevitably develop. This thinking led to the design of the long sweeping roof on the A. S. H. de Silva House in Galle (1959; p.71) and the adoption of a more traditional palette of materials for the Ena de Silva House in Colombo (1960; p.74), culminating in the design of the estate bungalow at Polontalawa, where the house was reduced to a simple roof spanning between two existing boulders (1963; p.93).

It is difficult to disentangle the work that Bawa and Plesner did together during this period. Later, after their acrimonious separation, they came to a gentleman's agreement that, amongst other things, attributed the Bandarawela Chapel and the Polontalawa Bungalow to Plesner and the two de Silva houses to Bawa. All the evidence suggests that they worked together on these projects and that each contributed in their different way. Plesner certainly played a crucial role in helping an inexperienced Bawa to find his feet and contributed enormously to the development of Bawa's design philosophy.

The Shell Ideal Home, Colombo, 1959
In July 1959 an Ideal Home Exhibition was held in the grounds of St. Bridget's Convent overlooking the south side of

the Viharamahadevi Park in Colombo. Inspired by similar exhibitions in Britain, it offered advice on modern living to Colombo's new middle class. The Shell Petroleum Company commissioned E. R. & B. to design an exhibition stand in the form of a prototype prefabricated house to be built on a plot of 19 perches (475 square metres), which at the time was considered small. The house would incorporate labour-saving devices such as a vacuum cleaner, a refrigerator and a kerosene cooker. The 72-square-metre plan incorporated a sitting room opening onto a covered verandah, two bedrooms, a bathroom, a kitchen and a prefabricated central storage and service core. A precast-concrete frame supported a roof of timber rafters, boards and half-round tiles, and the walls were standard timber-framed panels.

Top: Steel Corporation
exhibition tower, 1963
Middle: Pherooze Choksy
and Anura Ratnavibushana
on site at Beruwana in 1966

Bawa had not yet begun to formulate a response to the problem of the tropical urban house, and it could be said that this project represents a missed opportunity. The plan was similar to that adopted for British prefabs after World War II and made few concessions to conditions in Colombo: it was 'post-colonial' in spirit and offered a version of the bungalow dream that figured in Hollywood movies of the 1950s. Although a few examples were built on the outskirts of Colombo, the design had little impact and was soon forgotten. However, the project led to a further commission from Shell to design a company bungalow in Anuradhapura in 1960, as well as serving to bring the practice to the attention of the nuns of the Good Shepherd Convent.

Office colleagues

In the absence of an architectural school Bawa hired people who had trained at Maradana Technical College or who could demonstrate some talent for drawing. Amongst his early recruits were S. Narasingham, Laki Senanayake and Ismeth Raheem, the latter two both founder members of Colombo's 'Young Artists Group' who found casual work as draughtsmen in various architects' offices. Senanayake, a largely self-taught painter and sculptor, had enormous talents as a draughtsman and soon developed skills as a technician and designer, becoming one of Bawa's favourite assistants and working on all the key projects of the period.

In 1961, thanks largely to Justin Samarasekera, a school of architecture opened at Katubedde Technical College in Moratuwa, offering a three-year course leading to an intermediate diploma. Both Plesner and Bawa agreed to teach at the school, and Plesner in particular gave up much of his free time to help the students. The first batch included Ismeth Raheem

and Anura Ratnavibushana. It was usual at this time for students to pay their way by working as freelance assistants and both Raheem and Ratnavibushana moved promiscuously from one office to another, almost on a day-to-day basis. In 1963 when a number of offices were involved in designing pavilions for the Colombo Industrial Exhibition, Ratnavibushana was working simultaneously for two different architects on two separate pavilions. One of these, designed with Bawa for the Steel Corporation, took the form of a remarkable variant on the Tatlin Tower made from offcuts of steel section.

By 1965 the first students to finish the intermediate diploma at Katubedde were keen to complete their studies in Europe. Plesner persuaded the Danish government to provide three scholarships for students to study in Denmark and in 1966 Ismeth Raheem, Pherooze Choksy and Vasantha Chandraratne (later Jacobsen) were selected to study for two years at the Royal Danish Academy in Copenhagen, later to be joined by Anura Ratnavibushana. The combination of studying for three years in Colombo and two years in Copenhagen proved potent: all four acquitted themselves well in Denmark and returned to Colombo to rejoin Edwards, Reid and Begg as project architects in 1969. In the meantime Turner Wickramasinghe and Nihal Amarasinghe had both completed their studies in London. Bawa had now assembled a team of six talented and fully qualified architects.

Home and office

At the beginning of the 1960s Bawa responded instinctively to shifts in the spatial organization of Colombo and moved both his home in Galle Face Court and the E. R. & B. office in Prince Street away from the central business district into an area known as Colpetty on the landside of the Galle Road. Although the plots of

Colpetty's grand nineteenth-century villas had been subject to the subdivision spreading throughout the city, by 1960 the area still had the ambience of a garden suburb, with tree-lined streets running east–west between Galle and Thurston roads, serving a secondary grid of north–south lanes.

Bawa rented the third in a row of four small bungalows occupying a tiny cul-de-sac at the end of 33rd Lane off Bagatelle Road and converted it into a small *pied-à-terre* with a sitting room, bedroom and room for a servant. He later persuaded the owner, Harold Pieris, a wealthy patron of the arts, to sell him the whole row and set about remodelling all four houses to create the labyrinth of courtyards, rooms and verandahs that would become his town house.

In 1961 Bawa was commissioned to build a substantial house for a Burgher doctor called Bartholomeusz on land behind Alfred House in Colpetty that also belonged to Pieris (1961; p.84). When Bartholomeusz suddenly emigrated to Australia leaving Pieris with a half-completed shell, Bawa persuaded his partners to take over the house as their office. Consisting of a sequence of three pavilions separated by courtyards and connected by a central axial loggia and secret staff corridor, the house came to be known as 'Number 2'.

The relationship of the various partners was graphically expressed in the layout of the new office. The first pavilion served as a gatehouse and storeroom; the first courtyard was used as a car park for the partners and their clients; the second pavilion became the design office, and the pool court was used as a reception area. The ground floor of the third pavilion was allocated to Bawa and Plesner, while the upper floor was given over to the main drawing office. Bawa occupied a fixed

desk on the cross-axis of the main ground-floor room in a position that signified his seniority. This gave him an oblique view of all the comings and goings along the main axis of the pool court and enabled him to observe the waiting area without himself being seen. When unwelcome visitors appeared, Bawa would escape down the secret corridor. Plesner sat opposite Bawa in a position that implied a near equality of status, while Nilgiria occupied a small corner office on the first floor, and Valentine Gunasekera and his staff were relegated to a cramped room in part of the middle pavilion.

Bawa preferred to spend weekends at Lunuganga and would often invite friends down for Sunday or *Poya* lunch. Saturday, however, would be devoted to the garden: trees had to be pruned, new planting organized and projects hatched. During this period Bawa opened up the vista from the south terrace of the bungalow, cutting a swathe through the rubber plantation and lowering the summit of Cinnamon Hill to create a view across the lake

towards a distant Buddhist temple. He also remodelled the northern terraces to create the Middle Walk and the Scala Danese. This activity was described in great detail by Ulrik Plesner in his article 'A Ten-Year-Old Garden in Ceylon' (Plesner 1959b).

The tropical urban house

Bawa's move away from the Fort coincided with the beginning of a further wave of densification in Colombo's residential suburbs. The new middle classes wanted to be close to the centre of town and the elite schools and as demand for houses increased plot sizes shrank, making it more and more unfeasible to build colonial-style bungalows in the middle of generous gardens. Designed as it was originally as a house, Bawa's new office served as the flagship for a new style of urban living and demonstrated that high levels of openness, ventilation and privacy could be achieved when the traditional house was turned inside out and the garden brought to the centre of the

plan. The houses that Bawa designed for Ena de Silva and Chris Raffel (1962) drew on the forgotten traditions of the medieval manor house, the Dutch courtyard house and the Muslim row house to offer a new concept of urban living in a dense tropical city. The perimeter garden was replaced by inward-looking, open-to-the-sky courtyards with loggias and covered verandahs, balconies and roof terraces. Bawa's designs inspired other architects and, by the end of the 1960s, the courtyard house had been accepted as a prototype for urban living. With the process of densification continuing apace, by the end of the 1970s the inward-looking house had become so commonplace that few people could appreciate just how radical a proposition it had been only twenty years earlier. When the Ena de Silva House was built, a plot size of 30 perches (750 square metres) was considered small. By 1967 Bawa was able to demonstrate with the Keuneman House (1967; p.95) that a plot size of less than 10 perches (250 square metres) was perfectly feasible.

Artists and friends

Bawa and Plesner both sought to encourage young artists and designers and used every opportunity to persuade their clients to buy good paintings and well-designed fabrics. As Bawa's confidence increased he sought to influence, if not control, the way that clients lived in his houses, and as part of his 'after-sales-service' he would advise them on what furniture and paintings to buy and on how to arrange them.

Plesner was more gregarious than Bawa, who often seemed shy and reserved in public. Between them they gathered together a circle of young artists and designers and introduced them to a new generation of art lovers. Bawa was keen to use his expanding house in 33rd Lane as an informal gallery and it became the centre of an ever-changing group of like-minded people.

Soon after Plesner moved to Colombo he came to know the Australian painter Donald Friend, who was living in a small house on Bevis Bawa's estate. Plesner recognized Friend's special talent and persuaded the German Cultural Institute to sponsor an exhibition of his work in 1960. He also obtained a commission for Friend to create a huge glazed-tile mural along the front of Baur's new factory building in Jethawana Road – a project that, although never realized, led to further commissions for Baur's offices in the Fort and Mckinnon MacKenzie. Bawa bought a number of Friend's pieces for himself and persuaded his clients to do likewise.

Friend was experimenting with a range of new media in his work at this time, using gold leaf, aluminium and terracotta. His paintings ranged from huge city panoramas to delicate images of exotic birds and plants and included a series of exquisitely decorated door panels. He was a larger-than-life figure, a heavy drinker subject to wild mood swings, but he was a generous teacher, particularly helpful to Laki Senanayake and Ismeth Raheem, offering advice and technical guidance, and through them he influenced a whole generation of Sri Lankan painters. Laki Senanayake went on to become one of the most talented artists of his generation and adorned Bawa's buildings with an unending stream of sculptures, murals and paintings. Raheem inclined more towards a career in architecture, but he produced an arresting series of metal reliefs, many of which can still be seen in public buildings in Colombo. Friend's example influenced their paintings and sculptures and also led to the evolution of the draughting style that became the stock-in-trade of the Bawa office.

Another key figure in the circle of artists was Barbara Sansoni. In 1959 Bawa spent five months on a 'Leadership Scholarship' in the United States. He took advantage of this opportunity to travel, visiting buildings by Mies van der Rohe and Frank Lloyd Wright and spending six weeks in Mexico. During Bawa's absence Plesner designed an extension to the home of Barbara and Hilden Sansoni in Anderson Road and moved in as their tenant. This was the first of Plesner's simple 'roof houses': a double-pitched roof covered both the cellular two-storey living core and the double-height living room, with free-standing walls dividing the space into a variety of garden and pool courts.

Barbara Sansoni was a distant cousin of Bawa and a self-trained artist with a strong eye for colour and an interest in textiles. During the 1960s she established weaving factories with the nuns of the Good Shepherd Convent, and built up a highly innovative and successful design business in Colombo. She became a close friend of both Plesner and Bawa, and her company supplied the fabrics and fittings for many of Bawa's later projects.

Top left: Barbara Sansoni with
examples of her fabrics in 2000
Top centre: Drawing of Padeniya
Temple by Barbara Sansoni
Top right: Drawing of two
boys by Laki Senanayake in the
guest room at Lunuganga
Middle left: Batik ceiling
panel for the Bentota Beach
Hotel by Ena de Silva

The year Plesner had spent with Minette de Silva in Kandy had awakened an interest in the traditional architecture of Ceylon and in 1960, with the support of Barbara Sansoni, Laki Senanayake, and Ismeth Raheem he launched a project to identify and record the old architectural traditions of Ceylon. Over the next few years the four of them would set out on regular weekend explorations armed with cameras, sketch pads and surveying equipment. Together they recorded many forgotten buildings from the Portuguese, Dutch and British periods. Bawa occasionally accompanied them on their outings but he didn't participate in the work. He already knew some of the buildings and was slightly bemused by his friends' enthusiasm. However, there is little doubt that he took more than a passing interest in the results of their efforts, and that many of their insights later informed his designs.

The results of this work were first published by Sansoni and Plesner, under the names Simon and Claude in the *Ceylon Daily Mirror*. Later Sansoni published a collection of her own sketches and observations in a book, *Viharas and Verandahs* (Sansoni 1978), and later still she incorporated much of the original survey material in *The Architecture of an Island* (Lewcock et al. 1998). The project did much to draw attention to Ceylon's fast-disappearing heritage of buildings from many different periods, and may well have been instrumental in halting the destruction of at least a few of them.

The batik artist Ena de Silva entered Bawa's life as a suspicious client but she also became a close friend and collaborator. The house he designed for her in 1960 included a batik studio, and once it was completed Ena de Silva established herself as Ceylon's foremost batik artist and designer. She was later joined by Laki Senanayake, who had decided that architecture was not for him. Bawa used Ena de Silva's work in many of his buildings: her batiks covered the ceiling of the Bentota Beach Hotel and her huge flags, based on the traditional and *korale* flags, were hung in the piazza in front of Bawa's Parliament building in Kotte.

Office politics

Jimmy Nilgiria was increasingly forced to take a back seat in the practice and things were managed jointly by Bawa and Gunasekera. In 1961 Bawa invoked the partnership agreement and put pressure on Nilgiria to resign. Nilgiria demanded a termination payment of 100,000 rupees for his name and good will but, as neither Bawa nor Gunasekera could afford such a sum, he remained as a sleeping partner.

From the outset Bawa and Gunasekera had worked on separate projects and had built up their own teams within the office. Bawa belonged more to the functionalist wing of modern architecture, while Gunasekera, who had worked with Eero Saarinen in the United States, was more of an Expressionist. Bawa once said of Gunasekera: 'With Valentine there's always too much architecture between you and the landscape!', while Gunasekera felt that Bawa was using architecture to perpetuate the elitism of the '*walaawe* class'.

After 1960 Dr K. Poologasundram, a senior design engineer in the State Cement Corporation, began to moonlight for Bawa as a freelance structural engineer. In 1966 he resigned from the corporation and was about to emigrate to Malaysia when Bawa persuaded him to join E. R. & B. as his partner and office manager.

Poologasundram agreed on condition that he would be given a free hand to 'sort out' outstanding partnership issues with Nilgiria and Gunasekera and to 'regularize' the position of Ulrik Plesner.

The year 1966 also saw a cooling-off in the friendship between Bawa and Plesner that soured their working relationship. Bawa had become increasingly jealous of Plesner's popularity, his many friendships and his wide range of interests; Plesner resented Bawa's tendency to take all the credit for projects they had worked on together. Things were brought to a head by the arrival in Ceylon of Plesner's friend Tamar Liebes, whom he later married.

During 1966 Plesner worked on three ill-fated projects: a new television station funded by the East German government, a hotel design at Pegasus Reef for BOAC and a Hilton Hotel in Colombo. When the Hilton project was cancelled in mid-1967, Plesner quit E. R. & B. to join Arup Associates in London. Of his relationship with Bawa, Plesner has said:

Our partnership was like a marriage, a platonic marriage of minds, not one of use and misuse, of master and servant. It was choreographed like Laurel and Hardy. We were equals. Humour played a big part. We spent twelve to sixteen hours of every day in each other's company. Our success was based on Geoffrey's flair and my practical abilities. Few partners achieve such symbiosis. We had a shared view but different skills. We brought different things to the partnership. (Ulrik Plesner in conversation with the author, 1999)

There is no doubt that Plesner made a substantial contribution both to the office and to Bawa's personal development. He was the only colleague who became a close friend, and the only friend whom Bawa treated as a working equal. Though Bawa's jealousy probably provoked Plesner's departure – Poologasundram may well have oiled the wheels as well – Bawa was devastated when Plesner left and for a time lost all enthusiasm for his work.

Poologasundram was also concerned that the growing coolness between Bawa

and Valentine Gunasekera made their partnership unviable. He persuaded Gunasekera that it would be in his best interests to start his own practice, and even helped him to find new premises. Gunasekera finally quit in 1968, leaving Poologasundram and Bawa as sole and equal partners of Edwards, Reid and Begg.

The Catholic Church

Bawa's mother was a devout Anglican and his father was the son of a Ceylon Moor who had converted to Christianity, but Bawa himself was agnostic and seems to have had little time for organized religion. His office colleagues were of every religious persuasion and came from every corner of Ceylon's ethnic maze: Sinhalese Buddhists, Tamil Hindus, Muslims, Parsees, Catholics and Anglicans. During the 1960s, however, it was the Catholic Church that favoured Bawa with its commissions.

Barbara Sansoni, a devout Catholic, introduced Bawa and Plesner to Mother Good Counsel, the Good Shepherd Convent's Provincial for the Indian subcontinent. She first commissioned Bawa and Plesner to design the Bandarawela Chapel (1961; p.88) and later was the client for St. Bridget's Montessori (1963; p.68), the Yahapath Endera Farm School (1965; p.89), the Mahahalpe Silk Farm (1969) and the Wattala Convent (1970). It was also on her recommendation that Bawa was appointed by the German charity Misereor to design buildings for the de la Salle Brothers at the boys' orphanage or 'Boys' Town' near Ragama to the north of Colombo in 1963. This in turn led to his being commissioned in 1965 to design a new Boys' Town at Madurai in South India – Bawa's first commission outside Ceylon (1965; p.92). He subsequently designed an Education Centre for the Church at Piliyandela (1978, p.156).

An Irish nun from Tramore whose original name was Eileen Mills, Mother Good Counsel was a woman of enormous energy and conviction who generally succeeded in getting her own way through a combination of stubbornness and piety. She was one of the few people that Bawa held in awe, and the two became the best of friends. The long line of projects that Bawa built for the Catholic Church enabled him to experiment with cheap local materials and traditional building techniques. These projects serve to counter suggestions that Bawa designed only for the Colombo elite: much of the work for the nuns of the Good Shepherd was done for a minimum fee or for no fee at all.

Bottom right: Mother Good Counsel outside Bandarawela Convent Chapel, 1963

Hotels

Until the end of the 1950s Colombo was served by two traditional British hotels dating from the end of the nineteenth century: the Grand Oriental, which lay next to the harbour, and the Galle Face Hotel, which occupied the southern end of the Galle Face Green and framed the beginning of the Galle Road. Both offered that combination of dark polished panelling, white sarong-clad servants and bad food that still passed for British colonial hospitality. Similar hotels existed at Mount Lavinia, Kandy, Galle, Nuwara Eliya and Trincomalee. Outside the main towns travellers had to rely on a network of government rest houses and circuit bungalows, often situated in beautiful locations with breathtaking views. A typical rest house consisted of a line of rooms, each with its own verandah and bathroom, connected by a covered link to a central loggia and dining room.

The arrival of long-haul jet aeroplanes heralded both the end of long-distance sea travel and the beginning of a new kind of package tourism. Ceylon was earmarked by tour operators as an exotic holiday destination: it was still considered to be a safe and peaceful country; its people were literate, anglophone and low paid; it offered tropical beaches and cool mountain retreats, exotic food, mystic religions, lost ancient cities and wildlife parks. All it lacked was a well-developed infrastructure with modern hotels and properly trained staff.

The office's first design for a hotel in Colombo dated to 1961, when the government initiated the Hotel Colombo project in an unsuccessful attempt to persuade the Hilton Group to run a hotel in the city. It would have been located on the east side of the Galle Face Green on the site now occupied by the Taj Samudra. No drawings survive apart from a few sketches that appeared in the Danish magazine *Arkitekten* (Bawa and Plesner 1965b), showing a long, four-storey block emerging from a *piano nobile* of loggias and courtyards raised above a stone-clad podium–basement. The main dining and sitting rooms were placed at fourth-floor level under a vast floating roof similar to that used on St. Bridget's Convent. A further project launched in 1963 for a hotel in Hong Kong also came to nothing.

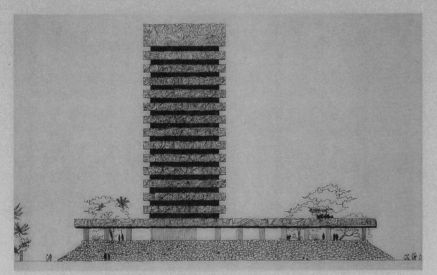

Top: Elevation of the Hilton Hotel, second project – the pavilion scheme of 1965
Middle: Elevation of the Hilton Hotel, third project – the tower scheme of 1967

Opposite
Top: The Blue Lagoon Hotel, Negombo, 1965–66
Bottom: Early elevational sketch of the Bentota Beach Hotel

Two years later a local developer called Cyril Gardiner tried to promote a second Hilton project and negotiated an option to buy a large piece of land between the Galle Road and the Beira Lake owned by the Bishop of Colombo. Bawa produced two alternative schemes, one a tower and the other a group of low hipped-roof pavilions. Of the latter only a set of pencil drawings has survived, revealing the first step in a line of development that led to the Bentota Beach Hotel (1967; p.96) and, many years later, to the Parliament building at Kotte. When the Hilton vice-president saw the designs he apparently pointed to the pavilion scheme and said: 'That's how all architects begin…', and to the tower scheme: '…and that's where we end up!'

The project was revived in 1966 and Cementation, a British developer, was invited to participate. Cementation stipulated that Bawa team up with a British firm of architects and Bawa proposed Maxwell Fry and Jane Drew, whom he had known during his time at the AA. Jane Drew worked in Colombo for a short period, and Plesner in turn worked in Fry Drew's London office. Together they produced designs for a massive twelve-storey slab block with projecting balconies decorated with relief patterns similar to those produced by Anil Jayasuriya for St. Thomas's Preparatory School. But when the scheme was finally presented to Gardiner in mid-1967 it was turned down on the grounds of cost. Fry and Drew were left to sue Cementation for unpaid fees and the site was eventually developed by the Oberoi Group with a design by Skidmore, Owings & Merrill.

The various ideas for a hotel finally came to fruition when in 1965 Bawa was commissioned by G. E. B. Milheusen to build a hotel on a spit of land across the Negombo Lagoon from Colombo's International Airport. The Blue Lagoon was Ceylon's first purpose-built tourist hotel and was designed like a traditional rest house with a central reception building overlooking the lagoon and rooms arranged in individual villas within a coconut grove that ran towards the sea. Although it was set in an ideal location and became a popular destination for day-trippers from Colombo, the hotel eventually failed, mainly because it was too small for package tours.

In 1965 the UNP government decided to play a direct role in the development of tourism and set up the Hotels Corporation as a state-owned enterprise to develop new infrastructure and build and manage

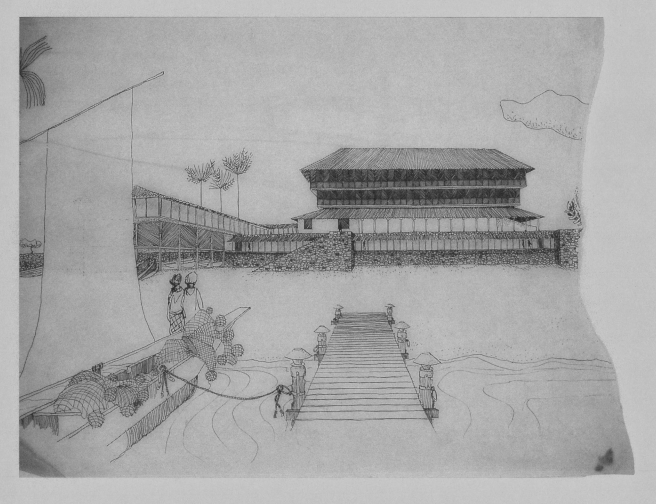

hotels in partnership with the private sector. The new minister for tourism was Bawa's old friend J. R. Jayewardene, and the chairman of the Hotels Corporation was another friend, Cecil de Soysa. Not surprisingly, therefore, Bawa was commissioned to produce a master plan for the first purpose-built resort, located on the west coast at Bentota, chosen because it was relatively close to Colombo and the international airport, lay well beyond the densely built-up coastal towns of Panadura and Kalutara and could offer long stretches of beautiful beaches that were reasonably safe for at least part of the year. The Bentota Beach Resort set standards that were sadly never emulated. Following Bawa's master plan the Hotels Corporation created a tourist village around a pond on the edge of the existing village and built a new railway station, shopping arcade, police station and restaurant. It provided the ideal setting for foreigners to mingle with local people and to buy their produce without hassle and confrontation. Bawa identified sites for half a dozen hotels on the spit of land between the sea and the estuary of the Bentota River and designed two of them himself in 1967. The first of these, the Bentota Beach Hotel, remained one of the most beautiful hotels in Asia until it was savagely remodelled by new owners in 1998.

Recognition

Bawa remained an inveterate traveller and his crowded passports bear witness to his regular visits to Europe and the United States. During the 1960s the architecture of E. R. & B. started to reach a wider audience. The first major article to feature the work of the practice appeared in 1965 under the names Bawa and Plesner in *Arkitekten* (Bawa and Plesner 1965b). After a brief account of Ceylon, its climate and its

architectural traditions, the piece went on to describe the major projects that the duo had completed during the previous eight years. In 1966 an article appeared in the *Architectural Review*, featuring seven of the early buildings, with texts by Bawa himself and photographs mainly by Plesner (Bawa and Plesner 1966a). It is interesting that the images were carefully chosen to emphasize the Modernist aspects of the work and played down its regionalist or vernacular characteristics. The same issue carried a photograph of the Steel Corporation Tower for Colombo's 1963 Industrial Exhibition alongside a set of Barbara Sansoni's drawings of old Ceylonese buildings, wrongly attributed to Bawa and Plesner. Recognition also came in the form of the Pan Pacific Citation of the Hawaii Chapter of the American Institute of Architects. The award was made in Bawa's name only and made no reference to the official title of the practice or to Plesner's contribution.

In the following year Bawa came as close as he ever would to publishing a statement about his design philosophy in an article that appeared in the *Times of Ceylon Annual* under the title 'A Way of Building' (Bawa 1968). He began with a reprise of the three great classical tenets – commodity, delight and firmness:

I have always found it difficult to write about architecture, particularly my own. There has been so much dogma and theory put forward over the centuries…that one is hesitant in stating a new set of rules…But there are rules, some old and strong ones. The first is that a building must, at the very least, satisfy the needs that give it birth…The second is that it must be in accord with the ambience of its place…And there is one more, a technical rule: there must be a knowledgeable and true use of materials.

There then follows a discussion on the lessons of history and the need to design

with climate. Finally Bawa suggests that architects must also transcend the rational and enter the realm of the emotions:

At this point the Architect becomes Artist and steps from the relative security of known and learnt things into the world of instinct, inspiration, talent, gift – a world inside his head and far outside it at the same time, almost sub- or super-conscious.

'One unchanging element is the roof – protective, emphatic and all-important – governing the aesthetic whatever the period, whatever the place. Often a building is only a roof, columns and floors – the roof dominant, shielding, giving the contentment of shelter. Ubiquitous, pervasively present, the scale or pattern shaped by the building beneath. The roof, its shape, texture and proportion is the strongest visual factor.'

the projects 1957–69

deraniyagala house

COLOMBO 1951–59

After his return to Colombo in 1957 Bawa quickly set about completing the house for Paul and Preeni Deraniyagala that he had begun in 1951. True to their word, the Deraniyagalas had waited for him to finish his studies and they now expected him to produce a design for a modern house that would echo the lost traditions of a pre-colonial past. Sadly for all concerned the final result was conventional and somewhat clumsy. Its various elements were first separated and then linked asymmetrically to create a series of loosely defined outdoor spaces. A pair of two-storey pavilions – one containing a library and bedrooms, the other a garage – is connected by a single-storey spine block housing the sitting and dining rooms under a large roof terrace to another two-storey pavilion to the rear, in which the kitchens and servants' rooms are located. A long loggia runs the length of the spine from an entrance porch between the two front pavilions to the service block at the back.

The house was built on a concrete frame that is clearly expressed in the bays of the main pavilion and in the cantilevered supports of the connecting spine. The façade bays are infilled with panels of glass, louvre or trellis. Floors are of quarry tile and the roof is covered with half-round tile. The free-standing spiral staircase leading up from the hall was considered daring at the time and offered an immediate clue to the Modernist aspirations of both designer and client. However, this was exactly the sort of gratuitous form-making that Bawa soon came to repudiate. He would later argue that a staircase should be conceived neither as a sculptural object nor as an excuse to perform structural gymnastics but as a spatial experience, the means to move in a significant way between one level and another.

In many ways both the plan and the elevation resemble an unrealized 1946 design by Andrew Boyd for a house in Kandy (Hollamby 1962), and suggest that Bawa was using Boyd's work as the starting point for his own explorations. Neither the architect nor his client was totally happy with the final result and they fell out over the design of the rear block. Bawa remained on good terms with the Deraniyagalas, however, and many of his later clients came from their relatives in the Bandaranaike and Obeyesekera families.

Top left: Front elevation of the Deraniyagala House in 1984

Top right: Spiral staircase in the Deraniyagala House, 1997

Bottom; Ground-floor plan of the Deraniyagala House

carmen gunasekera house

COLOMBO 1958

The brief for the Gunasekera House required the incorporation of a small private Montessori school. Bawa's proposal divided the house into two linked blocks displaced to define two open-sided garden courts. With bedrooms contained in a block to the rear, the school occupied the whole of the lower-ground floor of the front block. Above this was the main living room, which could be reached either from a formal entrance signalled by an elegant cantilevered canopy or via a flight of steps from the garden. An open wall in the living room was protected from rain by an innovative system of pivoting woven-rattan screens.

Bawa had difficulty designing the roof and finally placed opposing single pitches on each block. He was disappointed with the result, however, and as the house neared completion he hired an elephant to move fully grown clumps of bamboo into the front garden to hide the roofs from the street.

Top right: The entrance to the Gunasekera House in 2000

Bottom left: The junction between the two blocks

Bottom right: The tilting rattan screens seen from the living room

At the beginning of their collaboration, Bawa and Plesner worked together on a series of Modernist designs for town houses. Bawa still felt uncomfortable about using duo-pitch or opposed mono-pitched roofs on urban houses and the two architects embarked on a series of experimental frame designs using various types of breathing-wall construction combined with overhanging flat roof decks supported on deep reinforced-concrete beams. The roofs served as paved terraces or roof gardens. The use of 200–300 millimetres of soil added mass and insulation to the roof and planting added shade and induced cooling through evaporation.

Top left: The N. U. Jayawardena House in 1997

Middle left: Cantilevering beams and sun-breakers on the Kanangara House

Centre: The living room of the Kanangara House in 2000

Bottom left: The Wijewardene House seen from Thurston Road in 2000

Opposite: Drawing of the unbuilt Fernando House

jayawardena house

COLOMBO 1959–60

The first such project was a two-storey house that Plesner designed for the banker N. U. Jayawardena in Cambridge Place in Colombo at the end of 1959. This was an elegant essay in concrete-framed construction set behind a contrasting white-painted perimeter wall of rough stone. The flat roof decks were supported on clearly expressed beams and were covered with 250 millimetres of soil that was paved or planted. The house is still in excellent condition and its roof remains both cool and watertight.

wimal fernando house

COLOMBO 1959

The unbuilt Wimal Fernando House design of 1959 further developed the idea of accessible roof terraces, proposing a series of linked pavilions arranged on a loose chequerboard pattern of enclosed and semi-enclosed courtyards located to exploit existing mature trees. A staircase in the double-height living room led to shaded roof terraces and planted areas.

kanangara house

COLOMBO 1959–61

Later in the same year, Bawa designed a similar house for a lawyer called Aelian Kanangara on a tight site at the end of a narrow lane off Horton Place in Colombo. The building's footprint occupied a large proportion of the site and part of the first floor was designed to serve as a terrace and garden. Much of the ground floor was given over to an immense rectangular living area measuring about 9 by 27 metres, which incorporated two small atria and was sandwiched between a pair of bedrooms and the service areas. The roof of this monumental, column-free space was supported by deep lateral beams resting on a system of longitudinal beams and perimeter piers. The bays between the piers were infilled with panels of glass or timber, while the lateral beams projected out from the façade to support concrete sun-and-rain-breakers, the space between providing permanent ventilation. A staircase in the entrance hall rose to a first-floor gallery leading to the main bedroom and library and connected with an open roof terrace and a more enclosed inner courtyard.

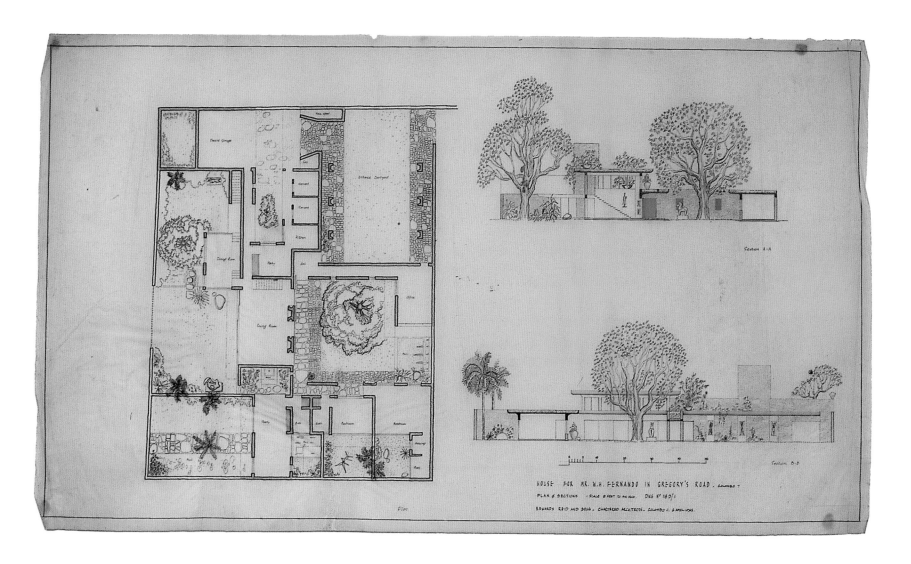

HOUSE FOR MR. W.H. FERNANDO IN GREGORY'S ROAD. COLOMBO 7

PLAN & SECTIONS - SCALE 8 FEET TO AN INCH.   DWG N° 183/1

EDWARDS REID AND BEGG. CHARTERED ARCHITECTS. COLOMBO 1. 3 APRIL 1958.

wijewardene house

The last of the series of 'frame' houses was in
Thurston Road, designed by Bawa in 1959 for Upali
Wijewardene, a wealthy newspaper proprietor and
politician. In this case the exposed concrete frame
was painted black while the infill panels were of
white-painted brickwork. Much of the ground floor
was given over to service spaces and offices, and
the living accommodation was situated at first-
floor level with direct access to the upper roof
terraces. The exposed concrete frames continued
above the second floor parapet to support pergolas
and loggias. The clients later extended the house
upwards to incorporate a rooftop swimming pool
and helicopter pad.

Bawa's designs for schools form part of a series of experiments to develop an effective system of breathing walls. The series begins with the perforated screened walls used at St. Thomas's Preparatory School and culminates in the outward cantilevering floors of the Bentota Beach Hotel and the Steel Corporation Offices. The aim was to find ways of using inexpensive local materials and traditional forms to achieve optimum levels of lighting and ventilation, while protecting the interior from rain and direct sunshine. Although all Bawa's classrooms were built for private schools in Colombo, his design experiment had a considerable influence on the government's school building programme and contributed to the thinking of the Asia Regional Institute for School Building Research, which was based in Colombo during the 1960s.

st. thomas's preparatory school

COLOMBO 1957–64

E. R. & B. received the commission to design new classrooms for St. Thomas's Preparatory School in 1957, before Bawa had joined the practice. The school occupied an exposed site in Colpetty between the Galle Road and the coastal railway line. A general site strategy had already been decided and the accommodation was to be divided between two blocks, one placed parallel to the seashore and the other at right angles. Bawa set himself the task of creating a cool and well-lit environment using a minimum of glass, and his general approach was influenced by the post-Corbusian school of what came to be known as Tropical Modernism.

The block next to the railway consisted of two lower floors of classrooms and an open upper floor that served as an assembly space. The structure was designed as a concrete portal frame with columns set well back from the façade and strongly expressed ridge and eaves beams. The lower floors were enclosed by a breathing wall of hollow concrete blocks – aligned north-west on the west façade and south-east on the east façade to minimize rain penetration during the two monsoons – topped by a glazed horizontal clerestory. Above, the top floor was clad with vertical concrete louvres

and sliding glass screens. The breathing wall functioned well for much of the year, but let in too much spray during the south-west monsoon; Murad Ismail, one of Bawa's later associates and a former pupil at St. Thomas's, recalls that he was often sent home on 'rain days'. The external walls have been replaced by conventional masonry and glass construction.

The second block consisted of two floors of classrooms, its façade given a strong horizontal emphasis by a deep overhanging beam at eaves level and a continuous horizontal spandrel panel at first floor. Bawa invited Ena de Silva's son, Anil Jayasuriya, to design a sculptural concrete frieze to decorate the spandrel and this was created by pouring concrete into sculpted clay moulds. The use of sculptural concrete was still in its infancy, however, and the panels eventually spalled as the sea air attacked the reinforcements, so that only the panels on the east-facing gable survive today. In conversation with Channa Daswatte in 1997, Bawa recalled:

At St. Thomas's there was the possibility of using reinforced concrete in a certain way and to decorate it in a certain way using people like Anil, who was a good sculptor. It was just a matter of using all of our knowledge and capabilities to the fullest extent...there was Sahabdeen, the master mason, there was Anil and there was concrete.

Bottom: An early view of St. Thomas's Preparatory School

bishop's college

COLOMBO 1960–63

In 1960 Bawa prepared a development plan for Bishop's College, a girls' school to the south of the Beira Lake in Colombo, and as a result was asked to build a three-storey classroom block. The new classrooms were placed at first and second-floor level behind a breathing wall, while the ground floor was left open as a covered activity and play area.

The structure was cantilevered outwards from an *in situ* concrete portal frame with exposed beam ends. The floor slabs ended on the line of the structural columns and concrete grilles were supported from the ends of the cantilevers at first and second-floor level so that a stack of air could flow up behind them. The delicacy of the grilles was accentuated by narrow vertical gaps between each panel and by clear horizontal openings running between the beam ends. This clear expression of structural and non-load-bearing elements marked the first appearance of an elevational ordering system that Bawa would return to in a number of projects. Over the years clumsy changes have destroyed the clarity of the structural expression and the efficacy of the ventilation.

When the building was nearing completion Bawa's close friend Lidia Duchini, an Italian sculptress, arrived in Ceylon on a two-week visit and Bawa persuaded her to create the sculpture of a bishop that still stands at the foot of the main staircase. Duchini applied the final layer of gold leaf on the last day of her visit before being rushed to the airport.

Top: The exterior of Bishop's College

Bottom left: The breathing wall at Bishop's College

Bottom right: Exterior view of the ground floor of Bishop's College

st. bridget's montessori school

COLOMBO 1963–64

The Montessori School for the nuns of the Good Shepherd Convent was built in the grounds of St. Bridget's Convent in Colombo in 1963. Bawa developed the design with Laki Senanayake and murals were added by Barbara Sansoni.

Although the rectangular two-floor building is strategically similar to Bawa's earlier classroom blocks, the design abandons white Tropical Modernism in favour of a witty reworking of a traditional 'wattle-and-daub' village school. The upper floor is covered by a huge umbrella of Portuguese tile on cement sheeting that cantilevers far out beyond the perimeter of the classrooms to protect the interior from driving rain and harsh sunlight, its rafters elegantly supported by an articulated concrete frame. The first-floor slab sits on mushroom-topped columns and its soffit is modelled to create a cave-like quality. Open sides and the high roof encourage natural ventilation, and surrounding vegetation helps to cool the air.

Teaching areas are delineated by low walls that create small-scaled enclosures within the megastructure of the roof and the floor slab, while toilet cubicles and storerooms occupy free-standing concrete cells with organic shapes that suggest hollowed-out boulders. Balconies and spiral staircases are cast in rough, curving concrete in a manner that is reminiscent of traditional *pisé* construction, and small openings and decorative features are placed at 'child's-eye level'.

Bawa's architecture was generally rooted in the traditions of functional Modernism and, in spite of his admiration for the Baroque and his love of decoration, he rarely strayed into the realms of Expressionism. Here, however, the skeletal structure, the organic forms and the naïve decorative patterns carry memories of Gaudí's Parc Güell in Barcelona. The classrooms are still in good condition after thirty-five years of constant use, though repainting has destroyed the harmonies of the original colour scheme.

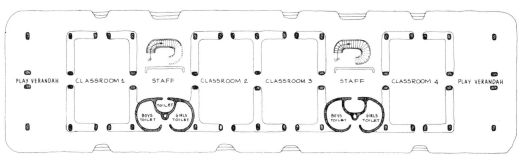

Opposite
Top: St. Bridget's Montessori
School in 1997

Bottom: Elevation and plan of
St. Bridget's Montessori School

This page
Top left: The upper classroom
level

Top centre: An early view
of the staircase with mosaic
decorations by Barbara Sansoni

Top right: The lower classroom
level

Bottom right: The staircase in
1997

ekala industrial estate

JAELA 1959–60

When Ulrik Plesner joined E. R. & B. in early
1959 he worked on a series of commercial
projects. His first job was to finish off a factory
and office building for Lever Brothers in Grand
Pass that had been designed by Morris Russell,
the last of the practice's British associates. He
then designed a warehouse and office building
in Jethawana Road for a Swiss trading company,
Baur & Co, proposing a long street elevation
with expressed beams projecting between
horizontal glazed openings and a blank panel
running the entire length of the façade at first-
floor level. A suggestion to cover this panel with
a glass mural by Donald Friend was scuppered
by a government ban on imports.

Later in 1959 Plesner and Bawa worked together
on Ceylon's first modern industrial estate, built
for the government, although the funding and
briefing came from the United States Agency for
International Development (USAID). The project
was located on a former coconut estate at Ekala
to the south of Katunayake Airport and the aim
was to create low-cost starter factory units in a
variety of sizes, each unit comprising a workshop
with screened cross-ventilation, an office annexe
and a walled yard. This was an essay in simple
clean-lined Tropical Modernism, a composition of
white prismatic with horizontal louvred openings.
It photographed well when it was new but it was
unsuitable for a hot–humid climate: the absence
of an overhanging roof increased solar gain in
hot weather and led to rain penetration during
the monsoons, while the pure white forms soon
developed unsightly stains.

Top right: Early view of the
Lever Brothers Factory

Bottom left: Breathing wall
detail at Ekala in 2000

Bottom right: A factory unit
at Ekala in 2000

a. s. h. de silva house

GALLE 1959–60

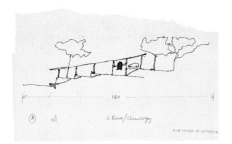

A. S. H. de Silva, a young doctor setting up a practice in Galle, wanted to build a house and surgery on a steeply sloping site on the northern edge of the town and picked Bawa's name out of the local telephone book. Bawa's design deconstructs the colonial bungalow and reassembles the parts in an apparently informal way to create a chequerboard system of linked pavilions trapping small gardens and courts between them. The separate elements are unfettered by a defined boundary but linked by a single roof plane and a long, raking spine wall. The roof design resembles the solution Bawa had recently adopted for a clubhouse at Ratnapura Tennis Club, also situated on a steeply sloping site.

At the foot of the slope sits the doctor's consulting room beside an open loggia that served as the patients' waiting room, connected to the house via a long staircase tunnel. This serves as the boundary to the garden, a pointer to the main entrance of the house and a device to lead the visitor up to the very heart of the design. On plan the main house appears to be a simple rectangle arranged around a central courtyard, though the section articulates the upper bedroom wing from the lower living area. A separate wing containing the kitchens, kitchen courts and servants' rooms between two parallel walls runs southwards from the living area along the contours of the site, while a pavilion to the north contains an independent flat for the doctor's sister. The house remains relatively extrovert: the internal spaces flow out into the gardens, which, in turn, reach out towards the surrounding landscape. The articulation of the plan elements and their disposition on the slope in relation to open courtyards and gardens

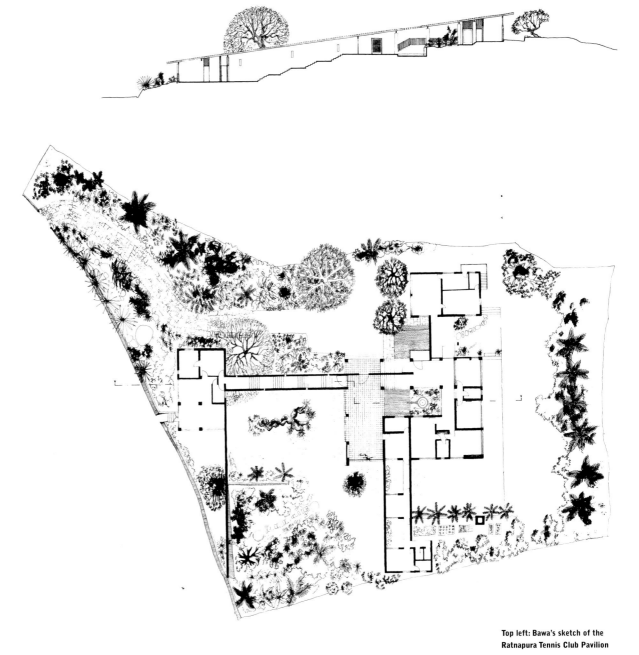

Top left: Bawa's sketch of the Ratnapura Tennis Club Pavilion

Top right: Cross-section through the A. S.H de Silva House

Bottom right: Plan of the A. S.H. de Silva House

makes good environmental sense: every room benefits from cross-ventilation or from a stack effect induced by the roof.

The plan can be compared to Mies van der Rohe's 1923 Brick Villa project, and there are certainly many similarities: both set out to deconstruct the traditional villa, both make a clear distinction between 'wall' and 'no wall', and both use continuing wall planes to link inside and outside space and to define outdoor rooms. But Bawa exploits the sloping site to create additional spatial effects, using the roof plane to anchor the elements to the site. He replaces Mies's solid hearth core with a void so that here, for the first time, an open courtyard occupies the very heart of the plan. While he has arrived at a solution that can be compared to the courtyard or *meda midula* of a traditional Sinhalese manor house, he has come to it on a fairly long and circuitous route. In typical fashion he has taken one idea – the Miesian pinwheel plan – and added others – the sloping roof, the central court – in order eventually to create something quite new.

This was a time of severe economic restraint, with imports strictly controlled. When Bawa wanted to line the central pool with blue glazed tiles Laki Senanayake achieved the desired effect with broken Milk of Magnesia bottles. However, the house's design achieved the synthesis for which Bawa had been striving: clean abstract forms are arranged in an informal way to embrace areas of landscape and to break down the separation of inside from outside.

Bottom left: The entrance to the A. S.H. de Silva House in 1997

Top right: Early view of the entrance

Middle right: Early view of the central court

Bottom right: The central court in 1997

manager's bungalow

STRATHSPEY ESTATE, UPCOT 1959–60

When they were asked to design a manager's bungalow in 1959 on the Strathspey Estate near Maskeliya, at the foot of Adam's Peak in one of the most remote parts of the Tea Country, Bawa and Plesner found themselves creating not a prototype but one of the last of its kind, a memorial to a fast-disappearing way of life.

A tea-estate bungalow can be compared to the concept of *villa suburbana* developed by Andrea Palladio; it is like a noble villa situated at the centre of a working farm. Indeed the design that Plesner and Bawa developed owes something to the Palladian tradition: the bungalow is contained within a formal perimeter of walls and outhouses, overlooking the estate but distanced from it and combining beauty with convenience. The atrium is employed not as a focus of peace in a hostile urban environment but more as a safe haven within a stockaded enclosure at the edge of a wilderness.

The plan was conceived as a rectangular enclosure, subdivided to create a hierarchy of three courtyards. The entrance gate is signalled by a tall square water tower of white-painted rubble at the south-western corner of the enclosure. It leads into an entrance court and is on axis with the main door to the house itself, which occupies slightly more than half the enclosure and focuses on an internal north–south atrium surrounded by a continuous loggia. The main rooms of the house are all arranged around the courtyard with views out towards the north, east and south, while the kitchens and service rooms are located in the west wing. Mono-pitch roofs slope gently in towards the atrium so that the external eaves cantilever up from the perimeter walls as if to draw in the vast panorama of sky and mountain. An open verandah between the dining and living rooms frames views towards the north and can be screened off from both rooms or from the outer garden by a system of sliding panels.

The bungalow was built by a local contractor and most of the materials were found on or near the site: the walls of white-painted rubble have large openings infilled with glass or timber and the floors are of polished black stone. Today the house is shrouded by trees and neat rows of vegetables have replaced the old croquet lawns.

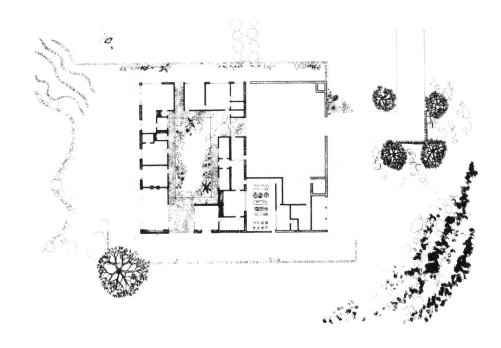

Top: Plan of the Strathspey Manager's Bungalow

Middle: Early view of the water tower and entry court

Bottom: Early view of the living room showing the sliding screens pulled back to create an open verandah

house for osmund and ena de silva

COLOMBO 1960–62

The de Silvas wanted to build a house on a corner site of 30 perches (750 square metres) in Alfred Place bought for 180,000 rupees. All their friends advised that it was too small and overpriced. Colombo was now growing quickly, however, and the price of land in good locations was rising as the gardens of nineteenth-century villas were divided and subdivided. But as plot sizes shrank, the inadequacies of the typical colonial bungalow plan became more and more apparent: it gave little aural or visual privacy and was difficult to ventilate.

Ena de Silva relates how she had interviewed four different architects before her friend Bevis Bawa finally introduced her to his brother. She had seen Bawa driving around in his Rolls with his scarf blowing in the wind and was repelled by his dilettante image. When they met, however, her prejudices evaporated and as the design developed they became the best of friends.

Like the Deraniyagalas, the de Silvas had one foot in the past and one in the future. Ena was conscious of the Aluvihara family traditions, though she hated the colonial-style bungalow that the architect Charles Gomez had built for her father at Aluvihara in 1956. She demanded a house that would incorporate traditional Kandyan features – an enclosing wall, open-

sided rooms, verandahs, courtyards, a shrine room – but she also wanted a modern house with an office for her husband, a studio for her son, and a guest wing for visitors. Inspired by these demands, Bawa responded instinctively to the problem of the compact site:

I remember talking to Ena, seeing her surrounded by all the things she liked. All she wanted was brick walls and a roof. The plan came about largely because she, and consequently I, wanted a private compound that would not be overlooked by the neighbours. (Geoffrey Bawa in conversation with Channa Daswatte, 1997)

The plan is introspective, forming a pattern of linked pavilions and courtyards disposed around a large central court or *meda midula* and contained within a limiting perimeter wall. It employs the same elements as the A. S. H. de Silva house – a workspace, a living pavilion, a service tract and a central courtyard – but these are brought together in a formalized arrangement within a finite boundary. The design may well have been inspired by Kandyan courtyard houses, by medieval manor houses such as the Eknelligoda *walaawe*, by Dutch town houses, or even by Roman atrium houses. Throughout his career Bawa would draw on a variety of sources, many of them noted during his travels, combining and developing them to create something both new and yet familiar.

The main elements are arranged in layers of increasing privacy as they progress away from

the street. First a long loggia, since removed, was formed by huge timber columns supporting a cane screen, recalling the front porches or *stoeps* of early Dutch houses. Behind this a high wall, broken only by openings for the main entrance and car port, defines a long garden court in front of the first pavilion, serving as a buffer zone between the house and the street.

The first pavilion, which contains the office and studio, the garage and a guest suite, looks onto a large central court occupying the heart of the plan, surrounded on four sides by an open loggia. The courtyard is finished in a combination of cobbles and gravel, with four huge grinding stones placed at each corner, and is shaded by a large mango tree and gnarled plumeria. Beyond is the main living accommodation: a two-storey pavilion with living and dining areas at the ground level separated by a stair tower and shrine room, with bedrooms above. Running down the side of the complex is the service tract: two long walls define the servants' rooms and kitchens, each separated by small courts, and, at the intersection with the first pavilion, the garage.

The visitor entered along one of Bawa's scenographic promenades. The front loggia was first encountered obliquely as part of the perspective of the street and gradually revealed the main entrance on the centre line of the second of its four bays. The solid wooden door, set back within the outer wall of the compound,

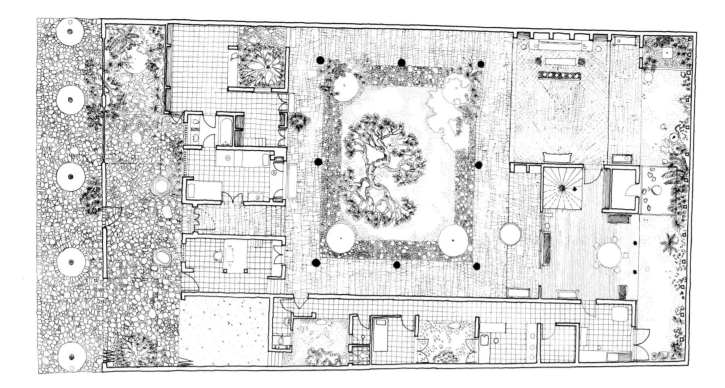

opened to reveal the long transverse courtyard bridged by a covered link. A second solid door, rescued from an old temple, opened into a narrow passage leading into the main courtyard. Interestingly the axis defined by these two doors fell neither on the centre of the courtyard nor on the line of the service tract loggia but at a point that gave a direct view across the courtyard to the dining room and beyond while leaving the open sitting room hidden from view. Bawa took great delight in setting up a system of formal axes and then deliberately knocking them out of kilter in a way reminiscent of old monastic plans.

Like all Bawa's early buildings, the house was built during a time of shortage and import restriction, when glass and steel were expensive and modern fittings were almost impossible to obtain. He used locally produced materials because these were all that were available but this restriction encouraged him to study how materials had been used traditionally, inspiring him to be innovative and inventive. He also successfully persuaded local craftsmen to cooperate in reproducing or 'pirating' standard designs of contemporary furniture and light fittings.

The overpowering presence of a tiled roof and the generally localized palette of materials give this house its vernacular feel, and yet the highly articulated and open plan is quite modern in its effect. Space flows from inside to outside and long vistas range across a series of indoor and outdoor 'rooms' to create the illusion of infinite space on a relatively small plot. Every room is naturally ventilated from two sides: Ena de Silva did not want air-conditioning, demanding a house without glass, with windows that 'could be used for serenading at night'. New devices are incorporated – projecting bay windows boxed out with diagonal timber lattice, raised ventilating ridges formed by extended 'cross-over' rafters, polished satinwood columns raised on elegant granite bases, deep overhanging eaves. The net result is something quite new: an inward-looking house on a restricted urban site in which workspaces, guest rooms, family rooms and service spaces are all clearly defined and separated but at the same time interconnected.

Ena took an active part in the design and building process. It was she who discovered some abandoned millstones on a roadside and it was she who organized an elephant to place them and the mature plumeria in the main courtyard. Her husband worried constantly about the expense of it all, but the final account came to 200,000 rupees, which was only 20,000 rupees over budget. In the final analysis the house cost little more than the site.

Soon after moving in Ena started her own batik business, developing a vocabulary of designs – used by Bawa in many of his projects – based on her wide knowledge of traditional Sinhalese and South Indian prints. After the death of her husband, she quit Colombo and returned to the family home in the Matale hills, where she built up a batik-making cooperative with local villagers. The house was rented during the late 1970s by Bawa, who used it as the design office for the Parliament project.

The de Silva House remains one of Bawa's most potent and beautiful designs. At the time of its conception the urban courtyard house was part of a forgotten tradition found only in the old Dutch and Moor streets of Hultsdorf, Galle and Matara. Coming at a time of growing urban congestion, this house more than any other was responsible for changing the perceptions of a generation of architects and ultimately of the entire urban population of Ceylon.

Opposite: Cross-section through the Ena de Silva House, copy drawing by Vernon Nonis, 1984

This page: Plan of the Ena de Silva House, copy drawing by Vernon Nonis, 1984

Top left and right: Views from the entrance towards the main courtyard

Opposite: View from the courtyard towards the entrance

Overleaf: The main courtyard

sleep sleep
sleep sleep
sleep
I'm falling
asleep

Frida Kahlo

Previous page: View from the living room towards the main courtyard

Left: The dining verandah

Bottom right: Courtyard detail

Opposite: View from the studio courtyard towards the main courtyard

Top left: An upper bedroom

Top right: The staircase

Bottom left: Detail of the dining verandah

Bottom right: One of a pair of inverted grinding stones used as entry portals

house for dr bartholomeusz

COLOMBO 1961–63

In 1961 the house in Alfred House Road that had been designed for a Burgher doctor called Noel Bartholomeusz was cancelled as it was nearing completion and Bawa persuaded his partners at E. R. & B. to take it over as their office. The original design was developed in the spirit of the Ena de Silva House, though the plot was narrower and longer. A first courtyard, separated from the street by a two-storey lodge containing garages, servants' accommodation and an entrance archway, faced a single-storey pavilion containing a dining room and kitchens. Beyond, a formal pool court led to the main pavilion, which was occupied by the principal living room with bedrooms on an upper floor. The living room opened via a covered verandah into a final garden court.

The change from house to office was effected with so little effort that one is left to wonder whether Bawa had prior knowledge of his client's intentions. With its courtyards, loggias and verandahs, the building created a pleasant and comfortable working environment that obviated the need for air-conditioning and offered a sample of the practice's work to any prospective clients. The design of the building incorporated two innovations: polished coconut trunks were used in conjunction with granite bases and capitals to protect them from termite attack, and the 'tile-on-cement' roof made its first appearance.

Bawa had already concluded that the roof was the critical element in tropical architecture and experimented with a number of alternative materials and methods of construction: flat roofs were difficult to seal and tended to get hot, though earth-covered slabs had yielded interesting results; interlocking 'Calicut' or

'Mangalore' tiles were lightweight and required relatively minimal timber support but offered little insulation; traditional flat Kandyan tiles needed high maintenance and had to be laid to steep pitches; corrugated cement sheeting was light, easy to support and highly waterproof but unbearably hot and totally unattractive; the half-round 'Portuguese' tile produced a pleasing texture and good thermal mass, but its double layering required a complex and costly timber structure of battens, close-spaced rafters, purlins and trusses. While seeking a solution for the roof of a house in Jawatte Road, Bawa hit upon the idea of laying Portuguese tiles in and over the corrugations of cement sheeting. This marriage combined the advantages of the two materials – excellent waterproof qualities, good insulation and attractive appearance – and minimized their disadvantages. Extra tiles were laid at the ridge and the eaves to prevent slippage and improved adhesion was achieved by adding cement fillets. The new office offered the perfect opportunity to try out the new idea on a substantial building, and its immediate success prompted its adoption for many subsequent projects.

The office was used until the end of the 1980s, when Bawa slowly withdrew from E. R. & B. and began to work more and more from his home off Bagatelle Road. In the summer of 1997, after eight years of disuse, Poologasundram and Bawa finally agreed to wind down the holding company that owned the office and Bawa became its sole owner. The house was then rented out to Shanth Fernando, the proprietor of a chain of design shops. A simple roofed pavilion was added to the furthermost garden to serve as an open-sided restaurant, and the rest of the ground floor was turned into a gallery and shop. This conversion has given a new lease of life to the complex, while respecting something of the spirit in which it was designed.

Opposite

Top right: View of the main office from the central court in 1984, showing the first use of tile on cement sheet

Middle right: The central courtyard in 2000

Bottom: Front elevation and long cross-section

This page

Top: Bawa's own office in 1984

Middle: Elevation from entry court and upper-floor plan

Bottom: Garden elevation and lower-floor plan

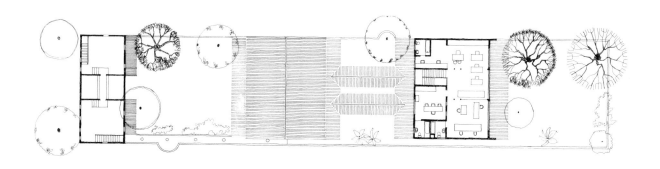

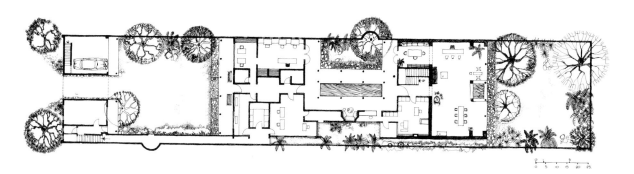

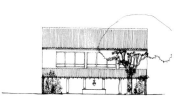

Left and opposite: Views
of the central courtyard
and pool in 1984

chapel for the good shepherd convent

BANDARAWELA 1961–62

In 1961 the nuns of the Good Shepherd commissioned a new chapel for their convent in Bandarawela. This small market town was situated at 1300 metres above sea level in an area renowned for its pleasant, dry climate and the convent was used as a training centre and a rest home. The original concept was developed by Plesner and Bawa with their friend Barbara Sansoni and the detailed design was then worked up by Laki Senanayake under Plesner's direction. Early sketch drawings by Plesner survive as well as Senanayake's final working drawings.

Lying beyond a group of older convent buildings, the chapel occupies a ridge that falls gently towards the east with steep slopes to the north and south. Its street façade takes the form of a long blank wall of grey rubble terminating in a squat square tower and is relieved by a series of five low recessed bays formed just above ground level by bearing arches. These serve to admit a trickle of ventilation along the inside wall of the chapel and are decorated with panels of patterned terracotta tiles. A small door in the façade – the public entrance to the chapel – opens into a wide vestibule connecting at its opposite end with the more private areas of the convent, and through two doors to the right into the chapel itself.

The chapel's granite floor follows the slope of the ground and falls gently away towards the altar, placed at the base of the tower and lit from an unseen glass roof. The roof of the chapel itself is made up of five angled vaults of red tuna wood. On the south wall of grey rubble stone abutting the road a series of terracotta reliefs depicts the Stations of the Cross, while the north wall carries four full bays of glazing incorporating three large crucifixes at their junctions and opening towards a thickly planted garden with views of distant hills. At night, spotlights illuminate the altar from the tower, while the body of the church is lit indirectly from the garden. Inspired by Donald Friend, Barbara Sansoni produced the terracotta *Rising Christ* that graces the solid bay in the north wall as well as the Stations of the Cross and the patterned tiles that line the bearing arches.

The chapel is one of the most impressive spaces for Christian worship to be found in Sri Lanka. The overall effect is one of focused calm and sanctity achieved through careful manipulation of space, juxtaposition of simple materials, and the careful control of light and shade. While it makes oblique references to the Romanesque–Gothic traditions of Western church building, the chapel has no direct precedents. It was built almost entirely from materials found nearby or manufactured in the vicinity, and seems to grow out of the ground, a building that has been 'unearthed' rather than designed.

Mother Good Counsel, the driving force behind the project, wrote to Plesner in 1965:

Today…I had a little private laugh in remembering the pre-building days when we each in turn went out to see if the rising sun would be unbearable…during Lauda. This morning it lighted the spirit of the Virgin, turning her into living flames and us poor mortals standing under her into creatures of light.

She then asked him to design a garage:

…or our long-suffering car will refuse to serve us… I must mention that we have not knitted enough to pay any money to the architect for the wonderful plan we want from him.

Middle right: The chapel exterior in 1984

Bottom left: Early view of the chapel interior

Bottom right: The interior of the tower in 1997

yahapath endera farm school

HANWELLA 1965–71

The idea to build the farm was the brainchild of Mother Good Counsel, who envisaged a centre where orphan girls could learn agricultural and homecraft skills. It was she who secured the land – a rubber and coconut estate near Hanwella – as well as persuading the German charity Misereor to finance the project and commissioning Bawa to be the architect.

The project confronted Bawa with the issue of how to place a disparate group of buildings within a large landscape, and formed the antecedent of his designs for Piliyandela Education Centre (1978) and Ruhunu University (1980). The various elements were located formally and orthogonally in plan but, following the precedent of classical Sinhalese architecture, were allowed to 'run with the contours' in section. Individual buildings were positioned carefully to define open spaces and axes and to regulate the vistas between them.

Anura Ratnavibushana, who acted as Bawa's principal assistant for the project, has described how Bawa generated many of his ideas while actually on site, developing them in the evening, in a series of detailed sketches – usually multi-layered plans and sections drawn with biro on squared paper. Often he would draw long vertical sections through the site and critical parts of the buildings. Although no models were made Bawa was able to visualize the three-dimensional complexities of the evolving design.

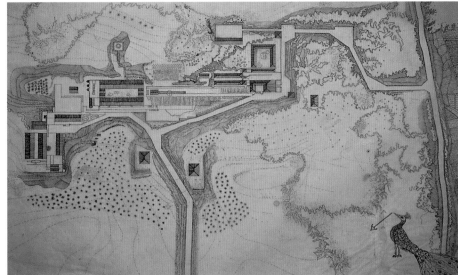

Top: Original plan of Yahapath Endera

Middle left: Early panorama view of Yahapath Endera

Middle right: Early view of the Priest's House

Bottom: Panorama drawing

Ratnavibushana would work the ideas up into more finished drawings that would then form the starting point for another round of discussions and sketches. Bawa had recently obtained a copy of *Arquitectura Popular em Portugal* (Sindicato 1961), a detailed survey of Portuguese vernacular architecture, and this was used as a source book and a means to connect the design back to an important influence on Sri Lanka's own indigenous vernacular traditions.

An early decision to keep an existing estate bungalow – located at the southern tip of a long north–south ridge and visible from the approach road in the valley below – became one of the generators of the scheme. The bungalow was converted to provide accommodation for the nuns and was extended northwards by a courtyard and eastwards down the slope by lines of chicken sheds and a group of farm buildings arranged around an open farmyard. These various elements were all located behind a long raking rubble wall. The visitor climbed the side of the valley to the foot of this wall and was then drawn up to the bungalow's entrance. Two balcony turrets were added to the bungalow as if to provide the nuns with defensive watchtowers, while a simple *ambalama* was placed at the extreme southern tip of the ridge to serve as a sheltered waiting room. Below this, hidden in the trees, was the priest's house, a symbolically isolated preserve for a solitary male, its steeply pitched thatched roof inspired by Ulrik Plesner's earlier studies of thatched brick kilns (Plesner 1959a).

The bungalow acted as a pivot: turning its corner the visitor joined the main north–south axis of the ridge, encountering the long perspective past the chapel towards the girls' dormitory and taking in the beautiful panorama of rubber plantations on the hills to the west. The original design for a *cadjan*-roofed chapel was never realized, and a more conventional chapel was added in the early 1980s. The girls' accommodation comprised two long buildings running either side of a garden court with a separately roofed entrance loggia at one end and a stage at the other. The west building contained the dining room and teaching area, the east the students' sleeping cubicles. Beyond the stage a smaller court was formed by a bakery with a huge tapering chimney and by a row of toilets and washrooms housed within apsidal cells. Finally, marking the north end of the ridge, a sickbay was combined with the main water tank to create an outward cantilevering watchtower. The cowsheds and farm buildings were located below the girls' block on the western flank of the ridge and three communal houses were later added nearby to accommodate groups of older girls.

All the buildings were simple and cheap and were constructed from locally available materials, including coconut timber, rubber wood, clay tile and coconut thatch. The section was designed with overhanging eaves and open trellis clerestories to protect the interiors from direct sunlight and driving rain and to encourage cross-ventilation, obviating the need for glass. Simply designed furniture was produced by

village craftsmen. The project offered a vocabulary for contemporary rural redevelopment projects and influenced the government's model village programme in the early 1980s.

The death of Mother Good Counsel robbed the farm school of its guiding spirit and it went into a decline during the early 1980s. The nuns sold the farm to the monks of the de la Salle Order, who ran it for a few years as a 'Boys' Town', but by the end of the 1990s the buildings had fallen into disrepair and the estate was sold to a brewery.

Middle right: The dormitory courtyard and stage in 1977

Bottom left: The water tower/ sanitorium in 1977

Bottom right: Early view of the chicken sheds

Opposite: The teaching area in 1997

madurai boys' town

SOUTH INDIA 1965–67

Having financed some of Bawa's work for the Good Shepherd Convent, Misereor insisted that E. R.& B. be employed in 1963 to design extensions to a 'Boys' Town' at Ragama run by the monks of the de la Salle Order. This led in 1965 to an invitation from Brother Vincent Gottwald, the Provincial of the de la Salle monks in India, to design a more ambitious Boys' Town at Madurai. The first of many projects that Bawa attempted in South India, this was one of the few actually realized.

The Boys' Town occupied 80 hectares of land in a valley hemmed in by steep rocky hills. It provided accommodation for four hundred boys as well as training facilities for farming, machine maintenance, carpentry and metalwork. The boys' accommodation occupied a corner of the site and was designed as a small township with an open space at its centre dominated by a steeply roofed chapel. A series of residential clusters, each containing four 'homes' within a high-walled compound, defined three sides of the central space; the fourth was formed by the monks' accommodation and administrative buildings, with classrooms, workshops and farm buildings located further up the hillside. The lower walls of the houses and the surrounding compound walls were built of random rubble. Upper floors and roofs were supported on simple *in situ* concrete frames and the roofs themselves were of tile on cement sheet.

Madurai seems close enough on the map but at the time it was still a remote destination: to travel there from Ceylon meant either enduring the discomforts of the ferry from Talaimannar or flying to Madras. Much of the preliminary design work was carried out in Ceylon and Brother Vincent travelled to take part in early discussions with the architects at Lunuganga. Plesner was responsible for developing the detailed design and carried out a number of site visits during 1966. But it was difficult to run a project on site from such a distance and after Plesner quit E. R. & B. in 1967 the office relinquished control of the project. Eventually the final supervision of the first phases and the design of subsequent phases were entrusted to the Trivandrum-based architect Laurie Baker. A number of the original buildings from the first phase have survived, however, and are still in use.

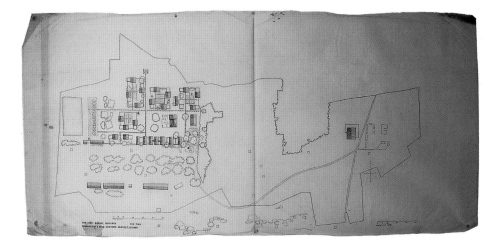

Top: Original drawing of a cluster of rooms for Madurai (compare with the plan of the Abhayagiri Monastery on p.30)

Middle left: A residential block at Madurai in 2000

Bottom left: The interior of a workshop block

Bottom right: The chapel

polontalawa estate bungalow

NIKARAWETIYA 1963–65

In 1963 the Swiss company Baur & Co commissioned a new manager's bungalow for a remote coconut estate near Nikarawetiya in the Dry Zone about 100 kilometres north of Colombo. Baur's Swiss director, Thilo Hoffman, wanted a prefabricated house similar to that built for the Ideal Home Exhibition in 1959. He provided a survey plan of the estate that identified a flat site next to the main estate road and the architects sketched out a first proposal based on the house they had built for Shell at Anuradhapura in 1960. When Plesner made an initial visit to Polontalawa, however, he made the radical suggestion of shifting the house into an area of large boulders. Hoffman then accompanied Plesner and Bawa on a working visit, when it was proposed that the house be built in the form of a cluster of pavilions inserted amongst the boulders. He seems to have warmed to the idea immediately and all thoughts of a low-cost prefabricated bungalow evaporated. The house was sketched out roughly on a piece of paper and then set out on the ground with sticks and string. Bawa later told Channa Daswatte:

We discovered a spot full of boulders and we all said how excellent and splendid it would be to build a house there. So we got sticks and string, brought some chairs and sandwiches, and set the house out with the contractor, who followed every gesture of our hands.

Ulrik Plesner remembered: 'Geoffrey stood in the middle, telling the jungle villagers what to do and keeping them giggling – he was always the star on site while I was the grey eminence' (letter to the author). The house was built without drawings by the local estate staff, acting mainly under Plesner's supervision.

The compound is defined by a high encircling wall of rubble entered through a lychgate. A small entrance court leads between two boulders into the main living area, an open pavilion defined by a roof spanning from one vast boulder to another. A grand piano was placed beside one of the boulders, perhaps to emphasize the civilizing effects of the house on this remote and inaccessible site. Beyond the living area are two rubble-walled pavilions, one for the manager and one for his guests. A third pavilion, set behind the living room and next to a service entrance, contains the kitchens and estate office and is signified by a rubble water tower. A system of detachable rattan screens could be hung on the appropriate side of the living area during the monsoons.

Employing materials from the site and its immediate surroundings, this is a house that grows out of the landscape. It belongs to a long Sri Lankan tradition of cave temples insinuated between boulders and tucked under cliffs, and indeed such a temple exists at Kadiyagawa, just a mile to the north-west of the site. Here for the first time Bawa and Plesner exploited and celebrated a natural landscape to the full and succeeded in expressing the roof as a totally autonomous element.

Middle: An early view of the main living space at Polontalawa

Bottom: A view of the entrance gate to Polontalawa

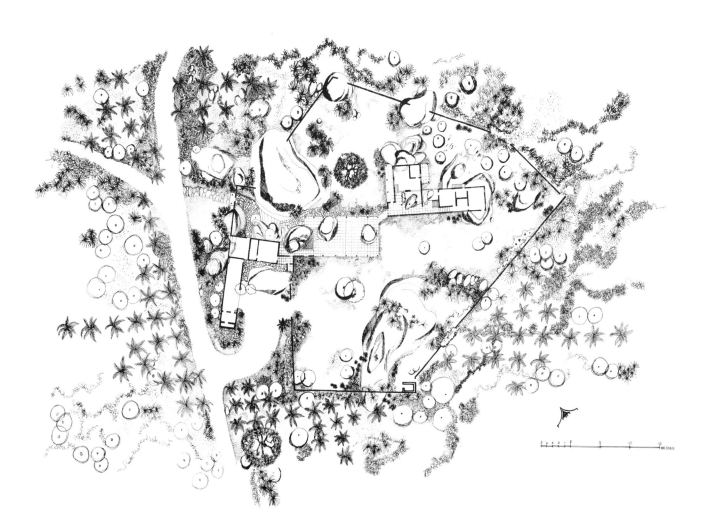

Top: Plan of Polontalawa

Bottom left and right: Views of
the main living space in 1997

Opposite
Top: Cross-section
and elevations of the
Keuneman House

Bottom: The top-floor pavilion
of the Keuneman House

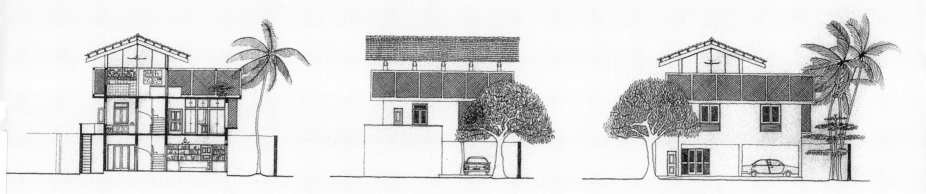

keuneman house

COLOMBO 1967–69

Peter Keuneman was a prominent Marxist member of Parliament and a leading figure in the Lanka Sama Samaj Party (LSSP). He and Bawa were distant cousins and had been near contemporaries at Royal College and Cambridge. Later, during the 1970s, he became minister of housing and local government and introduced a controversial floor area limit of 90 square metres on all new private houses. In 1967 Keuneman asked Bawa to design a house for him on a small leftover plot hemmed in by other houses in a lane at the back of Ladies' College. The new house replaced an older bungalow, though a rear section of servants' quarters would be retained. At the time Bawa was designing a three-story annexe to his own house off Bagatelle Road and he proposed a similar tower house for Keuneman.

The tower house type is the antithesis of the courtyard house and offers an alternative strategy for small urban plots. Bawa reversed the normal sequence of floors: the ground floor was taken up by a car port and the MP's office; the kitchen, dining room and main bedroom occupied the first floor; and the living room was placed under a simple twin-pitched roof on the second floor beside a large open terrace. This reversal made excellent environmental sense: the office and bedroom were protected from direct sun while the living room benefited from good cross-ventilation and enjoyed excellent views across the neighbouring rooftops towards the sea.

The total area of the house came to over 300 square metres but if the servants' wing, office, car port and open verandahs were excluded it could be passed off as a house of 100 square metres. Bawa later derived enormous pleasure from pointing out his friend's hypocrisy and during the 1970s became adept at designing houses with open verandahs, car ports and 'offices' to circumvent government restrictions.

bentota beach hotel

BENTOTA 1967–69

The Bentota Beach Hotel was arguably one of Bawa's most important buildings, and the one that, more than any other, encapsulated the achievements of the previous decade. As a scheme it seems to have emerged fully fledged from his fertile mind, resolving some of the key dilemmas facing the designer of a resort hotel: how to pander to the needs of global travellers while providing them with a memorable local experience and how to safeguard and celebrate the values of the host community.

Bawa was himself a seasoned traveller who had stayed in countless hotels in every part of the world and could empathize with both the visitor and the visited. He was therefore able to design a modern building that reflected something of the culture and traditions of its milieu without descending into parody or pastiche, a building that offered subtle hints of a lost world of ancient palaces, medieval manor houses and colonial villas while still addressing the needs of the modern traveller. The design treated the site and surroundings with respect and played on all five senses to capture the unique spirit of the place. As such it was one of the first hotels of its kind to be built anywhere in Asia.

The site itself was an inspired choice: on one side of a spit of land the white-topped waves of the Indian Ocean broke over a distant reef and rolled in towards a long sandy beach fringed with palm trees, while on the other the Bentota River slid lazily along its mangrove-clad banks towards the sea. Bawa placed the hotel at the neck of the spit, close to the point where

parallel rail and road bridges carried visitors from Colombo across the estuary, on a mound surmounted in earlier times by makeshift Portuguese and Dutch forts and crowned more recently by the Bentota Rest House.

The original brief asked for extensive public spaces but stipulated only thirty bedrooms. This was expanded during planning, however, and a further twenty rooms were contained in an additional wing to the north, with forty more rooms added later in a new southern wing.

The apparent simplicity of the plan belies its spatial complexities and the subtleties of its section. The mound was encased in a rubble podium that mimicked old Dutch fortifications and contained a shopping arcade and links to the service areas. The main reception spaces were placed on top of the mound and took the form of an enfilade of rooms around a square courtyard. Finally, two floors of bedrooms were placed in an L-shaped wing on adjacent sides of the square.

Bawa's architectural promenade began at the moment when, nearing the end of their journey from Colombo, visitors came suddenly to the edge of the Bentota River and caught their first view of the upper floors of the hotel floating above a canopy of palm trees on its further shore. Having crossed the river they were deposited at the foot of the massive stone bastion and encountered a yawning *porte cochère*, seemingly carved out of naked rock. Within this cavernous entrance, a stone staircase led up towards the richly coloured batik ceiling covering the reception area. Here they encountered the central courtyard with its gurgling pool framed by a trio of temple trees, where they caught their first tantalizing glimpse of the distant ocean through the columns of the main lounge and the coconut palms beyond. At

Top: The entrance façade

Middle: The entrance staircase

Bottom: Cross-section through the main hotel building

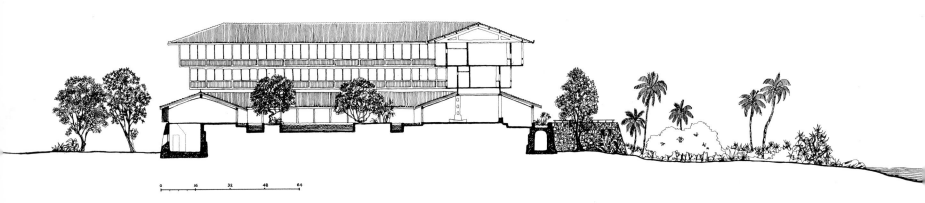

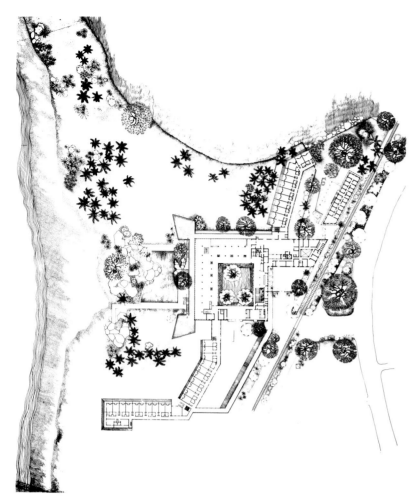

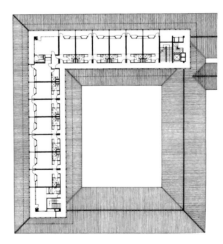

the opposite end of the reception area the decorated door of the hotel's only lift invited them up to the open balconies running around the courtyard at first and second-floor levels, giving access to the rooms. Every room had a private balcony, offering guests their own unique view across the palm trees towards the ocean.

The main courtyard functioned like the *meda midula* of a medieval manor house and echoed the courtyard of Bawa's house for Ena de Silva. Originally Bawa intended the reception rooms to remain open both to the courtyard and to the outer terraces of the bastion, but sadly the tour operators insisted that the dining and sitting rooms be air-conditioned. Above the courtyard, the bedroom floors cantilevered outwards in a manner reminiscent of Bawa's unbuilt design for the first Hilton project, recalling the palace at Padmanabhapuram and the tower of the Saman Devale temple at Ratnapura.

The plan differentiates clearly between the individual rooms and the communal areas in a way reminiscent of a monastery, with monks' cells clustered around a central cloister. In this

respect it can be compared to Le Corbusier's design for the Monastery of La Tourette, which placed two layers of cells on three sides of a central court above communal spaces. The hotel bedrooms offered the possibility of individual communion with nature, while the central court-yard functioned as the heart of the community. From their private balconies guests could experience the tropical landscape beyond the confines of the hotel – the thunder of the ocean, flashes of sunlight on the swaying palm fronds, the shriek of a peacock, the orange glow of the setting sun as it slipped below the horizon, the whiff of distant wood fires – but as soon as they quit their rooms they were confronted by the civilized landscape of the courtyard – the spices of the evening meal, the chink of glasses and babble of foreign tongues. For the determined individualist a pair of narrow winding staircases offered a hidden escape route down into the dungeon-like corridors of the bastion and out past the rock-lined swimming pool, across the boulder-strewn lawns and through the lines of coconut trees to the beach and the edge of sea. Back in the hotel, however, the stepped floor of the dining room presented the panorama of the estuary to every diner, while lines of chairs in the lounge invited visitors to share the experience of a glass of arrack and the view through the coconut grove towards the sea. Even when the hotel was new the choice of materials – rough granite, polished concrete, terracotta, timber – and the palette of colours – dark-stained timber, warm handloom ceilings, samara (ochre-coloured) soffits – gave it a well-worn and lived-in feel, and a strong sense of continuity with an unspecified past.

Like all Bawa's early projects, the Bentota Beach Hotel was built during a period when imports were restricted and building materials were in short supply. The architects had to use their imagination and rely on locally produced fixtures and furnishings. Almost all of the furniture was designed in the office and made by local craftsmen, and the fabrics were woven by Barbara Sansoni's convent girls. Bawa filled the hotel with artworks by his friends and collaborators, all executed in a sense of playful improvisation – making do with what was available: the batik ceiling that hovered like

a tent above the reception was made by Ena de Silva; the handloom ceilings of the dining room and lounges were the work of Barbara Sansoni; Laki Senanayake sculpted the peacock that guarded the staircase down to the pool bar; the doors to the lift were designed by Anura Ratnavibushana and executed by Bellic Baas; and the drawings that adorned the public areas were the work of Ismeth Raheem.

The hotel survived in its original form for nearly thirty years and brought immense pleasure to countless numbers of tourists. During the 1980s, the government divested itself of its hotel interests and Bentota passed eventually to John Keels Ltd. In 1998 the new owners undertook a drastic programme of 'modernization' that effectively expunged every element of quality from the building. The clay roof tiles were replaced by green metal sheeting, the courtyard was 'tidied up', the podium extended, and the reception areas remodelled. In a tragic orgy of developer madness, Sri Lanka lost the first, most significant and arguably most beautiful of its resort hotels.

Middle right: View from one of the rooms

Bottom left: View across the courtyard towards the sea

Bottom right: The dining room

Opposite: The beachside elevation

Left: Overhanging floors

Opposite: The central courtyard

serendib hotel

BENTOTA 1967–70

The Serendib Hotel was developed in tandem with the Bentota Beach Hotel, though it was completed a year later than its neighbour and conceived as a budget-priced rest house for travellers. Approached down a narrow road running beside the railway line, the hotel presents to the world a long blank wall broken only by a deep *porte cochère*. The plan consists of two long parallel buildings enclosing a string of courtyards, the building on the street side containing offices, kitchens and service spaces, while that facing the sea contains two floors of accommodation flanking a central dining room.

The layering of space is similar to that set up in the house for Ena de Silva. A series of longitudinal strata was established between the railway track and the ocean: the street, the *porte cochère*, the service wall, the garden, the access corridors, the lines of bedroom cells, the private verandahs, the coconut grove and the beach. A single cross-axis pierces these strata like a skewer, proceeding from the *porte cochère* across the central courtyard past a peacock pen to the reception desk and continuing along one side of the restaurant and beyond through the trees to the edge of the ocean.

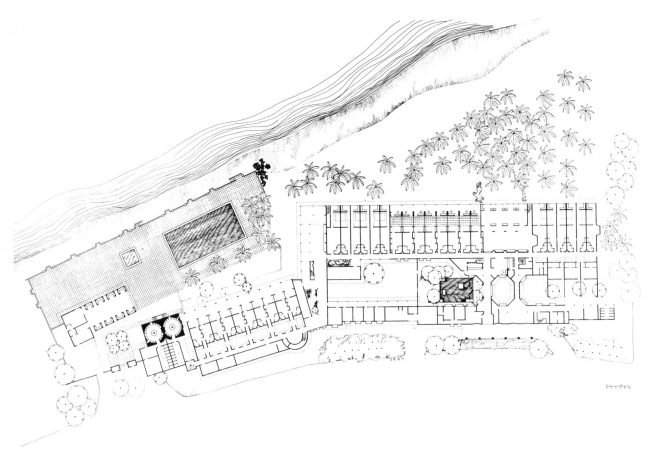

The original building has forty-four rooms, twenty on the ground floor and twenty-four above, the lower rooms opening into small courtyards with covered verandahs beyond, while the upper rooms open onto balconies. All were designed to function without air-conditioning and fitted with timber lattice louvres to encourage cross-ventilation, but this led to problems of noise transmission from the corridors and later the rooms were sealed and air-conditioned. A simple restaurant spills out onto the lawns, where open sitting areas are protected by triangular sails of orange and brown canvas stretched between the trunks of palm trees. The original design proposed roofs of coconut thatch and floors of raked sand, but the complete building employs roofs of clay tile on cement sheeting with terracotta floors.

The hotel proved very popular and it was extended towards the south in 1974 with a new block containing a further thirty rooms, a swimming pool and a poolside café. The link between new and old was formed by extending the gable of the original block to create a deep loggia facing the pool. The café is a masterpiece of sophisticated simplicity: its roof trusses sit on beams that cantilever out from the columns in a manner recalling the roofs of the *devale* at Embekke, while the glass screen wall dances in and out between the columns, creating a syncopation of internal and external space. Bawa also effectively solved the problem of noise transmission in this block: the corridors are enclosed and separated from the rooms by small open courtyards, with pairs of rooms connected to the corridor by narrow bridges and staircases.

Opposite
Top: Plan showing the 1973 extensions

Bottom left: An early view from the beach

Bottom right: The main block seen from the beach

This page: Views of the central courtyard

**Opposite
Left:** The poolside coffee
bar before it was glazed

Top right: A staircase in the
1973 wing showing the 'pine-
cone' lamp adapted by Bawa
from a design by the Dane,
Poul Henningsen

Bottom right: The poolside
coffee bar

This page: Interior views of
the poolside coffee bar

steel corporation offices

ORUWELA 1966–69

During the 1960s the Sri Lankan government signed 'aid-and-trade' agreements with countries of the Eastern Bloc. The steel-rolling mills at Oruwela were built with Soviet aid, their main function being to convert imported steel billet into reinforcing rod. The mills require water for cooling and a large reservoir was established on the site, set in an area of rubber and coconut plantation about 18 kilometres to the east of Colombo.

Bawa was commissioned to design the administrative building and an estate of staff houses. He placed the administrative building at right angles to the main rolling mill, projecting out into the reservoir. It adopts a simple rectangular form but has an outward cantilevering section, inspired by temple buildings in Kerala and Nepal, offering protection from overhead sun and monsoon rain and permitting the use of a breathing wall. The main structure is of framed reinforced concrete, while the external breathing wall is formed from precast rectangular concrete grilles diminishing in scale from floor to floor. The original design proposed open-plan offices in order to maximize natural ventilation and lighting, though these have now been partitioned.

The staff-housing scheme was designed as rows of back-to-back courtyard houses running along the contours of a neighbouring rubber estate. Each house occupies a rectangular plot of about 150 square metres, and the main habitable rooms open into a walled courtyard. This simple plan could achieve a density of about fifty dwellings per hectare and offered an interesting prototype for inexpensive medium-density urban houses, although the model was sadly ignored both by the government of the day and its successors.

Top left: The Steel Corporation Offices seen from across the reservoir in 1984

Top centre: The view from an office

Top right: The verandah of one of the staff houses

Bottom: Side elevation of the office block in 1997

ceylon pavilion

OSAKA 1969–70

Ceylon's pavilion at the 1970 Osaka World Fair in Japan was designed by Bawa in collaboration with Anura Ratnavibushana, who had recently returned to the office after completing his studies in Copenhagen. Built to a modest budget by the Japanese contractor Mitsui, the pavilion attracted considerable attention. Two steel-framed and glass-clad cubes were placed at a seemingly arbitrary angle to each other and connected at mezzanine level by a balcony. The entry cube and link contained Buddhist temple carvings and Ceylon gemstones, while the exit cube promoted Ceylon tea. The forecourt was dominated by a huge 12-metre-high bronze bo leaf designed by Laki Senanayake, and the interiors were hung with huge batik flags by Ena de Silva. The starkness of the interiors was relieved by clusters of paper lamps, of the type made for the Buddhist *Vesak* festival, while panels of glazing were decorated with translucent paper cut-outs.

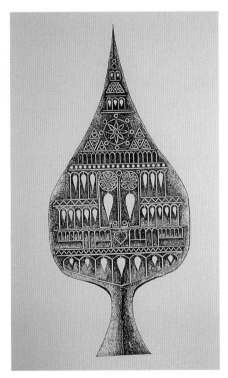

Top: View of the exhibition pavilions

Bottom left: Laki Senanayake's design for the *bo* tree sculpture

Bottom right: Interior of the first pavilion showing Ena de Silva's flags

A new government

The UNP was defeated in the general election of 1970 by a left-wing coalition headed by Mrs Sirimavo Bandaranaike's SLFP. The new government embarked on a programme of radical reform that included the nationalization of land, the introduction of strict import and foreign exchange controls and the adoption of Sinhala as the national language. In its external relations it followed a policy of non-alignment, interpreted in the West as a shift towards the Soviet Union. To signify a break with the colonial past, it dropped the name Ceylon in favour of Sri Lanka.

Within a year of coming to power Mrs Bandaranaike was confronted by a massive armed insurrection. This arose not from the ethnic minorities but from a grass-roots Maoist movement, the Janatha Vimukthi Peramune (JVP), which for some time had been covertly recruiting and training unemployed Sinhalese youth in the rural villages. The uprising came close to toppling the government and was eventually put down with great ferocity.

Bawa was always careful not to identify himself too closely with any one political party, though his sympathies probably inclined towards the UNP. As a member of the Western-educated elite he was worried by the government's lurch to the Left and by what he saw as the triumph of theory over common sense. The imposition of

currency controls curtailed his freedom to travel, while legislation to regulate building rents and peg the size of new houses discouraged new building and threatened to reduce his workload. The 1971 insurrection added to his feelings of insecurity. Having grown up within the Burgher community, Bawa watched with dismay as many Burghers responded to the government's flirtation with Sinhalese nationalism by emigrating to start new lives in Australia and Canada. For a time he too entertained thoughts of emigrating and even went as far as to apply to the Australian High Commission for a visa. He also began to look for work abroad.

Working for the government

Although the new government came with radical credentials, most politicians of the period were 'hewn from the same wood' and belonged to the land-owning, Western-educated class: Mrs Bandaranaike, for example, was a close relative of Bawa's first clients, the Deraniyagalas. Although during the 1960s Bawa had succeeded in re-establishing the reputation of Edwards, Reid and Begg and built up a solid client base, mainly within the private sector, after 1970 many of these sources of work dried up. At the time, however, the office was by far the most experienced in Sri Lanka and soon began to attract major commissions from the government.

Several government projects were introduced to the practice by Stanley Perera, who had entered the office in 1946 as a government-qualified draughts-man and was Bawa's senior technician. He was active in politics and a cousin of N. M. Perera, the minister of finance. Through him the practice was commissioned to build an industrial estate at Pallakelle near Kandy (1970; p.131) and a new campus for the Vidyodaya University on the outskirts of Colombo, as well as new office buildings in Colombo for the State Insurance Corporation and the State Mortgage Bank (1976; p.134). The design of the State Insurance Corporation was compromised by the client, who insisted on appointing a separate engin-eering consultant, but the State Mortgage Bank is a work of enormous significance.

Working abroad

Restrictions on foreign travel at this time were particularly hard to bear. It had become almost impossible for Sri Lankan nationals to obtain hard currency, except by paying extortionate rates on the black market: when Milroy Perera, later Bawa's friend and collaborator, flew to England to complete his studies, he took with him gallon tins of coconut oil to sell in Madras in order to raise foreign currency. Bawa looked for jobs abroad to enable him to travel and he was prepared to offer his

The Madurai Club

services in exchange for plane tickets, hotel accommodation and a small subsistence allowance.

The Bentota Beach Hotel had already established Bawa's reputation as a hotel designer and in 1971 he succeeded in obtaining a commission to build a new wing for the famous Connemara Hotel in Madras, on the strength of which he opened an office in Madras and began to shuffle staff backwards and forwards from Colombo. As well as eventually buying a substantial house called Keith Lodge to serve as both his office and his Madras home, he also, predictably, bought another Rolls-Royce, this time from a Maharaja, but was later frustrated when Indian export restrictions prevented him from shipping it to Colombo.

It was at the Connemara in 1971 that Bawa first met Martin Henry, the young general manager of Madurai Mills, who asked him to design a new company club in Madurai (p.119). This led to further commissions from Madurai Mills for mill buildings and staff housing, and procured an introduction to the Kumararaja of Chettinad, who commissioned Bawa in 1975 to prepare designs for the proposed Kumararaja M. A. M. Muttiah Hospital

at Adyar as well as for a house in Madras for Mrs Meenah Muttiah. Other hotel projects followed: the Connemara Group asked Bawa to remodel the West End Hotel in Bangalore, while the Indian Tourism Development Corporation commissioned studies for hotels in Pondicherry and Goa. The Madurai Club and Connemara extension (now largely destroyed) were the only substantial projects to get off the ground, however, and the Madras office closed in the late 1970s.

Bawa's other foreign work during these years came about as a result of personal contacts. In 1972 he converted an old sugar store on the island of Mauritius into a weekend villa for a planter called Peter White (p.127) and in 1973 he helped the Australian painter Donald Friend to develop a small beach resort on the island of Bali (p.123). It proved difficult to run jobs in faraway places, however, and as the political situation became more stable and the prospects for work improved, Bawa refocused his attention back on Sri Lanka.

The office
During the 1960s Bawa had gathered around him a unique group of highly qualified and talented young architects.

At the beginning of the 1970s he probably employed over a third of all the qualified architects in Sri Lanka. Although these collaborators were imbued with a sense of common purpose and method, they were all strong individual designers in their own right and made a significant contribution to the success of the office during this period. Bawa stood in their midst like the conductor of an orchestra or the director of a play. They had skills that he had never developed and that he relied on them to provide, but he was possessed of his own unique array of talents: wit, imagination, inventiveness, a vast store of ideas and observations gleaned from his travels, a highly developed sense of space and spatial theatre, a capacity for self-criticism, a sureness of touch and taste, an understanding of when to stop designing and, above all, a sense of the sheer enjoyment of making architecture.

His attitude towards his employees at times bordered on the feudal, however. Although he treated close colleagues as if they were members of his extended family, helping them through personal crises and joining in their social activities, he steadfastly refused to pay them an equitable

Left: Keith Lodge, Bawa's office in Madras
Centre: The drawing office in Alfred House Road
Right: The design studio in Alfred House Road

wage. His attitude seemed to be based in part on a belief that they were apprentices, learning at his feet, and in part on the idea that, because he had helped them to qualify and arranged scholarships for them to study abroad, they now had an obligation to work for him for next to nothing. When there were deadlines to meet, staff were expected to work all hours of the day and night, though if there was a lull they were free to work in the office on their own private jobs. It became normal for Bawa's assistants to run their own practices on the side in order to make ends meet. Stories illustrating the partners' parsimony are legion: in 1972,

when Ismeth Raheem was working in Madras on the Connemara Hotel, his wife Delini called at the office to collect his pay cheque to be told: 'But Delini, it's like a holiday for Ismeth in Madras, no? Surely he doesn't expect to be paid as well!'

There were perks, however. In 1971 Bawa rented a bungalow between the back of the office and the Galle Road and converted it into a small café. At the time Colombo had very few cafés or clubs for young people and Bawa's aim was to provide his staff with a place where they could eat, relax and entertain friends. Because the café was directly accessible from the office via a door

in the rear courtyard wall it was given the name 'Next Door'. The interiors were remodelled by Anura Ratnavibushana using shiny gloss-white surfaces relieved by areas of matt blue and mauve with reflecting pools, hidden lamps, and highly sculptural built-in furniture. Although it ran at a financial loss, the café served as a focal point for the social life of the office.

One by one, Bawa's trusted assistants left him to set up their own practices or to work with other architects. In 1971 Nihal Amarasinghe went to Mauritius to work with two friends from the AA before setting up his own office in Colombo. Soon after,

Turner Wickramasinghe joined the newly formed State Engineering Corporation, where he was later responsible for designing many public buildings and housing projects. Pherooze Choksy and Ismeth Raheem both quit in 1976 to start their own practice, going on to produce a portfolio of innovative work that included the celebrated Habarane Lodge Hotel. Anura Ratnavibushana was probably Bawa's favourite assistant and the one to whom he gave the greatest degree of design independence. He recalls:

I was a specially privileged 'student', whom Geoffrey took under his wing. The dedication in a book he gave me, which reads 'to Anura – first among equals', is a reminder of my lifelong association and friendship with a unique guru. (Anura Ratnavibushana, letter to the author, 2001)

In 1971 he became a partner in a new office called DG5 but continued to work with Bawa until 1978, when he left Sri Lanka to work in Nigeria. By the end of the 1970s, therefore, Vasantha Jacobsen was the only one of Bawa's original team who remained and she became his principal assistant.

Bawa looked back on the 1960s as a golden age; a time when there were few rules, when things were simple and everything was improvised, when he was surrounded by a group of young and unselfconscious designers. He felt betrayed by their departure and experienced difficulties finding replacements of the same calibre. The dispersal of his team helped to broadcast his ideas, however, and all of his former employees went on to produce interesting buildings under their own names. Their absence also encouraged him to reinvent himself and he soon demonstrated that he could function without them.

Friends

Bawa appears to have become more and more aloof and solitary during the 1970s. Although he was a well-known figure in Colombo society and had a wide circle of acquaintances, he had few close friends to whom he could relate intellectually, and no close colleague who could fill the void left by Ulrik Plesner. He threw himself into his work, taking solace from the rebuilding of his Colombo home, his regular weekend visits to Lunuganga, and his occasional solitary trips abroad.

However, in 1976 new friends appeared from an unexpected quarter: the London architects Chamberlin, Powell & Bon were coming to the end of their marathon Barbican project in the City of London and Joe Chamberlin, his wife Jean – the office manager – and his Swiss partner Christoph Bon decided to devote more time to travel. They set off on an exploration of India in the company of the former editor of the *Architectural Review*, Jim Richards, and his wife Kit. Richards had already published an article on Bawa's work (Bawa and Plesner 1966a) and had visited him in Colombo in 1970. The group met up with Bawa at his home in Madras, where he persuaded them to accompany him on a visit to the Madurai Club. They were so impressed that they accepted an invitation to visit Colombo the following year to see more of his work and in 1977 the Chamberlins and Bon spent three weeks in Sri Lanka, staying in Colombo and the Bentota Beach Hotel and managing to visit a number of Bawa's buildings. Jean, Joe and Christoph already operated as a close triangle and they now adopted Bawa as a fourth member of their group. When he next visited London early in

Opposite
Left: Jean Chamberlin, Jim and
Kit Richards and Joe Chamberlin
arriving at Madurai in 1976
Right: Joe Chamberlin at the
Bentota Beach Hotel in 1977

This page: Bawa with Jean
Chamberlin at Yahapath Endera
in 1977

Below left: Design for a resort hotel
at Yala – the 'dune village', 1975
Below right: Design for a resort hotel
at Yala – the 'rock village', 1975

Opposite: Seema Malaka, Colombo

1978 he stayed with them in their home in South Edwardes Square. The initial bond of friendship was forged with Joe Chamberlin but after Joe's sudden death at the end of 1978 Bawa became his replacement in the triangle. He was encouraged to treat South Edwardes Square as his London home, while Jean and Christoph became regular visitors at 33rd Lane and Lunuganga. Bawa no longer went off on trips by himself, but joined Christoph and Jean on their elaborate foreign journeys.

Hotels

During the 1970s Bawa and his colleagues produced a total of fourteen unexecuted designs for hotels in Sri Lanka and India. These included two proposals for an extension to the Mount Lavinia Hotel, south of Colombo, which were developed in collaboration with Wimberley, Whisen, Allison, Tong and Goo. Ratnavibushana made drawings for a fantasy beach resort in the extreme south of Sri Lanka at Yala, with rooms built into caves and under sand dunes; Ismeth Raheem produced a detailed feasibility study for a visitor centre at Kadagannawa with views towards Bible Rock, as well as designs for resort hotels in Goa and Pondicherry in India and for a 'Club Mediterranée' on a site at Nilaveli on Sri Lanka's east coast; Vasantha Jacobsen worked up a proposal for a village hotel at

Panama in the south-east of the island, but the project provoked protests from environmentalists and was cancelled after work had started on site. While this lack of success was certainly demoralizing, Bawa treated each of these projects as a challenge and an opportunity to develop ideas.

Reputation

Although his designs of the 1970s lacked some of the creative exuberance of the previous period, Bawa gained valuable experience during these years of working on big projects with complex briefs, tight deadlines and strict budgets. His international reputation was finally confirmed by an article in the *Architectural Review* in 1978 by Michael Brawne, who had first encountered Bawa's architecture when invited to Sri Lanka in 1977 to design a new National Library in Colombo. Brawne's article ignored the government projects of the 1970s and featured the Yahapath Endera Farm School, the Bentota Beach and Serendib hotels, and the Madurai Club, using photographs by Christoph Bon. The author was responding to what Bawa had shown him and, through no fault of his own, presented an image already nearly ten years out of date. His perceptive text stressed Bawa's position as a Modernist with strong regionalist tendencies, while emphasizing the neo-vernacular character

of his architecture. Brawne's piece featured beside an article by the British architect Richard MacCormac entitled 'Housing and the Dilemma of Style', which carried illustrations of buildings by David Lea, Edward Cullinan and MacCormac's own practice, all of which bore a strong affinity with those of Bawa. It was almost as if the editors were using the article on Bawa as ammunition in a growing debate about the future of modern architecture in Britain. A caption for a photograph of Cullinan's Minster Lovell project could equally have been applied to any of the Bawa illustrations: 'the force of a lively constructional aesthetic seems to break out of a vernacular crust…the ingredients are conventional but their assembly unprecedented' (MacCormac 1978).

'In each project one finds oneself unconfined. With the particular needs of the building at the back of one's mind one sees the solution as a totality – the site being all-important – and one sees whatever vision is granted one of the building set in its surroundings – the building seen from outside, movement through the building, the whole picture as seen by anyone using the building.'

the projects 1970–77

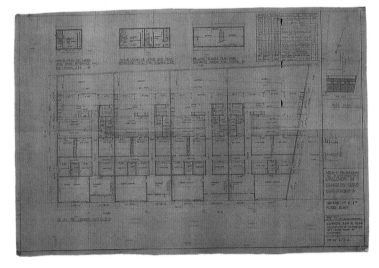

Left: Street elevation of one of
the P. C. de Saram row houses

Top right: Roof detail

Middle right: Internal courtyard with 'burglar pergola'

Bottom right: Original
drawing for the P. C. de
Saram row houses

four houses for p. c. de saram

COLOMBO 1970–73

Government restrictions brought private housebuilding to a near standstill during the early 1970s and Bawa's only domestic commissions came from the de Saram family. P. C. de Saram was a member of the Illangakoon family, for whom Bawa had designed his very first house, on Charles Circus, with H. H. Reid in 1951. In 1970, when de Saram asked him to design houses for each of his four children on a site on 5th Lane at the rear of the Illangakoon block of land in Colpetty, Bawa proposed a line of four row houses, each conceived as a mini version of the Ena de Silva House, with strong references to the Dutch–Muslim tradition of urban courtyard houses.

Sited on plots measuring about 15 by 35 metres (about 20 perches), each of the houses is set back to create a parking bay with a small planting bed, presenting to the street walls of white plaster with window and door reveals picked out in Corbusian primary colours, a different colour for each house. The houses comprise three transverse pavilions separated by courtyards and linked by a spine corridor. The first pavilion contains a garage, office and entrance hall, with staff accommodation on the first floor; the second contains bedrooms and bathrooms; and the third contains the dining and sitting rooms. The internal courtyards are protected by parallel pre-cast concrete beams that break up the light, diffuse heavy rain and provide security against rooftop burglars, hence earning the name the 'burglar pergola'. The interiors are cool and well lit, offering a strong sense of space and privacy on a compact plot. Surprisingly, this interesting and apparently successful experiment in urban living was never properly recorded or published.

The following year Bawa designed a single house for another member of the de Saram family in Cambridge Place, which took the form of an atrium house enclosed within a monumental blank wall.

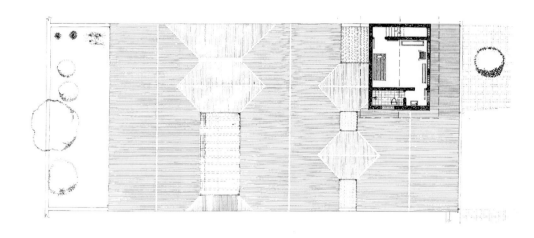

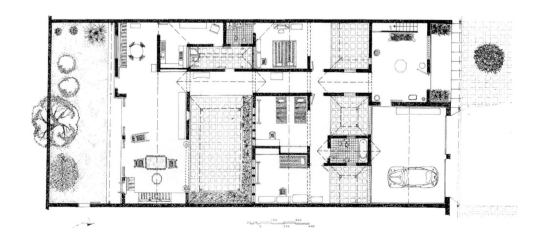

Top left: Plan of the Stanley
de Saram House

Top right: The central loggia
of the Stanley de Saram House

Bottom: Street façade of the
Stanley de Saram House

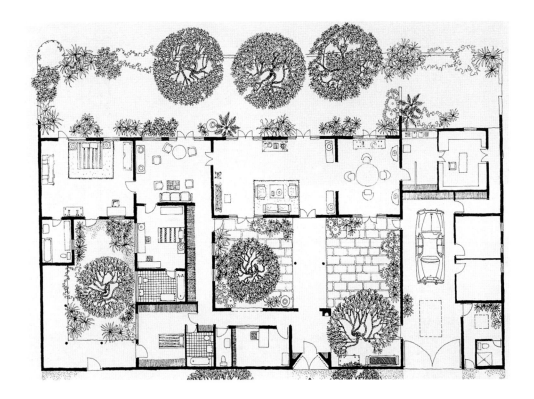

the madurai club

MADURAI, INDIA 1971–74

Martin Henry was appointed general manager of Madurai Mills in 1970. At the time the large thread-making company based in and around the South Indian city of Madurai ran two staff clubs: the Madurai Club in the centre of the town was an exclusive European preserve offering 'chambers' to outstation members and visitors, while the Garden Club in the suburb of Kochidi was for Indian staff and consisted of a simple bungalow with billiard room, card room and a verandah for dancing. Henry resolved to sell the old Madurai Club, using the proceeds to turn the Garden Club into a single meeting place for all his senior staff, and after sharing a drink with Bawa, asked him if he would be the architect for the new club. Bawa travelled to Madurai on 24 July and stayed two nights with the Henrys, visiting the site, collecting survey drawings of the existing buildings and subjecting Henry to twenty-four hours of intensive grilling. Three weeks later he returned to Madurai with a full set of design proposals.

At this point Henry added one further stipulation: the new club should be built entirely from materials found within 10 kilometres of the site. Bawa rose to the challenge and proposed that the structural columns should be of honey-coloured stone quarried from the local Nagamalai Hill and that stone slabs from an old mill should be used for the floors.

The project went on hold for almost a year while Henry wound up the old club and disposed of its buildings, so Bawa's next visit to Madurai took place in April 1972. On this occasion he and the Henrys travelled up to Karaikudi, where they agreed to break their self-imposed 10-kilometre rule and bought two old Chettinad doors, a set of four old carved stone columns and a miniature temple cart, all of which were incorporated into the new club. Bawa had occasionally used salvaged elements in his work before – the old temple door in Ena de Silva's house was an early example – but this was the first time he had used *bricolage* on such a scale and in such a deliberate way. Work finally started on site in January 1973 and the completed building opened in January 1975.

The merging of the two clubs brought Western and Hindu traditions into direct confrontation and was not without its complications. A mixed

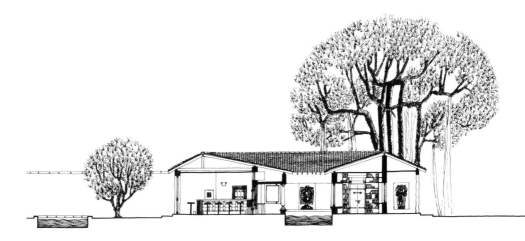

Top: Cross-section through the bar and the library

Bottom: The sitting room seen from the bar court

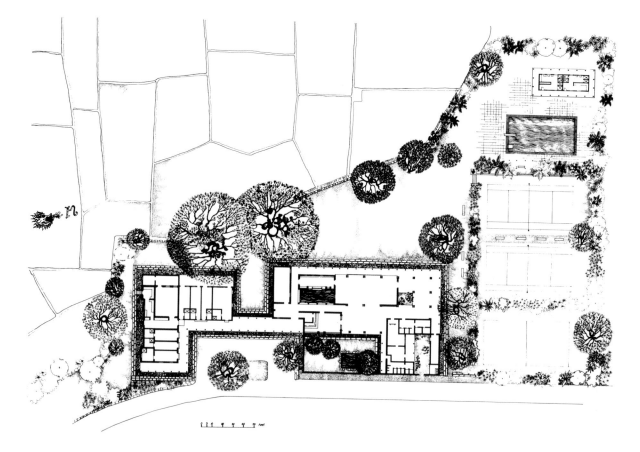

club needed a bar but this had to be hidden from the direct view of the teetotal members, while the restaurant needed two kitchens, one for vegetarians and one for non-vegetarians. The residential accommodation had to be segregated from the club proper, and the billiard room was to be treated as an inner sanctum. In response to these requirements, Bawa's design converted the old Garden Club into a set of seven 'chambers' grouped around the billiard room. A new wing containing the bar, a lounge, a restaurant, a library and a dance floor comprises a group of pillared pavilions placed around three internal courtyards under overhanging pitched roofs. Although the design is deceptively simple, it succeeds through the subtlety of its spatial organization, the care with which spatial hierarchies are set up and the connection of exterior, interior and semi-interior spaces through axial views.

The approaching visitor follows a narrow driveway into a small courtyard, where an entrance loggia connects the old Garden Club

to the new wing. The entrance, marked by a pair of wrought-iron gates and offering an immediate cross-vista through the club towards the garden, leads into a lobby where the visitor turns to encounter the long vista past the pool court through the restaurant towards the ping-pong verandah and the tennis courts. The pool court is punctuated by a set of old Chettinad columns and the pool is fed from a small fountain that gurgles from under the hood of an Indian temple cart. From the restaurant the bar is reached through an old Chettinad door set between two full-length mirrors that poke fun at the invisibility of the evils that lie within. Children, of course, are not allowed into the bar, so Bawa thoughtfully provided them with a small low-level window in the entrance loggia through which to order their soft drinks.

The walls are of random rubble, the columns of rough-hewn stone from a local quarry and the roofs of clay tile on corrugated cement sheeting. Close inspection reveals a minor order of single columns supporting the outer

Top, middle and bottom left: Details of the roof, walls and sliding screens

Top right: Plan

Opposite
Top right: View towards the bar and the central pool court

Bottom right: The central pool court

Bottom left: Bawa's design for a dressing table drawn by Ismeth Raheem in 1973

verandahs and a major order of composite columns made up of four quadrants of split stone set around a reinforced-concrete core and acting as the main structure. Large windows are set within stone jambs and sills, while smaller windows sit in monolithic stone frames, and glass door panels run on large brass wheels. The vaulted ceilings of the main restaurant and lounge areas are formed from coloured panels of locally produced handloom.

In 1974 Bawa opened a permanent office in Madras, and K. D. Schroff, a Parsee who had been Madurai Mills' factory engineer, joined the design staff. E. R. & B. continued to work for Madurai Mills, building a number of production buildings and a group of staff houses at Ambasamudrum.

Bawa, meanwhile, had grown fond of the Henrys and in 1973 designed a dressing table for Margaret Henry as a Christmas present. Made of rosewood with brass and ivory handles, it comprised three sections – two solid plinths spanned by a top with a mirror – and was intended as a travelling case. In what was later to become a characteristic gesture, Bawa added a personal message to the drawing: 'Dear Margaret – here's a non-Christmas present – it's designed so you can travel with it – you can pack it like two trunks – and there's a collapsible lamp to hang near it – the lamp is for your birthday – Geoffrey Nov 1973.' The Henrys subsequently moved to Bangalore and in 1979 Bawa remodelled their house in Edward Road.

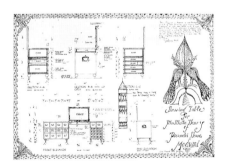

Left: View along the entrance
verandah towards the apartments

batujimbar pavilions

BALI, INDONESIA 1972–75

Geoffrey Bawa's brother, Bevis, had met the Australian painter Donald Friend in 1949 on a ship sailing from Colombo to Italy and had casually invited him to come and stay at Brief when he was next in Ceylon. Friend finally took up this invitation in 1957 and stayed for four years, building a studio for himself in Bevis's garden. This was a prolific period for Friend, as he experimented with a number of different media: *bas relief* tiles, aluminium sculptures, painted doors, murals, gold-leaf paintings. While Friend received help and encouragement from Plesner, he and Bawa were not especially close; Friend was a bit of a rough diamond who would alternate periods of hard work with bouts of heavy drinking. He probably found Geoffrey altogether too genteel and too 'pom', while Geoffrey was probably overawed by this rip-roaring Aussie.

In 1967, Friend made a first visit to the island of Bali and was immediately captivated. The following year he returned and started to build a house for himself on a large plot of land next to the sea at Batujimbar, on the south-east corner of the island, at a point where the coral reefs 'divide Asia from the Antipodes'. While passing through Ceylon in 1971 he visited Lunuganga. He was planning to build a development of beach villas at Batujimbar and he wanted Bawa to be its architect. The development would include a museum to house Friend's collection of Balinese sculpture and an amphitheatre for performances of music and dance. It would be built by local craftsmen and incorporate salvaged artefacts from old Balinese palaces.

Bawa visited Friend in Bali and spent some time contemplating the site, gathering information about Balinese architecture and meeting local craftsmen. From Friend's description of this visit in his book *The Cosmic Turtle* (Friend 1976, pp.12–15), one senses the tensions in their relationship:

Before the building at Batujimbar arose, the architect used to stand (immensely tall) in the grateful shade of the breadfruit, and direct at the sun-drenched distances a gaze both cynical and visionary. The look, in fact, that the creative artist bestows on his subject before disintegrating it and reconstituting it as a work of art. Next came an airy gesture that conjured the horizontals and verticals of terraces and walls.

'Some stairs. Certainly some stairs. Malachite. You have malachite quarries nearby?'
'The nearest are in Russia.'
'How tiresome. Honey-coloured marble?'
'In Isfahan. Transport would present a problem.'
'Would it be extravagant to propose a lake? – rather a large lake – with a sort of Chinese island and a pavilion from which to view the reflections of passing clouds in a mirror of water?'
'But Geoffrey the cost…'
'It would be simple enough to make the lake. All you'd have to do is build a bund linking those two ranges of hills.'
'It's not my land.'
'Then you must buy it immediately. This very day. How strange that you should own this piece of land and not that. So now you shall have both. It will provide a modicum of elbow room.'
'It would cost millions.'
'Not that many millions. Besides, think of what pleasure it will give you. To have something uniquely beautiful and completely useless.'
'Really, Geoffrey…'
'What in fact I was seriously proposing is a moat along three sides of the inland border. Water lilies. Ferns. Golden carp fish.'
A moat! – the relief was immense. That lake would have beggared me for life; the moat only for a couple of years. After the torture of the slicing knives, a blow on the head is a positive pleasure.

Friend set up a development company with a Balinese partner in 1972 and appointed Bawa lead consultant with a local practice in support. Back in Colombo, Bawa drew up a master plan identifying fifteen plots, each with an area of about 4,000 square metres and a beach frontage of about 30 metres. The scheme had to include Friend's existing house on plot 5 and that of his business partner, Wija Waworuntu, on plot 7. Work began the following year on plot 5 – which would contain Friend's private museum, the open-air theatre and a visitor centre – and on plots 6 and 11, while detailed designs were also produced for plots 8, 10 and 12.

The houses were designed individually but each conformed to a basic pattern: an entrance court with garages and servants' quarters next to the

Top right: Drawing of Batujimbar by Donald Friend

Bottom right: Plan of plot 6

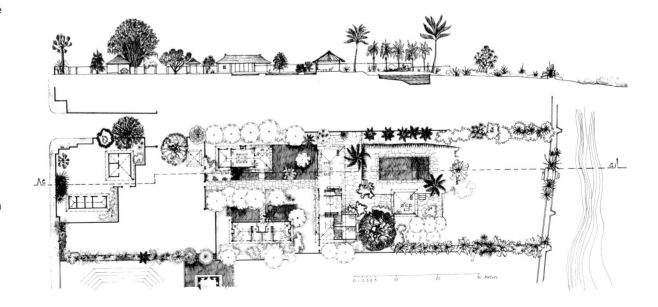

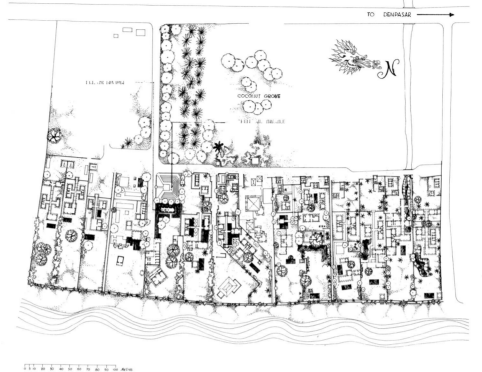

road; a walled area with residential pavilions grouped around a pool at the centre of the plot; and a garden area with smaller pavilions that led finally, via a small opening, to the beach and the sea. The main pavilions were set on raised stone plinths and consisted of open loggias with thatch roofs supported on slender teak columns, leading to enclosed rooms with thick walls of plastered rubble and coral. Bawa was able to tap directly into Friend's extensive knowledge of Balinese architectural traditions to develop designs that reflected the methods of local craftsmen. The overall concept was inspired by the nineteenth-century palaces at Klungkung and Amlapura, which Bawa visited with Friend, but the asymmetrical arrangement of raised pavilions within a walled compound also recalls Sinhalese monasteries of the Anuradhapura period.

Top left: Friend's self-portrait in the Lunuganga visitors' book, showing him staring at Bawa's design for the museum

Top right: Plan of the whole development with designs for fifteen plots

Middle and bottom: Cross-section and plan of plot 11

Opposite

Top: A Bawa sketch of traditional Balinese pavilions

Bottom: Friend's museum on plot 5 in 1979

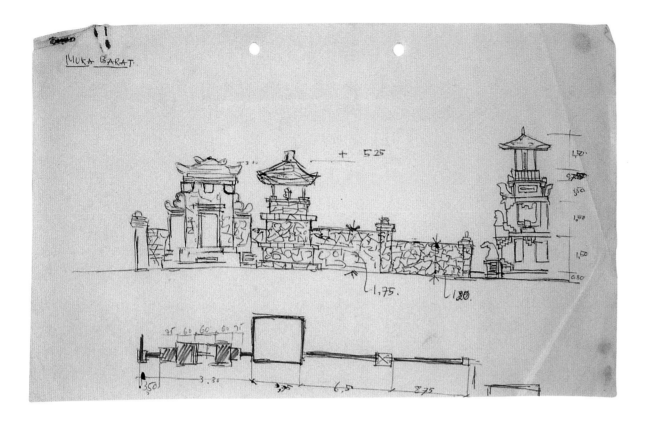

MUKA BARAT.

Bawa supplied general design drawings for the various buildings, backing these up with a library of standard details, but supervision was entrusted to the local architects, while building work was carried out by local contractors and detailed embellishments were carved by local craftsmen working under Friend's direction. Bawa pursued his new interest in *bricolage* and incorporated Friend's collection of old doors, windows and stone carvings into the designs. Because the project had to be managed from afar, it was difficult for Bawa to control the site work and he also had to contend with interference from Friend and his local collaborators. Only the museum pavilion on plot 5, with its moat and stone terracing, and the houses on plots 6 and 11 were built to his designs.

In *The Cosmic Turtle* Donald Friend offers a glowing testimonial to his architect (Friend 1976, pp.15–27):

Today this moat reflects a building of faded rose brick and grey mauve stone. A flight of stone steps rises to the upper storey – a wide, long, open platform with a forest of slim pillars supporting the thatched roof. Warm yellow–grey thatch in the sunlight – silver–grey where the palms throw shadows...

Once inside it, one finds that its ten lofty windows are deeply embrasured, conveying the illusion of being protected by walls six-feet thick...the room's classically elegant proportions define an environment of aesthetic self-indulgence from which one may look out on all sides to vistas of moat, garden and plantation. It is one of Geoffrey Bawa's architectural masterpieces.

Sadly Friend fell out with his local partners and lost control of the development. Batujimbar passed into the hands of Waworuntu and the remaining plots were developed in piecemeal fashion without adhering to the master-plan principles. Part of the estate was later leased to the Indonesian hotelier Adrian Zecha, whose in-house designer Ed Tuttle revamped plot 5 in 1985. A number of the other gardens were extensively remodelled by the Australian garden designer Made Wijaya, while some of the interiors were fitted out by Bali-based decorator Linda Garland. The estate became a favourite haunt of the rich and famous and only a small part of Friend's vision and Bawa's architecture has survived. However, Batujimbar was an early example of a tourist development that sought to capture the spirit of Bali and respect local traditions of making and doing and it exerted a considerable influence on later developments on the island.

Top left: Roof detail

**Bottom left: The main pavilion
of plot 11**

**Top right: Plans of the main
pavilion of plot 11**

peter white house

PEREYBERE MAURITIUS 1973–74

The opportunity to convert an old sugar mill on the island of Mauritius presented Bawa with a fresh challenge but also served to underline the difficulties that working outside Sri Lanka inevitably entailed. Although Mauritius has much in common with Sri Lanka and on the map seems to be only a short hop across the Indian Ocean, communications between the two islands were not easy.

Peter White, the client, had spent part of his childhood in Ceylon before the war and had returned there in 1946 to work in an agency house called Boyce Brothers. He had been a friend of Bevis Bawa and was an admirer of the Ena de Silva House. White moved to Mauritius in 1964 to take up an appointment as manager of the Lonrho sugar plantations. His office was in Port Louis but he lived for most of the year at Phoenix on the Curepipe Plateau. In 1972 he discovered a ruined mill on an old sugar plantation at Pereybere near Grand Bay and resolved to convert it into a weekend house.

Bawa's former colleague, Nihal Amarasinghe, had recently arrived to work in Mauritius and White learned from him that E. R. & B. was short of work and asked Bawa to be the architect for the mill conversion. Exchange control restrictions made it difficult for Sri Lankans to travel abroad and Bawa agreed to undertake the design in exchange for an air ticket and his board and lodging. He flew out to Mauritius via East Africa in May 1973 and spent three weeks contemplating the site, taking photographs, making sketches and formulating proposals.

Working from such a distance was not without its problems, however. Back in Colombo the survey plans, sketches and photographs were handed over to Ismeth Raheem, who worked up the design to the level of detail that would normally have sufficed for a project in Sri Lanka, where most of the critical design decisions would be made on site. It had been agreed that the building work would be carried out by Lonrho contractors and that Bawa might pop over for a couple of site visits as the job progressed. When the drawings were sent to White, however, he felt that they were not sufficient for the contractors to work from and the office had to supply more detailed

drawings. White arranged for much of the specialist wrought-iron work to be executed in his own estate workshops. The project was completed in nine months. Bawa was unable to visit the site during construction and in the event Amarasinghe acted as the site architect.

The design respected the integrity of the existing buildings. The main store consisted of two long vaulted rooms and was designated as the main pavilion, with a kitchen and store-room inserted under a mezzanine bedroom at the end of one of the vaults. A second, smaller building was converted to a guest wing.

White never actually lived in the house and used it mainly for entertaining. When he finally quit Mauritius in 1995 the land was divided into parcels and sold off. The old mill is now used as a private house.

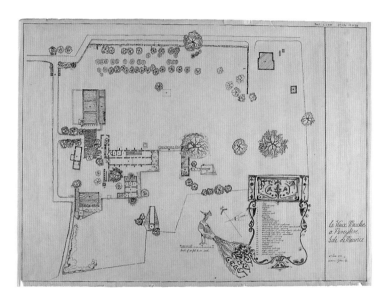

the neptune hotel

BERUWELA 1973–76

The Neptune Hotel, commissioned by the Hotels Corporation, was Bawa's only hotel design in Sri Lanka to be realized during this period. The site occupied a long and narrow strip of land running between the main road and the sea within a fairly densely populated area to the south of the old Arab port of Beruwela. Bawa, perhaps unconsciously, used a strategy similar to that he was developing on a much smaller scale at Batujimbar to create a totally intro-spective composition. The hotel was planned in the form of a huge H, the arms forming an entrance court to the east while to the west was a large pool court. The reception area was raised to first-floor level so that visitors moved from a *porte cochère* to a reception loggia and terrace with an elevated view over the pool court towards the ocean. The main restaurant was located beneath the terrace, beside the pool. To form ramps up to the *porte cochère* earth was excavated from the entry court and the resultant pit was flooded to create an exotic wildlife pond. Hotel bedrooms were arranged on two levels around the three sides of the pool court, with balconies angled to face the sea.

Bawa had recently remodelled the house of his neighbours, Herbert and Norma Tennakoon, for which Laki Senanayake had sculpted a plaster *bas relief* of swirling vegetation. This served as a trial for a much larger series of reliefs that Senanayake carved in the Neptune's reception loggia. Bawa also liked to adorn hotel bedrooms with paintings, handlooms and batiks by his various friends and collaborators, though, in time, many of these beautiful objects departed in the guests' suitcases. To counter this, when the Neptune came to be refurbished in the early 1990s, Senanayake was asked to produce an individual mural on the wall of every single bedroom, which he did by working in relays with a team of assistants.

Opposite: Aerial view

This page
Top right: A bedroom wing

Bottom: Cross-section

Top left: The *porte cochère*

Top right: View of the upper sitting room showing a sculpture and wall relief by Laki Senanayake

Bottom: The pool seen from the dining room

pallakelle industrial estate

DIGANA 1970–71

Bawa's first commission from the new government in 1970 was to build a small industrial estate for the Department of Industries at Digana near Kandy to provide simple low-rental factories in an area of high unemployment. The site occupies the sides of a flat valley running towards the Mahaweli River a few kilometres upstream from the future site of the Victoria Dam.

The design proposed a series of standard units, each with a simple square plan under a stepped pyramidal roof of clay tile on concrete sheet. Units were built in two sizes and could be subdivided or connected. In each unit the roof is supported on elegant lightweight steel trusses spanning an outer and inner square of concrete columns, while the section admits natural light and breezes from the perimeter and from a step halfway up the roof. The double roof skin and generous height reduce the effects of internal surface radiation and the section encourages both stack and wind-induced ventilation.

In their final form these industrial units bear an interesting resemblance to traditional Buddhist teaching halls. After more than thirty years of use with little or no maintenance, the estate is still in reasonable condition and today accommodates a number of garment factories.

Top: A Buddhist preaching hall at the Dowa Temple

Bottom: The interior of a factory unit at Pallakelle

agrarian research and training institute

COLOMBO 1974–76

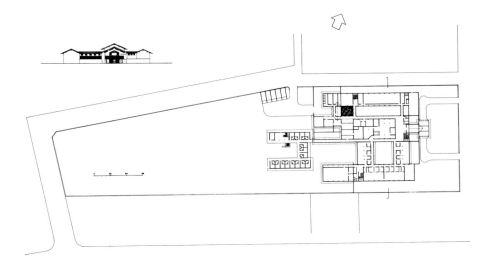

The Agrarian Research and Training Institute is situated at the southern end of Wijerama Mawatha, a broad avenue of large villas mainly housing official residences or government offices. The institute was built for a government department during a time of austerity and strict import control. The brief called for a range of large and small offices, a lecture hall, a library and a residential hostel and challenged Bawa to work within a low budget and with local materials to create a pleasant, naturally ventilated working environment.

Working with Ismeth Raheem, Bawa created a tight group of two-storey pavilions arranged in chequerboard fashion around a collection of carefully planted courtyards. In deference to the scale of the surroundings, the buildings are set back from the road behind a front garden and a simple *porte cochère*. In typical Bawa fashion the initial impression of axial symmetry is gently dispelled as the visitor penetrates the building and discovers the unique proportions of each successive space. Corridors are open-sided and serve single banks of rooms, encouraging cross-ventilation and removing all need for air-conditioning.

Bawa used his now familiar palette of materials with great assurance: a crisp concrete frame with neatly articulated concrete purlins and rafters supports a roof of tiles on corrugated sheeting; broad overhanging eaves cast deep shadows on the white plastered walls; access balconies are protected by chunky coconut balustrades and surfaced with polished clay tiles. Today, after nearly thirty years of use, these buildings are still in excellent condition and offer a potent exemplar of sustainable and energy-conscious design to a new generation of architects.

In the following year Bawa designed another experimental office building for the National Institute of Management Studies on a site immediately behind the ARTI. This five-floor pavilion adopted the stepped-out section developed for the Bentota Beach Hotel, making it possible to insert a surprising open courtyard at fourth-floor level.

Top: Plan

Middle: The *porte cochère*

Bottom: View of the main courtyard

Opposite
Top left: Upper verandah

Top centre: The side court

Top right: A typical office

Bottom: The National Institute of Management Studies

state mortgage bank

This uncharacteristic twelve-storey office building was commissioned by the government of the day to house the State Mortgage Bank, but when it was completed after the UNP's election victory in 1977, it was redesignated the main secretariat of the Mahaweli Development Ministry. It has never been published and was omitted even from Taylor's 1986 monograph, probably because its uncompromisingly geometric form did not accord with that book's emphasis on the vernacular and picturesque aspects of Bawa's work. This fact did not prevent Ken Yeang from observing: '[Bawa's] Mahaweli Headquarters Building is probably the best example of a bioclimatically responsive tall building to be found anywhere in the world' (Keniger 1996).

The restricted site is wedged between Darley Road and the southern tip of the Beira Lake and overlooks Colombo's Hyde Park Corner.

This busy commercial district was in former times a residential suburb and the vestiges of Bawa's childhood home can still be seen on the other side of the road. The lozenge-shape plan was developed with Anura Ratnavibushana and results in a profile that changes dramatically according to viewpoint, appearing slender towards the junction and much flatter towards the park and the lake. It is capped by a floating concrete canopy that reveals the geometric logic of the concrete structure below.

The objective was to provide a working environment that could be lit and ventilated by natural means in a building of moderate height that did not impose undue strains on the immediate urban infrastructure. The main elevations face north and south in order to reduce solar gain and catch the main breezes; windows are set back from deep spandrel panels designed as air-intake louvres. Appearing just as Colombo was about to experience an unprecedented building boom in its central business district, this design offered a prototype for office building in

a tropical city. Sadly no attempt was made by the client to monitor its performance or modify its details and the demands of offshore property developers and international clients prevailed in Colombo, giving rise to a crop of sealed-glass, energy-guzzling towers in the main business district.

Ratnavibushana has said that Bawa initially proposed to paint the render black. 'Alas, the superstitious bankers would have none of it but I managed to get them to agree to what I called "elephant grey"' (Anura Ratnavibushana in a letter to the author). Although the office floors were intended to be open, they were soon partitioned by the second client, whose expatriate consultants and managers demanded air-conditioning. While some initial problems had been experienced during monsoons, these could easily have been solved by sympathetic building management. Today the ground floor has been enclosed by walls and barbed wire for security reasons, ugly air-conditioners dot the façades and the render has been painted a gaudy mixture of turquoise, pink and brick red.

Bottom left: Plan at ground floor and a typical upper-floor level

Bottom right: Cross-section through the State Mortgage Bank showing the breathing wall

Opposite
Top left: The tower seen from Darley Road

Bottom left: The staircase

Right: The tower seen across Hyde Park from Union Place

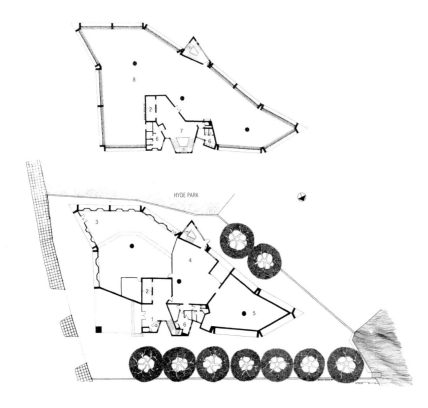

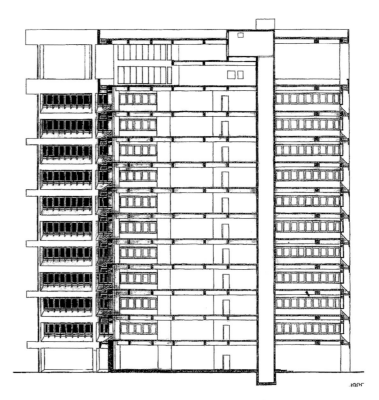

a buddhist temple

seema malaka

COLOMBO 1976–78

The Seema Malaka is the only modern Buddhist temple in Sri Lanka to have been built to a non-traditional design. It floats on Colombo's Beira Lake and is used as an inauguration hall for the monks of the nearby Gangaramia Temple. The idea to build a new temple came from a priest called Podi Hamudrua and it was he who raised the money and invited Bawa to be the architect. The main benefactor was a prominent Bora Muslim businessman called Moosajee, who had been ostracized by his own community and consequently decided to give his money to support a Buddhist foundation. Bawa was initially reluctant to accept the commission, though he may have been persuaded by the fact that Moosajee's son, Asker, was both a client and a friend.

The temple consists of a central plinth connected to the lakeside by a causeway and to two lesser plinths by short bridges. The main plinth carries a preaching hall, the northern plinth a small inauguration room and the southern plinth has a *bo* tree at its centre with *devales* at its four corners. While the design is quite revolutionary it recognizes a number of precedents and reveals the depth of Bawa's interest in classical Sinhalese archi-tecture. The idea for the overall form may have been taken from the forest monasteries of Anuradhapura – the subject of a study by the archaeologist Senake Bandaranayake (1974).

A typical forest monastery consisted of a walled enclosure containing a group of raised plinths supporting wooden pavilions with tiled roofs. Bridges connecting the plinths suggest that the enclosures were flooded with water.

The main preaching hall of the Seema Malaka seems to float above its plinth on massive cross-beams in a manner reminiscent of early *ambalama* such as that at Panavitiya near Kurunegala. Its pyramidal roof was originally double-pitched with clay tiles laid on corrugated sheets, but it has recently been reclad with blue glazed tiles. The interior is enclosed by a screen of inward-sloping carved rafters inspired by temples in Kerala and Nepal. The *devales* are designed as four small cubicles with granite corner posts and panelled timber walls, and they house the Hindu gods Saman, Kataragama, Nanba and Pattini. A small *stupa* has been added on a projecting platform to the eastern side of the plinth.

Bawa was not consulted over the choice of statuary and the temple has been subject to a number of small changes. However, the simplicity of the Seema Malaka has enabled it to absorb extraneous elements and it remains a place of astonishing peace and harmony. The design can be compared with the earlier factory units at Pallakelle (1970) and it also seems to anticipate the final design for the Parliament building at Kotte (1979), illus-trating the way in which Bawa would take an idea and develop it over time in a number of apparently different situations.

Middle right: Plan

Bottom: View from the lakeside

Opposite
Top left: View over the lake with the Colombo Fort in the background

Bottom left: The *bo* tree plinth with its four *devales*

Top right: View from the main preaching hall towards the inauguration cell

Bottom right: A traditional *ambalama*

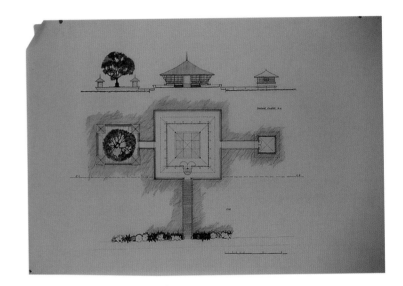

A change of government

In the 1977 elections the UNP swept back into power in a landslide victory and a new government under prime minister J. R. Jayewardene embarked on a massive development programme that included huge hydroelectric and irrigation schemes, social housing, village redevelopments and an expansion of higher education. A free trade zone was opened to encourage inward investment in industry and every effort was made to revive tourism. Following a change in the constitution in 1978, Jayewardene became Sri Lanka's first president, and his popular minister of housing, Ranasinghe Premadasa, was made prime minister.

The architectural profession had grown in leaps and bounds over the preceding twenty years and was now well established. The school of architecture at Katubedde, now incorporated into the University of Moratuwa and recognized by the RIBA, produced a steady stream of about thirty graduates a year. A plethora of architectural practices had come into existence, some of them quite large and several run by Bawa's former employees. The Sri Lanka Institute of Architects (SLIA) could now boast more than a hundred members; Bawa had been its chairman in 1969 and received its Gold Medal in 1982. The government invited the SLIA to play a major role in its new

development programme and projects were channelled through the institute to its members, though Bawa remained aloof from this process, preferring to receive his commissions directly from government.

As ever, Bawa maintained political neutrality in public, but privately he welcomed the change of government. Jayewardene was an old friend: he had been a contemporary of Bevis Bawa at Royal College and was responsible for commissioning the Bentota Beach Resort when he was minister of tourism in the 1960s. In 1979 Jayewardene entrusted Bawa with the project closest to his heart – the building of a new Parliament at Kotte (p.146). Other important public commissions followed: the remodelling of the old Parliament buildings, the refurbishment of offices for the Greater Colombo Economic Commission, the planning of the new University of Ruhunu (1980; p.158) and the design of a new rest house at Anuradhapura.

Bawa also received a phone call from the new prime minister one day in 1978. Premadasa was a unique figure in Sri Lankan politics: he had been born into a working-class family in Hultsdorf and had risen through the rough-and-tumble of Colombo municipal politics. He and his wife had just moved to Temple Trees, the prime minister's official residence and,

finding the place a little daunting, wanted advice about how best to settle in. Bawa spent a day with the Premadasas, placing furniture, hanging pictures and advising on new decorations. At one point he seated himself at the centre of the main reception room while the prime minister and his wife shifted furniture around to his bidding. Premadasa appreciated Bawa's help and later asked him to refurbish his official secretariat in Flower Road.

Bawa's success in avoiding being identified with any one political group was well illustrated by various private commissions he received over the next few years. In 1978 he designed a house with Vasantha Jacobsen for Anura Bandaranaike – the son of the former prime minister and an opposition MP in his own right – next door to Mrs Bandaranaike's home on the family plot in Rosmead Place. In the same year he designed a house with Anura Ratnavibushana for the UNP's minister for Mahaweli redevelopment, Gamini Dissanayake, and in the mid-1980s he designed a house at Mrs Bandaranaike's country estate at Horagolla for her daughter, Sunethra (p.172). Later commissions included houses for Premadasa's daughter, Dulanjalee Jayakody (1991; p.221), and Jayewardene's grandson, Pradeep (1997; p.223).

The de Soysa House, Colombo

Jayewardene and Premadasa united two opposing wings of their party and won enormous popular support for their policies. During the first five years of their mandate they achieved much of what they had promised and created a new sense of optimism and purpose in the country. Inexplicably, however, Jayewardene cancelled the elections scheduled for 1982 and substituted a referendum that allowed the UNP to appoint new MPs. This undermined Parliament's power at exactly the moment when its new buildings were due to open, paving the way for all sorts of political chicanery. MPs became fiefs in their constituencies and the UNP started to split into factions.

The government's successes on the economic front were tarnished by the deterioration of relations between the different ethnic communities. Tragically, UNP politicians failed to respond to signs of discontent among the northern Tamils or to appreciate the significance of growing calls for Eelam – an independent Tamil homeland. In 1983 a bloody ambush of an army patrol by Tamil Tiger rebels sparked off a week-long orgy of anti-Tamil violence across the south-west of the island, which in turn ignited a full-scale civil war in the north and east, forcing communities apart and slowly strangling the economic and social life of the country.

Working life

Most of the team of young designers that Bawa had assembled during the 1960s had now departed and he relied more and more on the support of Poologasundram and Vasantha Jacobsen. Although he missed the stimulus and friendship of his earlier colleagues he was now in his sixties and at the height of his powers: what he needed was not creative designers to help him work out new ideas but competent technicians to

do his bidding. The design team for the new Parliament included a group of architects from Bombay and was headed by Vasantha Jacobsen, while Ruhunu University was run almost single-handedly by Nihal Bodhinayake, a young architect who had studied in Belgrade and Australia.

Bawa increasingly relaxed and discussed evolving ideas with friends from outside the office. During the 1980s the architect Anjalendran became a regular companion and confidante, joining Bawa for weekends at Lunuganga and sometimes accompanying him on trips abroad. Anjalendran had studied at Moratuwa and graduated from the Bartlett in London in 1977. Having briefly worked at E. R. & B. at the end of the 1970s he left to start a small practice of his own from his mother's verandah and soon established himself as one of the most talented architects of his generation. He was also an inspired teacher and had a deep knowledge of architectural history and theory. Worried by the lack of any systematic recording system in the E. R. & B. office, he started to build up a unique archive of documents relating to the work of the practice.

Another close friend was Milroy Perera, an architect who had qualified at North London Polytechnic in 1975 and worked freelance for the next fifteen years, dividing his time between London and Colombo. When Bawa was in London, Perera acted as his companion and organizer, but he also took on an increasingly important backroom role in Colombo. Although Perera was employed directly by E. R. & B. only for short periods, Bawa frequently consulted him on technical matters and they would often work together at 33rd Lane, where the guest flat came to be used more and more as an informal office, its location close to the main office making it a convenient bolt-hole for Bawa.

Other friends offered support and advice from time to time. Ena de Silva continued to produce work for the office, designing the massive banners that were hung in the piazza of the Parliament building on state occasions, but she was also a regular visitor to Bawa's home. At one point, when he was worried about certain aspects of the Ruhunu design, she went with him to Matara and spent two days helping him on site. Barbara Sansoni, now the proprietor of a highly successful design business in Colombo specializing in modern handlooms, remained a close friend and also gave advice on colour schemes. Jean Chamberlin and Christoph Bon were frequent visitors to Colombo: Jean would offer advice on office management, while Christoph often acted as an outside critic.

Bawa enjoyed very little private life during this period: weekdays were dominated by office work and evenings were often given over to diagnostic discussions with Milroy or Anjalendran; weekends were usually spent at Lunuganga working in the garden and plotting new pavilions and planting schemes. However, Bawa's retreat now boasted an office on the eastern terrace and a guest wing for office staff in the valley next to the ha-ha, and it was not uncommon for Bawa to bring colleagues down with him to work over the weekend.

Bawa still enjoyed getting involved with small projects, particularly when he needed an antidote to the work of the office. For some time he had his eye on Mohoti Walaawe, an elegant but dilapidated nineteenth-century villa overlooking the beach from across the railway track on the southern edge of Bentota. Typically he tried to persuade various friends to buy it so that he could first enjoy the pleasure of remodelling it for them, then share their pleasure in living in it. One candidate was the Italian sculptress Lidia Duchini, who had carved the bishop for Bishop's College. She was now married to a Sri Lankan called Dallas Gunasekera and wanted a house near the sea where she could work. She wasn't interested in Mohoti Walaawe but Bawa did succeed in persuading her to buy two old houses nearby that faced each other across the busy Galle Road. Bawa first reversed the house on the east side of the road so that it faced inland onto an enclosed garden and then demolished the house to the west and rebuilt it within the garden at right angles to the first house. A third entry pavilion was added to complete the composition and a high boundary wall was built to keep out the noise of the traffic. The result was a subtle grouping of three pavilions around a partly enclosed garden that looked eastwards across an overgrown swamp. After Lidia Gunasekera's death the Gunasekera House, which came to be known as 'Number Eighty-Seven', fell into disrepair, but was rescued and lovingly restored in 1996 by Rohan Jayakody, who added a secluded lap pool to Bawa's design and later began to transform the swamp into a landscaped wilderness.

Another candidate for Mohoti Walaawe was Bawa's friend S. M. A. Hameed, who had been the manager of the Serendib Hotel since it had opened but had long entertained ambitions to own a hotel of his own. When Bawa suggested that he convert Mohoti Walaawe for this purpose, Hameed, doubting the viability of the proposal, bought the land immediately south of the villa instead and persuaded Bawa to design a row of small beach villas for him.

Having failed to persuade any of his friends to buy the villa, Bawa finally bought it for himself and set about

converting it into a small hotel. Initially he added a wing of bedrooms and an enclosed courtyard with a dining loggia and pool. Later a second wing of rooms was added to the north. The hotel was managed during the 1980s by Hameed who incorporated his own row of beach villas and gave the whole complex the name Club Villa. When Bawa sold his part in 1990, Hameed enlarged his villas, adding wings to designs by Anjalendran and Channa Daswatte, and continued to use the name Club Villa.

A book and an exhibition

Christoph Bon and Jean Chamberlin were keen to present Bawa's work to a wider public and in 1983 they started to make plans for the publication of a book, collecting material with the help of Anjalendran in Colombo. Unfortunately Bawa's office had never kept complete records of projects and many drawings and photographs of the early work had been either lost or destroyed by white ants. A draughtsman called Vernon Nonis was

hired to produce new drawings for publication and, in a bizarre attempt to give them greater authenticity, Bawa signed the drawings with dates approximating those of the originals. By chance the editors of *Mimar*, a quarterly journal supported by the Aga Khan, embarked on a similar project at about the same time and Bon and Chamberlin joined forces with *Mimar*, which agreed to publish the book through a Singapore-based firm called Concept Media. The American writer Brian Brace Taylor, an associate editor of *Mimar*, was asked to write the introductory essay for the book and responded well to a difficult challenge, in spite of having to navigate a way around Bawa's reluctance to discuss work in theoretical terms.

The book was pulled together from a number of sources and assembled in the London home of Chamberlin and Bon. As well as Taylor's essay, there was a fairly equivocal statement by Bawa, a description of Lunuganga by Ulrik Plesner that had first appeared in a Danish magazine in

Opposite
Top: A palm-leaf *pandol* depicting J. R. Jayewardene
Middle: President Jayewardene and Geoffrey Bawa during a site visit to Parliament in 1982
Bottom: Anjalendran in his 'verandah office' in 1987

This page
Top: Bawa on the eastern terrace at Lunuganga with his friends Dr Raheem and Jean Chamberlin
Middle right: Number Eighty-Seven at Bentota
Bottom right: The Mohoti Walaawe at Bentota

Bottom left: Bawa at work
on a drawing of Number Eighty-
Seven for the 'White Book'
Bottom right: Laki Senanayake's
original 1961 drawing of the
Ena de Silva House

1959, and an idiosyncratic background sketch by Barbara Sansoni. Photographs were begged and borrowed from friends.

Bawa's own piece was largely a reprise of an article he had written in 1968 for the *Times Annual of Ceylon* (Bawa 1968). Indeed almost half of it is taken word-for-word from the earlier article. It ends, however, with an important statement:

When one delights as much as I do in planning a building and having it built, I find it impossible to describe the exact steps in an analytical or dogmatic way…I have a very strong conviction that it is impossible to explain architecture in words…I have always enjoyed seeing buildings but seldom enjoyed reading explanations about them…architecture cannot be totally explained but must be experienced. (Taylor 1986, p.18)

In spite of being produced like a patchwork quilt on Jean Chamberlin's dining table, the book – the first of its kind to deal with the work of a 'Third World' architect – was a great success when it appeared in February 1986. It may be that its overall flavour was to some extent determined by the material to hand, though Bawa certainly kept a strict control on what was included. Looking back, it seems that, in spite of Taylor's attempts to tease out other issues, Bawa was happy to present an account of his work that was easy on the eye and emphasized its vernacular content. The book showed the selected projects in a way that stressed their scenographic qualities at the expense of any discussion about their social or cultural implications and did little to provoke any serious discussion about the real significance of Bawa's work. It also omitted projects such as the A. S. H. de Silva House, the Polontalawa Estate Bungalow, the State Mortgage Bank or the Martenstyn House, that addressed important issues or opened up interesting new debates. The 'White Book', as it came to be known, did succeed, however, in bringing Bawa's buildings to the attention of a wider public, helping to enhance his growing international reputation and eventually bringing new clients to his door.

The *Mimar* book and articles of this time in journals from around the world were influential in another respect: they introduced a style of drawing so widely copied that it became almost standard throughout tropical Asia. The copy drawings made by Vernon Nonis were the distillation of a house style that had evolved over many years. During the 1960s drawings were ascribed little value in Bawa's office, because so much was decided with the craftsmen on site. Often the first set of coherent drawings would be produced after the building was completed. What then emerged was a style of presentation drawing that lavished almost as much attention on trees and shrubs as on the buildings themselves, showing not 'how to build this design', but rather 'what this design will look like when the planting has taken over'. The first exponents of this style were Laki Senanayake, S. Narasingham and Ismeth Raheem, inspired in part by the example of Donald Friend and Ulrik Plesner. Senanayake recalls the time when he stopped drawing just 'any old tree' and started drawing precise tree species. His 1961 drawings of the Ena de Silva House provide a good example of the evolving house style. Drawn in an expressive and relaxed way with varying line thicknesses and hatching, the temple tree and jak tree are accurately represented and a tiny

Top left: A view of the 1986
exhibition at the RIBA in
London's Portland Place
Top right: Bawa supervising
the assembly of the exhibition

tortoise is shown walking along the verandah. The Nonis copies of these drawings in the White Book follow the original Senanayake drawings in every detail, right down to the tortoise, but are drawn with a controlled and constant line almost like Mogul miniatures.

At around the same time that the book was being prepared, a young British architect called Christopher Beaver, acting quite independently, had hatched his own plan to organize an exhibition in London of Bawa's work. Beaver had been introduced to the work by Ulrik Plesner when they were both working together at Arup Associates in London during the early 1970s. Having obtained the RIBA's agreement to stage the exhibition in their Portland Place headquarters, Beaver visited Sri Lanka early in 1984 to canvass Bawa's support. While there he managed to win official backing from President Jayewardene and the British Council and to obtain offers of financial support. At Bawa's suggestion he joined forces with the group working on the book in order to avoid duplication of effort, and the two projects developed in tandem.

The exhibition opened in London on 6 March 1986 and ran for four weeks. It followed the same general structure as the book, illustrating the same projects, but was more coherent. However, British architects at the time were still preoccupied with debates about Post-Modernism, and the exhibition attracted little attention, receiving only one rather mean-spirited review from Shanti Jayewardene, a London-based Sri Lankan architect (Jayewardene 1986b). Later in the same year it was shown in New York, Boston and Colombo before being stacked away in the attic in Alfred House Road. Ten years later, however, it was revived following the publication of a new edition of the *Mimar* book (Taylor 1995), the old panels dusted down, and a few new ones added, before being shown to large audiences and enthusiastic reviews in Brazil, Australia and Singapore.

Although Bawa had practised under the title Edwards, Reid and Begg since 1957 and had been in partnership with Poologasundram since 1966, both the book and the exhibition were presented under the name Geoffrey Bawa. While the book included a brief acknowledgment of Poologasundram's contribution, all mention of his name was omitted from the exhibition credits.

Foreign travel, lectures and interviews

Bawa had inherited a love of travel from his mother and he never forgot their trip to China in 1934. However, during the 1980s, foreign travel became something of an obsession: he travelled to be with friends, visit clients, sit on juries, give lectures, buy antiques for himself or his clients, receive awards; there were even times when he travelled alone simply to gain some time to himself. Although a seasoned traveller he was not good at looking after himself and enjoyed being spoiled in luxury hotels or friends' homes. Anjalendran recalls accompanying him to Moscow where, because the extreme cold forced them to wear several shirts at once, they soon ran out of clean linen. Bawa, who confessed to never having washed clothes before in his life, hung his shirts on a line above the bath and tried to wash them by spraying them with the shower.

During the time when the book and exhibition were being planned he made regular visits to London and stayed with Jean Chamberlin and Christoph Bon. He would also visit them at their home near Uzes in the South of France, and accompanied them on trips to Portugal, Spain, Italy, East Africa and India.

The *Mimar* book opened a link with the Aga Khan Award for Architecture: Bawa taught on the Aga Khan Programme at Massachusetts Institute of Technology in 1986 and was a member of the award jury in 1989. He was also invited to report on a number of hotels in East Africa that belonged to the Aga Khan's hotel group and to give his comments on two sets of architects' proposals for a new hotel at Mangapwani on Zanzibar:

I have to agree that neither of the design projects set out the full potential of the site, which…is magnificent. I may be prejudiced, but I would so like to have the enjoyment of doing the design myself. I would vastly enjoy putting on paper and ultimately seeing in reality the arrangements, shapes and forms that already fill my imagination…on a project of this importance there must be a sensitive understanding as well as ability. (Letter to Rudi Baur accompanying report, 19 March 1987)

His letter won him the commission but the project was later shelved.

Of Bawa's lectures, that given to a regional Aga Khan seminar in Dhaka, Bangladesh in 1985 is the only one that survives on tape. He confines himself to fairly straightforward descriptions of projects from the previous two decades, answering questions in a matter-of-fact way, and is surprisingly nervous and uncomfortable with the paraphernalia of lectures – microphones, projectors and pointers. Interestingly he always uses the second person plural – not an affected

'royal we' but a genuinely inclusive 'team we'. When asked why for the Club Villa project he had built a wall that cut off the view of the sea from the main courtyard but then inserted a window, he replied:

You can look out through the window towards the sea – it's just a window. But you can see how the outer landscape enters through the window and meets the landscape of the courtyard and becomes part of the building. You don't want to see the whole of the view all of the time… you should only see controlled bits…nor do you always want to see the same view. You need to frame views, to put the view to people in different ways. They know it's there so they can go through the door on the left whenever they want to see the whole view.

An extract from a symposium of the Regional Council of Architectural Institutes in the Asia Region (ARCASIA) in Bali in 1987 on the theme 'My Architecture' offers a further insight:

In each project one finds oneself unconfined. With the particular needs of the building at the back of one's mind one sees the solution as a totality – the site being all-important – and one sees whatever vision is granted one of the building set in its surroundings – the building seen from outside, movement through the building, the whole picture as seen by anyone using the building.

The end of an era

The heavy workload of the early 1980s took its toll on the main players in Bawa's office. The strain of running the Parliament project turned Vasantha Jacobsen's hair from jet black to snow white and in 1984 she quit the practice. Both she and her husband were devout Buddhists and they disposed of all their property and turned their backs on the world, each retiring to separate monasteries in the hills above Kandy. Although Poologasundram's

immediate family had not been directly affected by the 1983 riots, like so many successful Tamils he began to question his future in Sri Lanka. He was bitterly disappointed by Bawa's failure fully to acknowledge his contribution to the work of the practice in either the White Book or the London exhibition. Running the Parliament and Ruhunu projects as office manager had taken its toll on his health and he decided to devote more time to organizing his family's future. Relations with Bawa became increasingly strained and Poologasundram slowly withdrew from the practice.

Bawa was also exhausted. He derived little personal satisfaction from working on large projects and felt less and less at ease at the Alfred House Road office. As work on Ruhunu drew to a conclusion he spent less time in the office and more time at 33rd Lane or Lunuganga amusing himself with designing houses for friends. He was now approaching seventy, and many assumed he would retire and spend time travelling or working on his garden.

In 1987 the practice completed the Royal Oceanic Hotel in Negombo. Crammed into a narrow site between beach and road, it is one of a long line of hotels littering the shoreline of this once picturesque fishing village. Its design fails to dispel Negombo's depressing ambience and reflects the mood of exhaustion and disagreement that gripped the office at the time. Projects for a Winged Bean Research Centre in Kandy and headquarters building for the UN on the Maldives came to nothing. The rather nondescript City Dispensary Building in Union Place, completed in 1990, was the last project to be built under the name Edwards, Reid and Begg. From that moment the office in Alfred House Road, which had gradually been coming to an end, effectively closed its doors.

'We have a marvellous tradition of building in this country that has got lost. It got lost because people followed outside influences over their own good instincts. They never built right "through" the landscape... You must "run" with site; after all, you don't want to push nature out with the building.'

the projects 1978–88

new parliament

KOTTE 1979–82

Sri Lanka's original Parliament building dated from 1929 and had been built to accommodate a legislative assembly of fifty members. Occupying a long strip of land running between the southern edge of the Colombo Fort and the Beira Lake, it had been designed in the Anglo-Palladian style by Austin Woodeson, chief architect of the PWD, with highly modelled façades embodying a continuous double-height Ionic order above a rusticated podium. The Assembly was placed with its entrance portico facing towards the Indian Ocean, while the debating chamber occupied a double-height volume above a *piano nobile* and was arranged as a hemicycle with its seats focusing on the Speaker's chair. Behind the Assembly the Secretariat was housed in a separate block with its own entrances, connected to the Assembly by a recessed link.

The Colombo Fort had always been a foreign bastion, facing the sea and turning its back on the interior of the island. During the British period it gradually lost its residential function and became predominantly a centre for government and commerce. Parliament's position in relation to the Fort symbolized

the very limited powers of the new legislature: the real power was still vested in the British governor, whose base remained inside the Fort. The building's orientation towards the Indian Ocean and ultimately towards Europe served as a further reminder that the sun had still to set upon the empire.

After independence in 1948 the debating chamber was rearranged along Westminster lines with the government and opposition benches facing each other across the axis of the Speaker's chair. However, the chamber was too small to seat the number of elected representatives and during the 1960s there was increasing pressure to build a new Parliament. In 1974 the Bandaranaike government commissioned a detailed study by the PWD and a site was selected to the immediate south of the old building on the opposite bank of the Beira Lake. A design by PWD architect Pani Tennakoon proposed a circular building in a pseudo-Kandyan style with a roof in the form of a Kandyan 'hat'. Bawa was also invited to submit a scheme at this time and proposed a linear building running parallel to the old Parliament, echoing its strong horizontal lines and subdued vertical rhythms. The debating chamber was planned as a symmetrical rectangle based on the Westminster model with side galleries for MPs, upper galleries for the public and views towards the old

building and out across the Galle Face to the ocean. In an early version the chamber was given an outward-cantilevering form, sheltered by a heavy, overhanging, flat concrete roof supported on giant free-standing columns rising out of a massive tiered podium. On one surviving print Bawa has superimposed ballpoint sketches of a vari-pitched roof with a large exclamation mark. Eventually the project was cancelled and another surviving print carries the rueful comment 'shelved for lack of funds'.

One of J. R. Jayewardene's first acts after becoming president in 1978 was to decree that a new Parliament be built at Kotte, about ten kilometres inland from the Colombo Fort, at the centre of a new capital city. The choice of site seems to have been made by the President and his immediate advisers and was driven primarily by political and historical considerations. The Kotte citadel had been established during the fourteenth century at a time of great political confusion, when the island was divided into a number of rival kingdoms and was continually under threat from South India. In 1391 a chief minister of the Gampola kingdom called Alakesvara had inflicted defeat on the armies of the Jaffna kingdom. Descended from a clan of South Indian merchant adventurers who had Sinhalized by converting to

Buddhism, Alakesvara proclaimed himself king and shifted the capital to Kotte, which was given the honorific title of Sri Jayawardhanapura or 'resplendent (*Sri*) city (*pura*) of victory (*jaya*)'. For a brief time in the fifteenth century Alakesvara's descendant Parakramabahu VI managed to extend the power of the Kotte kingdom over the whole island for what was to be the last period of unified and autonomous government until Ceylon regained its independence in 1948.

President Jayewardene may have been swayed both by the historical resonance of the site and by its fortuitous connection with his own name. Many commentators, notably Vale (1992), have made much of this, suggesting that the shift of the capital could be interpreted as a direct provocation to the minority Tamil community. This criticism ignores the irony that Kotte was actually ruled by a line of kings of mixed Indian and Sinhalese descent at a time when political boundaries often obscured the clear distinction between Tamil and Sinhalese and when the biggest threats to security came from the Vijayanagar empire of South India and from China. It could equally be argued, therefore, that Kotte represented a last period not of Sinhalese hegemony but of Sri Lankan unity, before the onset of European colonization.

Left: Aerial view of the Colombo Fort showing the old Parliament building

Right: An early elevational study for the Beira Lake project with flat roofs (1974)

Opposite
Left: An elevational study for the Beira Lake project with pitched roofs (1974)

Right: Bawa's initial concept sketch for the Kotte site (1979)

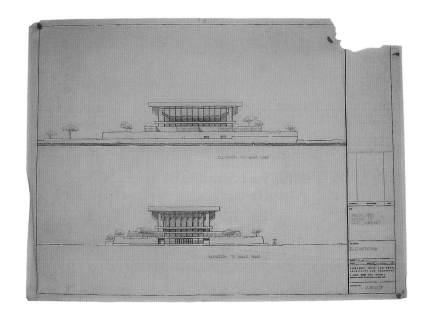

There were also good practical reasons for moving the Parliament to Kotte. Colombo was still governed as if it were a small municipality with half a million inhabitants, when in fact it had become an unplanned and chaotic metropolis of almost three million, restricted by the sea and by the marshes and lagoons that had once protected it. Its total primacy posed a serious threat to the balanced development of the whole country, economically, socially and communally and there were those who argued more radically to shift the capital to Kurunegala, Dambulla or even Trincomalee. But the move to Kotte, only ten kilometres as the crow flies, represented a sizeable conceptual shift. In practical terms it leap-frogged the main belt of marshland to the immediate east of the Baseline Road and opened the possibility of new urban development on a massive scale in an undeveloped area of about 150 square kilometres, bound to the north by the Kalani Ganga and to the south by the High Level Road. But it also offered the chance to orientate the capitol away from the Indian Ocean and the West and back towards the interior of the island.

Bawa was invited to be the architect of the new Parliament early in 1979. A morning phone call from a permanent secretary led to a brief lunchtime meeting with the

President, who offered Bawa the job on the spot. He was prepared to give Bawa a free hand in the design and his only stipulation was that the project be completed by April 1982. Whilst Bawa may seem with hindsight to have been the obvious choice, his practice had no experience of building on such a scale and it would hardly have been surprising if the commission had been given to the PWD or to a foreign firm of architects.

The newly created 'Urban Development Authority' (UDA) was responsible for drawing up a master plan for the new city of Jayawardhanapura-Kotte but it was Bawa who actually determined the precise location of the parliamentary capitol. Having viewed the area on the ground and from the air he proposed that the marshy Diyavanna Oya valley be flooded to create a lake of 120 hectares and that the new Parliament be built on a knoll of high ground two kilometres to the south-east of the ruins of the fifteenth-century citadel, on what would become an island at the lake's centre.

Bawa wasted little time in developing an overall design concept. He used his earlier Beira Lake scheme as a starting point and adapted it to fit the new site and meet the new programme requirements. One important idea carried forward was that the main debating chamber would be a symmetrical hall with government and opposition benches

facing each other across the axis of the Speaker's chair. This could be interpreted as a return to the Westminster model or as a reference to the royal audience halls of Kandy and Polonnaruwa. Whichever, Jayewardene accepted the design without reservation, even though at the time almost 80 per cent of members belonged to the government party. Another idea retained from the first sketch designs was that the chamber be flanked on each side by glazed lobbies so that the members could both see out and be seen. The expanding schedule of accommodation later forced Bawa to abandon these lobbies at the lower levels so that in the final design only the upper-most public galleries have direct views to the outside.

Poologasundram took charge of the management of the programme and it was at his suggestion that the construction project was let as a negotiated contract to the Japanese firm, Mitsui. Having built the Ceylon Pavilion at the Osaka Expo in 1970, Mitsui had already worked with Edwards, Reid and Begg. Once an outline design had been developed Bawa and Poologasundram spent four weeks in Japan in late 1979 working out the details of the contract with contractors.

Poologasundram realized that in this instance Bawa would not be able simply

to produce a few outline drawings and then work everything out on site as work progressed. The brief called for buildings with a total area of over 40,000 square metres, to be designed and built within a period of three years. It was agreed that E. R. & B. would produce all necessary design drawings and specifications and that Mitsui would produce detailed working drawings. Mitsui opened its own office in Colombo, while Bawa set up a project office in Ena de Silva's house in Alfred Place, where a special team of architects, several of them recruited from Bombay, was established under the leadership of Vasantha Jacobsen. Eventually the two teams produced more than five thousand drawings – a far cry from the days of the Bentota Beach Hotel, which had been built with only thirty. Brian Brace Taylor later observed:

The trauma of Bawa's life was having to work with a Japanese construction firm for the new parliamentary complex, where tight schedules had to be met and few changes could be made as one went along. (Taylor 1986, p.15)

Bawa conceived the Parliament as an island capitol surrounded by a new garden city of parks and public buildings. It would form the end point on a long promenade, beginning 8 kilometres to the west in Colombo's Viharamahadevi Park and

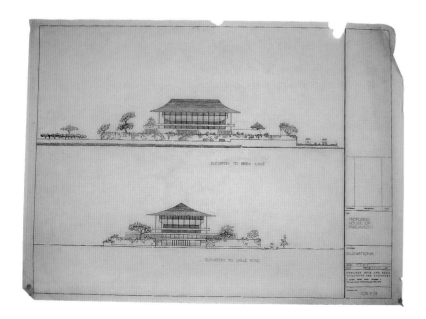

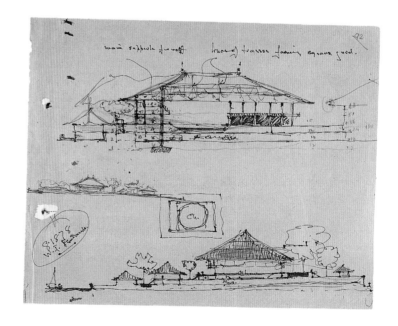

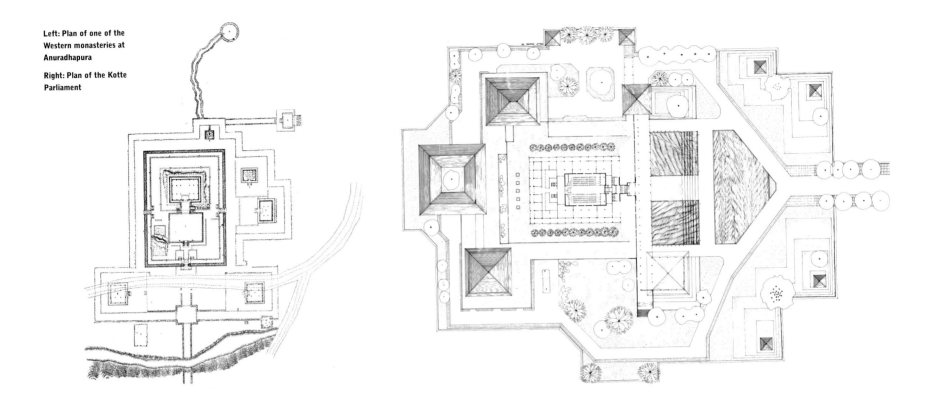

Left: Plan of one of the Western monasteries at Anuradhapura

Right: Plan of the Kotte Parliament

following the grand west–east axis formed by Ananda Coomaraswamy Mawatha, Horton Place and Castle Street before swinging southwards at Rajagiriya. Its cascade of copper roofs would first be seen from the north at a distance of two kilometres, floating above the new lake at the end of the Diyavanna Valley. The final approach would be over a tree-lined causeway to a public piazza punctuated by pools and water cascades with steps and ramps rising to the entrance loggia, from which a formal entrance and staircase would link directly on axis to the main chamber towards the Speaker's chair. As was so often the case with Bawa's designs, the starting point, the main *parti*, was an experiential journey, a controlled sequence of happenings, which in this case was focused on the annual state opening of Parliament.

The design placed the main chamber in a central pavilion surrounded by a cluster of five satellite pavilions, each defined by its own umbrella roof of copper and seeming to grow out of its own plinth, although the plinths are actually connected at ground and

first-floor level. This compositional device had first been used by Bawa in his Hilton Hotel project of 1965. The main pavilion is symmetrical about the debating chamber, but its axiality is diffused by the asymmetry of the arrangement of the lesser pavilions around it. As a result, the pavilions each retain a separate identity but join to create a single upward sweep of tent-like roofs.

Bawa remained typically reticent about the possible sources of this design strategy and it seems likely that, as was so often the case, he drew a number of memories together to produce a new hybrid idea. The lake itself can be read as a tribute to Sri Lanka's two millennia of tank building, recalling the Sea of Parakramabahu at Polonnaruwa and the tree-lined lake at Kandy. The plan and the asymmetrical arrangement of the pavilions might equally be said to recall Mogul lake palaces, South Indian temples, Chinese palaces or Sri Lankan monasteries of the Anuradhapura period.

Detailed plans of the Anuradhapura monasteries had long been in the public

domain (Smithers 1894, Hocart 1924), but renewed interest was sparked by the publication in 1974 of Senake Bandaranayake's analysis of the Western Monasteries at Anuradhapura in *Sinhalese Monastic Architecture* (Bandaranayake 1974). Bandaranayake categorized a number of monastery types in terms of plan form and speculated about possible roof forms using evidence from cave paintings and drawing parallels with the traditions of Kerala. He recalls that at this time he regularly met Bawa, who borrowed a copy of the book in 1977 and kept it for several years. During an interview in 1980 Bawa observed:

[Kotte] is a sort of design continuum, reflecting the visual formalities of the old Sinhalese buildings, grand but not pompous, like what you see in Senake Bandaranayake's book. Really it will be a set of pavilions with asymmetry of planning. (Roberts 1980)

Bawa has also said:

We have a marvellous tradition of building in this country that has got lost. It got lost because people

followed outside influences over their own good instincts. They never built right 'through' the landscape. I just wanted to fit [Parliament] into the site, so I opened it into blocks. You must 'run' with site; after all, you don't want to push nature out with the building. (Aung-Thwin 1984)

The main pavilion and its five satellites define a series of separate outdoor spaces between the building and the lake. Arriving in the ceremonial piazza the first satellite pavilion to the east takes the form of a large open-colonnaded audience hall for public meetings and spontaneous gatherings; to the west a second pavilion contains the public entrance and security checkpoint. On the western side of the island a less public square is defined by a third pavilion, which contains staff facilities. On the south side a fourth pavilion contains the service court and is connected by its own causeway back to the shore. A fifth pavilion at the south-east corner contains the MPs' dining room above a covered car park and defines a large garden court facing east across the lake, connected to the members' terraces by a monumental open staircase.

Top: Aerial view of the Kotte Parliament in 1982

Middle: Cross-section through the debating chamber

Bottom: View of the Kotte Parliament across the lake

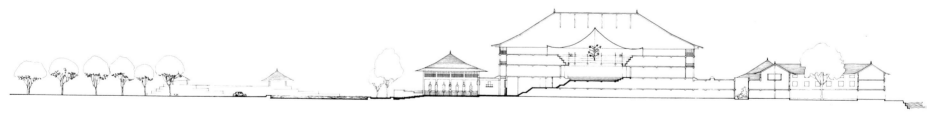

Traditional 'Kandyan' roofs were made from flat clay tiles laid to a shallow pitch at the eaves and a steeper pitch at the ridge. The form was appropriated by architects in the 1940s and 1950s for use at Peradeniya University and the Colombo Independence Memorial in an ill-conceived attempt to create a new national architectural style using pastiche historical forms. Bawa himself had used a vari-pitched roof in 1976 on the Seema Malaka, the lake temple in Colombo that appears almost to have served as a scale model for Parliament. But the vari-pitch roof is not endemic to Kandy: similar roof forms are found throughout the island, as well as in other parts of monsoon Asia. Bawa has said:

A roof is a covering and its shape suggests itself at some point, some stage of the design, which is what happened to the [parliamentary] complex. (Fernando 1982)

He has also written:

One unchanging element is the roof – protective, emphatic and all-important – governing the aesthetic whatever the period, whatever the place. Often a building is only a roof, columns and floors – the roof dominant, shielding, giving the contentment of shelter. Ubiquitous, pervasively present, the scale or pattern shaped by the building beneath. The roof, its shape, texture and proportion is the strongest visual factor. (Taylor 1986, p.16)

In their final form the Parliament roofs are an abstraction of the traditional Kandyan roof. The use of copper in place of tile gives them the thinness and tent-like quality of a stretched skin, transporting them far from the realms of historical pastiche while recalling the fabled 'brazen roofs' of Anuradhapura.

In contrast everything below the roof has been designed in an abstract Modernist mode with a simple elegance that follows the discipline imposed by a 6 x 6-metre structural grid. The pavilions are supported on two levels of plinth, expressed as a trabeated system of concrete columns at 6-metre centres, behind which the building skin is recessed within slender dark metal frames. The upper plinth steps back on the east, south and west sides to form a continuous upper terrace linking all the pavilions, but on the north side a double-height order of columns rises through both levels to mark the entrance loggia.

Rising out of the upper plinth, the main pavilion houses the debating chamber. A further row of concrete columns on its lower floor creates a continuous 3-metre-deep arcade in front of the members' lobbies, while an arcade on the middle floor is formed by composite teak columns at 3-metre centres and on the top floor

a perimeter ambulatory is enclosed by a fine timber screen. Above this, the roof cantilevers out 3 metres. The layering of the three levels produces a differential rhythm, while the timber lattice of the top floor exaggerates the shadow of the roof overhang and reinforces the impression that the roofs are floating above the buildings.

The ground floor, set within the plinth, contains a multitude of offices arranged around a central plant room. Ministers' and whips' offices are located at first-floor level on three sides of the main block and the chamber is on the second floor, with members' lobbies to the east and west and suites for the prime minister and the president to the north overlooking the piazza. The third floor accommodates translators and journalists and the fourth is given over to a public gallery.

Much of the interior is finished in a plain and matter-of-fact manner, with white polished terrazzo floors, off-white walls and dark timber furniture. The members' dining room offers views across the lake on three sides and, with its clay-tiled floors and sloping timber ceilings, has the ambience of a restaurant in a resort hotel. Rupert Scott, a former E. R. & B. assistant writing in the *Architectural Review*, compared the Parliament building with Bawa's favourite Keralan palace at Padmanabhapuram, peevishly bemoaning the lack of 'tortoiseshell floors, carved thrones and delicately pierced screens' (Scott 1983). In part this restraint was due to budgetary limits, and in part to the tight programme. In the main chamber, however, no expense was spared.

At the opening of Parliament the president, accompanied by the thunder of drums and the shriek of conch shells, crosses over the piazza between a phalanx of richly decorated banners designed by Ena de Silva, and passes through the loggia to a pair of heavy bronze doors. These slide open to reveal an austere stone staircase lined with murals by the artist Manjusri depicting the history of Kotte. At the landing a pair of silver doors engraved with the preamble of the constitution in Sinhala, Tamil and English, opens to reveal the short final staircase leading up into the chamber. The dignitaries ascend to appear before the Speaker's chair between the opposing ranks of members. Above them the ceiling seems to hover like a drooping tent of chain mail, with Laki Senanayake's massive chandelier of silver palm fronds hanging from its apex.

The ceiling is made from square tiles of aluminium, which, for reasons of safety, are each hung individually from the supporting roof structure. Poologasundram, who designed the structure, remembers that Bawa produced a silver chain-link purse of his mother's to demonstrate the effect he sought to achieve. The lower part of the chamber is contained within walls of rich dark timber panelling lit from concealed uplighters that act as supports for the metal flags of the eighteen *korales*. Above, four steeply tiered rows of visitors' seats rise towards an upper windowed gallery.

The chamber is thus more grand and ornate than the surrounding accommodation, recalling the Music Room in Brighton's Royal Pavilion with its ceiling of dragon's scales and its hanging gasoliers, as well as the British House of Lords, Indian palaces and ceremonial marquees. Scott was finally moved to declare that 'there is an enrichment [in the chamber] that, if applied to the whole building, would place it among the great monumental buildings of the world' (Scott 1983).

The new Parliament was completed within the allotted three-year period and opened on schedule in April 1982. Ironically a stone set in the wall of the main entrance loggia records that the architects were Edwards, Reid and Begg, adding, almost as an afterthought, the names of Geoffrey Bawa, Poologasundram and Vasantha Jacobsen – a Burgher–Moor, a Jaffna Tamil and a Sinhalese Buddhist. The plaque offers a reminder that Sri Lanka's various communities were all represented in Bawa's office and that, whatever the intentions of the politicians, the design for Parliament was conceived as an inclusive expression of the aspirations of the whole nation.

The opening of the new Parliament was staged against a background of rising communal violence that escalated into a bitter civil war. The continuing troubles necessitated the introduction of strict and highly visible security measures in and around Colombo. Little of the development proposed for the area around Parliament was realized and the Parliament building itself now stands forlorn, a remote citadel on an impregnable island, its approaches punctuated by checkpoints, lines of metal barrels and barbed wire. In August 1987, as if to underline the need for this isolation, a disaffected UNP fanatic penetrated the security system and carried out a grenade attack on a meeting of the Party's inner council, injuring a number of leading politicians.

Although the new garden city capital never materialized, Parliament's transfer to Kotte did encourage the growth of Colombo towards the east. Most of that growth was, however, the result of unbridled private investment and land speculation, neither subject to planning controls nor supported by infrastructural investment. Even the first tantalizing glimpse of the Parliament building that Bawa orchestrated at the turning of the road at Rajagiriya is now obscured by unauthorized developments on the edge of the lake in which it stands. Neighbouring Bataramulla, a remote and sleepy village in 1979, is now a congested urban centre, while uncontrolled suburban development has spread more than 10 kilometres further to the east. Sadly, a unique opportunity to plan a new city has been squandered.

Sri Lanka's parliamentary traditions are part of a colonial inheritance that was espoused by a Western-educated elite. The Parliament building is by necessity a national monument but it also exists in an international arena and reflects Sri Lanka's position in the modern world. It was financed partly with foreign aid and the Japanese contractors that built it used the latest 'fast-track' techniques. Bawa's own background – his mixed family, his Colombo childhood and his Cambridge education – made it possible for him to operate within a post-colonial context and to act as an intermediary between local and global cultures.

In designing the Parliament his aim was to create an accessible monument, a potent symbol of democracy that would transcend differences of community or religion. To this end he used historical precedents in an ambiguous and abstract way, drawing on a number of sources. As a result, the building has become an instantly recognizable icon that is identifiably 'of Sri Lanka' and 'of government', although there is nothing in the design that is specifically Sinhalese or Buddhist. However, the fact that Bawa's intentions have been subverted by political events supports his assertion that buildings cannot be pre-loaded with meanings: meanings develop through time and with use.

It would be wrong to hold the architects responsible for the present isolation of the complex or the fortress-like air it has assumed. The island was intended to serve as the focal point of a city park, its lawns dotted with groups of picnicking citizens, its waterside pavilions sheltering earnest debates between parliamentarians and their constituents. For the moment, however, the image is of a Parliament under siege: the lawns are empty and the lakeside pavilions are used by armed sentries. In another time, perhaps, when peace and communal harmony prevail, the terraces, gardens and pavilions will be thrown open to the people and the Parliament might finally become what it was intended to be: the expression of many different but overlapping cultures and traditions and a symbol of open, accessible and democratic government.

Right: The east façade

Opposite
Top left: The members' garden
Top right: The public assembly hall
Bottom: The entrance piazza

institute for integral education

PILIYANDELA 1978–81

The Institute for Integral Education was created by the Catholic Church to offer facilities for intensive residential courses aimed mainly at school-leavers and young people. Its founder, Dr Mervyn Fernando, having identified a suitable site on the road between Moratuwa and Piliyandela, persuaded the German charity Misereor to fund the project. The charity had supported the convent's farm school at Yahapath Endera (1965) and the silk farm at Mahahalpe (1969), and it was they who insisted that E. R. & B. were appointed as architects.

The site was on part of an old rubber estate called Brookside and occupied a steep valley running down through a grove of rubber trees to the edge of the Bolgoda Lake. The first phase was built between 1978 and 1981 and comprised a central conference and teaching centre with dining and residential facilities. The general layout and the form of the individual buildings were established by Bawa on site in response to the exact shape of the opposing valley sides, and the design was conceived as a promenade through an ever-changing sequence of loggias, links and open spaces. The buildings are modest and simply built, but demonstrate Bawa's growing skill for manipulating elements in a landscape to exploit the terrain and the potential views.

Visitors arrive at an entrance pavilion on the southern edge of the site and then plunge into a subterranean route excavated through the laterite hillside to emerge at the institute's centre. This trick was a favourite Bawa device that he had used in his own home and would later use to good effect at the Kandalama Hotel. The main conference room occupies a pavilion that spans the valley and gives views through the rubber trees towards the lake. The residential wings run along the contours on the northern flank of the valley and are connected by covered staircase links.

A second phase of building in 1986 added a raked auditorium and a library near the entrance on the southern side of the valley and extra wings of bedrooms to the north.

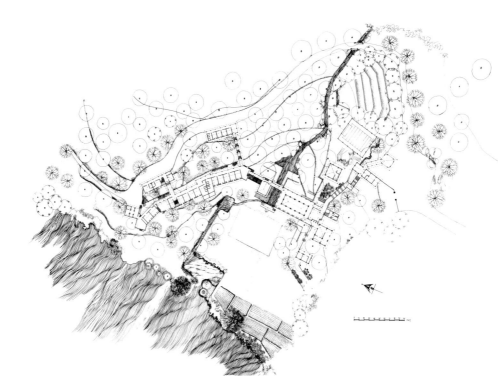

Top: General plan of the institute

Bottom left: The main bridge link spanning the valley

Bottom right: The underground approach corridor

Opposite
Top left: The main bridge link

Top centre, top right and centre: The staircase link to the residential blocks

Bottom: Cross-section showing the underground corridor

ruhunu university

MATARA 1980–88

The commission for a new university campus arrived in April 1979 soon after that for the Parliament. Suddenly Bawa and his colleagues were faced with designing and running two huge projects simultaneously, each involving more than 40,000 square metres of building.

Ruhunu University was established in the Matara constituency of Ronnie de Mel, the minister of finance, on three separate campuses: a general campus located on the south coast close to Matara town, and separate medical and agricultural campuses located on inland sites. Bawa was invited to design the general campus, which comprised science and arts faculties and central administrative facilities. It was planned to accommodate an initial three thousand students rising ultimately to a total of four thousand.

The 30-hectare site straddled three steep hills, the westernmost overlooking the sea and separated from the other two by a low-lying valley that carried the main road from Matara to Hambantota. Bawa placed the vice-chancellor's lodge and a guest house on the western hill and flooded the intervening valley to create a buffer between the road and the main campus. He then wrapped the buildings of the science faculty around the northern hill and those of the arts faculty around the southern hill, using the depression between them for the library and other central facilities.

A building project that in Europe would have been handled by a large team of architects and specialist consultants was run largely by an individual job architect: Nihal Bodhinayake. In typical fashion many of the important initial design decisions were taken by Bawa on site but he was happy to leave much of the detailed planning of the various buildings to Bodhinayake,

though Milroy Perera came to play an important role behind the scenes. What preoccupied Bawa was the siting of the buildings in relation to each other, the fixing of their relative levels, and the development of the spaces between them. He therefore, unusually, had a site model made and used this to work out detailed level relationships between buildings. The model was located not in the main office where Bodhinayake worked but in the new 'home office' in 33rd Lane. It was here that Bawa would ponder the scheme and discuss its finer points with Perera, or Christoph Bon and Jean Chamberlin when they were in town.

Bodhinayake's problem was that he had to translate Bawa's ideas into the language of the building contractor. To this end he set up a strict grid based on 3 metres horizontally and 1.5 metres vertically in an attempt to fix the various pavilions on a system of coordinates and to standardize all junctions. Bawa grudgingly recognized the need for such a discipline, but reserved for himself the right to break it whenever he saw fit.

His overall strategy was developed from that used in earlier projects such as the Yahapath Endera Farm School and the Piliyandela Institute for Integral Education. Buildings were planned orthogonally on a north–south grid but were allowed to 'run with site'. Natural features such as rocky outcrops were incorporated into the bases of buildings or became focal features of the open spaces. Although there is nothing that connects the design in a literal way to historical precedents, the limited architectural vocabulary clearly derives from Porto–Sinhalese traditions and the topographical approach is reminiscent of that employed in the building of Kasyapa's Palace on the rock at Sigiriya.

The design exploits the site to make every part of the campus seem unique. Pavilions, varying in scale and extent, are connected by covered links and separated by an ever-changing succession of garden courts. Everywhere there are places to

pause and consider, to sit and contemplate, to gather and discuss. The main routes either cut uncompromisingly across the contours or meander horizontally along them. Views are carefully orchestrated in a scenographic sequence that conceals and reveals in turn, playing the northern views of jungle and distant hills against the southern views of the lake and the ocean beyond, always referring back to the picturesque hump-backed bridge that connects the entrance across the lake to the central valley and acts as the linchpin of the whole composition.

Top: View from the south across the lake

Bottom: North elevation

Opposite: General plan of the Ruhunu campus

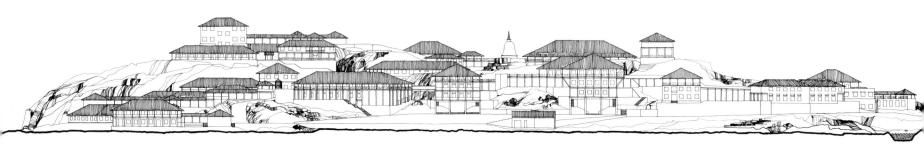

Ruhunu is remarkable in that it is composed from a series of fairly simple and, in the main, unremarkable buildings – about fifty in total – all built with a limited palette of materials and a limited vocabulary of standard details. The construction is straightforward, comprising walls of plastered brick on a concrete frame and roofs of half-round tile laid on corrugated cement sheeting. Buildings are aligned carefully to minimize solar intrusion and mitigate the effects of the south-west monsoon. Few of the spaces are air-conditioned and the buildings rely for the most part on natural ventilation.

The project was let to Ballast Nedam, a Dutch firm of civil engineering contractors, though the subcontractors, craftsmen and labourers were all local. Work started on site in August 1980 and the final arts faculty buildings were handed over in July 1986, with the project continuing to final completion in 1988. The total cost, including site works and furnishings, came to 450 million rupees, equivalent at the time to about 9 million pounds sterling. The result is a modern campus, vast in size but human in scale. As Bawa wryly observed: 'If this place doesn't turn students into civilized beings, nothing will!'

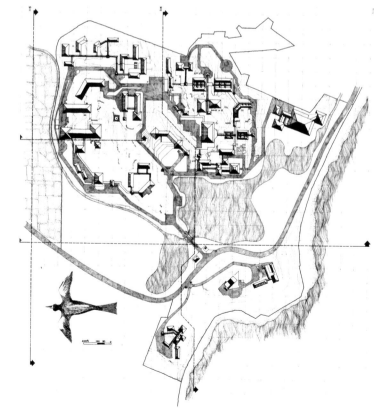

Top: Exterior view of the pavilions

Opposite
Top left and right: Views of the physics building

Bottom: A covered link

triton hotel

AHUNGALLA 1979–81

The new UNP government instated in 1977 sought to extricate itself from the system of state-run tourism that had operated during the previous fifteen years and started to sell off its main resort hotels, offering generous tax breaks on new private hotel developments. One of the commercial companies that moved into tourism and hotel management was Aitken Spence and Bawa's cousin and close friend Michael Mack was one of its directors. On his recommendation Bawa was invited in 1979 to design a new 125-bedroom hotel on the west coast at Ahungalla between Bentota and Galle. The site was located in a fairly heavily populated area but it boasted a long beach frontage and was connected to the main road by a corridor of land that ran through a grove of coconut trees.

Bawa's starting point was to adopt a fairly conventional rest house form similar to that he had used for the Serendib Hotel – a line of rooms facing the sea with the reception and restaurant at the centre. But he divided the rooms into small clusters, some of which he turned through 90 degrees to form projecting wings. This simple move had two immediate consequences: internal courtyards were set up to enliven the corridors, and three large garden courts were formed along the beach frontage. The central garden court, containing the swimming pool, would lie opposite the main reception area, mirrored on the land side by an entrance court with coconut trees standing like sentries in a large reflecting pool. Bawa had assembled the ingredients for his scenographic plot. Visitors would approach the hotel from the main road down a long walled driveway to arrive suddenly at the end of the entrance court, where they would see the reflecting pool with its captive palms, the reception loggia with its columns and polished floor, the surface of the swimming pool and a distant glimpse of the ocean. As he observed in a lecture at Dhaka in 1985: 'Everything is at the same level: if the world were only flat you'd

see Africa on the horizon.' Moving to the reception loggia, visitors would discover a cross-axis leading outwards and upwards past a sequence of courtyards and covered verandahs at different levels and finally to the rooms. What could have been straightforward and banal was thus transformed into a magical sequence of vistas and spaces.

The open reception hall, serene on a summer's evening, can be ravaged by wind and rain during the monsoon. For this Bawa was unrepentant:

In the monsoon it's very dramatic when all the wind from the whole south-west coast seems to blow through the lobby and you see people running horizontally to and fro, and their bills are blown into the reflecting pool. (Geoffrey Bawa, lecture in Dhaka 1985)

This approach corresponded to Bawa's belief that buildings should be experienced through all the senses. The monsoon was a part of the drama of nature and the lowering of the tats to keep out the rain was a welcome ritual.

The Triton's architecture is restrained: its plain elevations advance and recede under the constant horizontal line of the overhanging eaves. Apart from the roofs, which are clad in half-round clay tiles, Bawa eschewed the traditional materials and romanticized vernacular details of his earlier hotels. Everything is simple, uncluttered and unostentatious: a modern seaside palace filled with light and air and the sound of the waves.

At a moment when Bawa was heavily preoccupied with Parliament and Ruhunu, the Triton provided him with light relief and signalled the beginning of a move away from his earlier vernacular phase. The Bentota Beach Hotel had inspired an army of imitators, both in Sri Lanka and throughout Asia. When friends expressed surprise that he was abandoning the style he had helped to create he accused them of trying to straitjacket him and claimed the right to explore new ideas.

Unlike the Bentota Beach, the Triton retains some of its original atmosphere, though sadly the court-yards have been stripped of their planting. In the early 1990s Bawa added an extra wing of rooms and a new pool, fully in the spirit of the original.

Top: Aerial view

Bottom: South–north cross-section

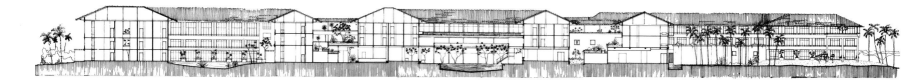

Top: View of the reception from the entrance court

Bottom: View through the reception area to the sea

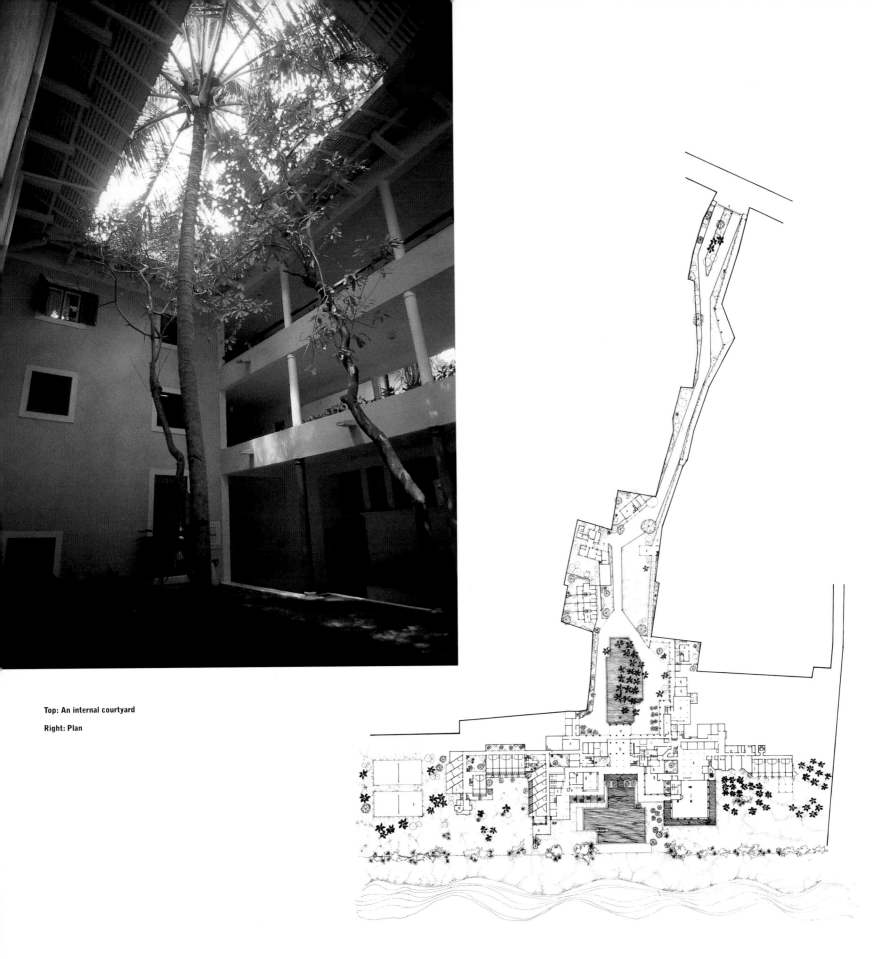

Top: An internal courtyard

Right: Plan

Top: The view from the upper
lounge towards the pool

Bottom: An upper-level lounge

martenstyn house

COLOMBO 1977–79

At the beginning of the 1960s Bawa had built a simple pavilion house for Pin and Pam Fernando on a fairly small plot in a short cul-de-sac off Kannangara Mawatha, and in 1977 they called him back to design a second house on the same plot for their daughter. Bawa had been experimenting with tower houses ever since completing the house for Peter Keuneman and had recently added a tower to his own house in 33rd Lane. He tucked the new house into a corner of the Fernandos' garden and let it grow up between the branches of a tall bo tree. Visitors arrive at a porch at the end of the cul-de-sac and are led via a long toplit tunnel past the front of the Fernando House to the base of the tower. Kitchen and dining room are on the ground floor, the sitting room is on the first floor, two bedrooms are on the second floor and the top floor is given over to a roof terrace nestling into the uppermost branches of the tree. All four levels are linked by a simple concrete staircase with metal handrails, and a double-height void connects the dining and sitting rooms.

As well as offering an alternative prototype for the tropical urban house, the Martenstyn House is important because it is spatially innovative. It is also an example of a new 'stripped-down' aesthetic that would reappear in Bawa's work with increasing frequency, signifying his growing irritation with being pigeon-holed as a vernacularist.

Right: The Martenstyn House seen from the garden

Opposite
Top left: The approach corridor and staircase

Top right: Ground-floor plan showing the neighbouring Fernando House in outline

Bottom: Cross-section through the house and the approach corridor

Left and opposite: Views
of the staircase

sunethra bandaranaike house

HORAGOLLA 1984–86

Bawa had previously renovated a house in Guildford Crescent for Sunethra Bandaranaike and in 1984 she asked him to convert into a house an old stable block on the Bandaranaike family estate at Horagolla. Dating from the mid-nineteenth century, the stables were located behind the main *walaawe* and Bawa separated the two by a high wall to create a large garden court. The stable block itself houses a double-height sitting room with a bedroom and study, while a new wing at right angles contains a kitchen and entrance along with guest rooms, forming the side of a second garden court that is closed by a screen of huge hora trees. A long loggia connects the two wings and runs from the *porte cochère* along the north side of the stable block, terminating at each end in a blank wall with an oculus, formed by Sahabdeen Baas, a master craftsman, who was instructed by Bawa to make 'two holes, one the size of a cartwheel, the other the size of a bicycle wheel'.

Sunethra Bandaranaike and Bawa became close friends and she has acted as one of his trustees and helped him during his illness.

Top: View of the main house, a former stable block

Middle: View from the garden court

Bottom: Cross-section through the main house

Top left: The sitting room

Top right: The oculus

Middle left: View across the courtyard

Middle right: The main verandah looking towards the entrance

Bottom: Elevation

fitzherbert house

DODAMPAHALA 1985–86

Richard Fitzherbert Brockholes was an estate agent from the north of England who had bought a piece of land next to the sea at Dodampahala near Tangalla to build a holiday villa. Bawa designed the house as a mini-Triton Hotel with three suites of rooms, each with its own bathroom and private courtyard, attached like satellites to a double-height loggia that served as the main dining room and lounge. A paved staircase wound its way down through the coconut palms to a small swimming pool perched on a headland above the sea. Like the Triton Hotel, the house responds dramatically to changes in climate and during the monsoon resembles a windjammer rounding Cape Horn.

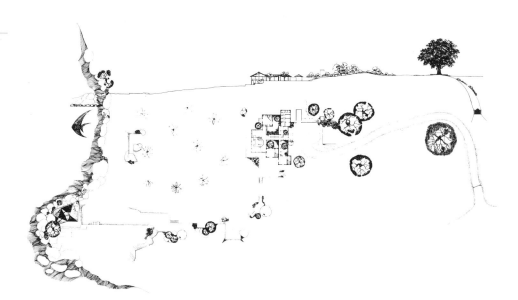

Top: Plan

Bottom left: Entrance

Bottom right: Main loggia

Opposite
Top left: View from the pool towards the house

Top right: View towards the pool

Bottom left: The main loggia

Bottom right: The northern bedroom

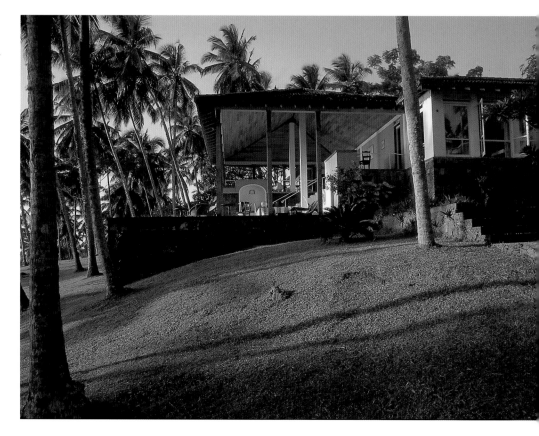

the de soysa house

Cecil and Chloé de Soysa were old friends of Bawa. Cecil had been chairman of the Ceylon Hotels Corporation when the Bentota Beach Resort was built at the end of the 1960s and had later become a private hotel developer, while his wife Chloé ran a boutique and gallery on Wijerama Mawatha in Colombo. The de Soysas owned an old house with a large garden that stretched between Wijerama Mawatha and Boyd Place. The garden was subdivided to create plots for the de Soysas' daughters, and one final plot was earmarked for the parents. The project to build a house on this plot was delayed by Cecil's sudden death but was completed by Chloé in 1991.

The house belongs to Bawa's canon of tower houses. A drawing dated 1985 carries a scribbled note from Bawa to his client:

Dear Chloé,
- an office on the ground floor 65 feet long by 14 feet [later a verandah for the house] looking over the garden and expandable into what is now the car port and, as a car port, not counted in the calculation of the 3,000-square-foot maximum area.
The first floor needs no explanation.
The main bedroom on the second floor is surrounded and shaded by planting in a 3-foot-wide trough. Windows on all three sides with white curtains. A 7-foot-high cupboard separates sleeping from dressing. This would need careful detailing later.
The roof is part pergola and part open to the moon and stars – and a view over the neighbouring trees.
Hope you like it!
Geoffrey, 6 July 1985

The main living room and bedroom are glazed on three sides using dark anodized aluminium sliding sashes. The house is surrounded by tall trees and dense vegetation and the narrow window frames seem to melt into the background of branches and creepers. This is a far cry from earlier, apparently more traditional, designs: the deceptively simple plans, the white walls and the contrasting frames represent a further move towards the minimalism to which Bawa was increasingly drawn.

Opposite: Entrance

This page
Top and bottom left: views
of the sitting room

Bottom right: Façade detail

currimjee house

FLORÉAL MAURITIUS 1986–94

The Currimjee House was the first in a long line of foreign commissions that came to Bawa during the ten-year period from 1986 to 1996, though it was the only one to be fully realized under his supervision. It also marked the beginning of Bawa's withdrawal from the office in Alfred House Road and his move to establish an independent office at his home in 33rd Lane.

Bashir Currimjee, a Mauritius-based business-man whose family came to East Africa from Gujerat at the end of the nineteenth century, bought an acre plot of land for a house at Floréal near Curipipe on the Mauritius Plateau. Acting on the suggestion of his friend Peter White he phoned Bawa in Colombo and asked him to be his architect. In October 1986 Bashir and his wife Najma sent Bawa a set of site photographs and a detailed contour survey along with a three-page brief. Bawa flew out to Mauritius in December for what the Currimjees expected to be a preliminary site visit: in fact he arrived with a fully worked-out sketch design that was hardly to change during the long years of building. An immediate bond of respect and friendship was forged between the Currimjees and their architect. Bawa's design proposed a house of 1,000 square metres consisting of a cluster of pavilions on different levels following the slope of the site and enclosing a series of outdoor courts and pools. It exceeded the Currimjees' expectations in terms of area and cost by a factor of three, but they were happy to tighten their belts and proceed.

Bashir Currimjee wanted to take a close interest in the construction and opted to build the house in stages using small local subcontractors. The design specified a number of finishing materials that had to be imported and called for the incorporation of antique doors. Marble was brought from Carrara, window frames from the Far East, furnish-ings from India. All of this needed time and the house took eight years to complete.

The Currimjees' enthusiasm for the project was fully matched by Bawa, who made a total of seven site visits to Mauritius during the construction period. When he came across an old door in a prison in Zanzibar he rang Bashir Currimjee and suggested that he should fly across to see it. 'Buy it!' was the response.

Top: The Currimjee House seen from the garden

Bottom: Plan

Opposite
Top: The pool court from the hall

Bottom left: The hall

Bottom centre: The library

Bottom right: The pool court

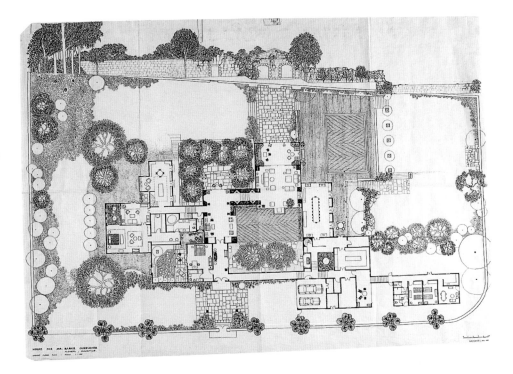

In Port Louis he found two old gables to incorporate into the outer compound wall. In Bombay, Christoph Bon and Jean Chamberlin were enlisted to help choose old doors and window frames. This scavenging had a purpose: the various items help to tell the story of the Currimjee family, of their origins on the north-west coast of India and of their trading along the coast of East Africa. When Bashir suggested that he might hire the services of a French landscape architect, Bawa was horrified and flew out immediately to forestall them so that he could supervise the setting-out of the garden himself. When Najma mentioned a plan to buy paintings from a young Delhi artist to cover the long dining-room wall, Bawa resisted and instead proposed a patchwork mural of Kashmiri rugs.

The house contains many echoes from earlier projects: the asymmetrical arrangement of solid and void on the sloping site recalls the A. S. H. de Silva House, while the use of courtyards and pools is reminiscent of the Madurai Club and the Club Villa. But it is quite un-Sri Lankan in spirit and incorporates a sense of timeless modernity with echoes of a North Indian and Muslim past.

Civil war

From 1983, politics and daily life in Sri Lanka were dogged by the endless civil war in the north and the east, which brought untold misery to all affected communities. President Jayewardene sought to end the conflict in 1987 by inviting the Indian government to send in a peacekeeping force, but the Indian army was inexorably drawn into the conflict and its presence was seen by many Sinhalese as a threat to national sovereignty. Jayewardene stepped down at the end of 1988 and was replaced by Ranasinghe Premadasa, who negotiated the withdrawal of the Indian force from the north but was suddenly faced by a terrorist threat in the south from the JVP, the same group that had shaken Mrs Bandaranaike's government almost twenty years earlier. Government forces succeeded in putting down the rebellion at the end of 1989 only by resorting to widespread and indiscriminate force.

The situation was forcibly brought home to Bawa late one afternoon at Lunuganga. He was sitting on the terrace with his colleague Dilshan Ferdinando and his family when a servant brought news that a gang of armed JVP terrorists was approaching. The group demanded money, but there was none in the house and it was agreed that they would return the following day to collect 20,000 rupees. The next morning Ferdinando borrowed money from Bawa's friend Hameed and left it at the house before returning with Bawa to Colombo. When he drove back to Lunuganga to check that the staff were safe he was horrified to come across the charred bodies of the three terrorists on a pyre of burning tyres at the roadside.

After the withdrawal of Indian troops the civil war in the north was reignited with far-reaching consequences: in 1991 a Tamil separatist assassinated the Indian prime minister Rajiv Gandhi, and two years later President Premadasa was killed by a Tamil suicide bomber at a May Day rally in Colombo.

The 1994 parliamentary elections were won by the People's Alliance, a loose coalition led by Chandrika Kumaratunga, the daughter of S. W. R. D. Bandaranaike. Later in the same year Mrs Kumaratunga went on to win the presidential election with a promise to seek an accommodation with the Tamil separatists. Sadly her efforts met with little success, and although her mandate was renewed in 2000, the civil war has continued to rumble on.

33rd Lane

During the course of 1988 Bawa and Poologasundram began to wind down their partnership. The office in Alfred House Road was owned by a subsidiary company in which Poologasundram and Bawa each held a 50 per cent share. They agreed to keep the office open with a skeleton staff to handle ongoing administration, and long-standing employees such as Stanley Perera, a technician who had worked in the office since the 1960s, continued to use it for their private work.

Rumours that Bawa had retired from architectural practice, however, were unfounded and he now began to work from home, converting the guest flat at the front of his house in 33rd Lane into a small drawing office. There were a number of jobs on site to keep him occupied, such as the de Soysa and de Saram houses in Colombo and the Currimjee House in Mauritius, but on the strength of the *Mimar* book he was also beginning to receive a steady stream of enquiries from new clients.

Sumangala Jayatilleke, a young graduate from the University of Moratuwa, known simply as Sumangala, was employed by Bawa in 1986, becoming the first architect to work exclusively from 33rd Lane. He was joined the following year by Dilshan Ferdinando, who had previously worked alongside Anjalendran in the office of Surath Wickremasinghe and had recently enrolled in a new part-time course in architecture being run by the Institute

The Jayewardene House at Mirissa

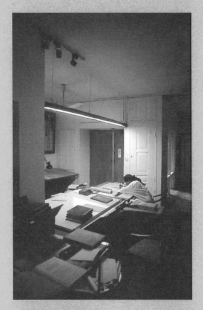

Top: The office at 33rd Lane
Centre: Bawa at work

of Architects. Administration was still handled by Janet Kanageswaran, who had worked in E. R. & B. since 1969 and was, in Bawa's own words, 'the hub of the turning wheel of my office'. She continued to work from Alfred House Road until 1992, when she also moved across to 33rd Lane.

Was there a grand plan? One suspects that, as so often in the past, Bawa was simply going with the flow, living each day as it came. He was happy to have extricated himself from what had become for him the oppressive machine of Edwards, Reid and Begg, and happy to be able to start again from scratch with a small team of young, fresh designers. What he now built up was more an architectural studio than an office, more concerned with design and the development of new ideas than with execution.

$10,000 Projects

In 1988 Bawa embarked on a remarkable series of fantasy designs that came to be known as the $10,000 Projects. Suddenly developers and clients from all over Asia were queuing up to employ him as their architect. With hindsight it would seem that in most cases they were simply interested in using his name to promote their developments to financiers and planning authorities and probably had no intention of ever building his designs. But it also seems likely that Bawa was perfectly aware of this and happy to play along. All that he demanded was prepaid air tickets, accommodation in good hotels, a basic consultancy fee – usually $10,000 – and a free hand to design whatever he thought appropriate. If a project went ahead he would hand it on to a local executive architect while retaining some degree of design control; if it foundered he would still have had the pleasure of designing something extraordinary. And so between 1988 and 1992 Bawa travelled incessantly,

sometimes accompanied by Dilshan Ferdinando or Milroy Perera, but often alone, meeting potential clients, visiting sites, producing endless sketch designs.

In 1988 Bawa was asked by the Singapore Tourist Promotion Board to design a new glasshouse to accommodate a simulated tropical rainforest in the Singapore Botanical Gardens. There was growing concern at the accelerating destruction of the country's architectural heritage and the Tourist Board wanted a building modelled on the great Victorian glasshouses of Kew in London to reflect Singapore's colonial past. They chose Bawa because the *Mimar* book suggested to them that he was the man for the job. In fact what he proposed was not a piece of Victorian pastiche but a contemporary cluster of glass pyramids. The four pyramids were of different sizes and were connected by ramped walkways in a manner reminiscent of the pavilion at the Osaka World Fair (1969). Bawa carefully choreographed the experience so that visitors moved through clouds of steam from pyramid to pyramid, descending into grottos, clambering under waterfalls and climbing rocky crags. When Bawa presented his design to the clients, however, it was not at all what they had expected and they rejected it out of hand. Christoph Bon, who had built a similar tropical glasshouse in the Barbican in London, was convinced that, had it been built, the Singapore Cloud Centre would have been one of Bawa's finest achievements.

A second project in Singapore was commissioned in 1989 by a Singaporean developer called Albert Teo for a row of four houses on a site overlooking one of the last surviving areas of natural forest on the island of Singapore. The design was sketched out in considerable detail by Bawa with each house occupying a

long, narrow plot sloping down from the access road. The houses all conformed to a general pattern of linked pavilions of varying heights alternating with court-yards. Eventually Teo sold the site with the design to another developer and nothing more was heard of it.

Shortly after delivering his lecture to the ARCASIA conference in Bali in 1987 Bawa was invited to design an extension to the Bali Hyatt Hotel, located on the south-eastern tip of the island close to Sanur and not far from Batujimbar. Bawa proposed clusters of pavilions arranged with semi-formality around a system of courtyards and alleyways. These were laid out along either side of a grand central avenue that formed the backbone of the scheme. An immense swimming pool ran down this avenue, linking an entrance pavilion to the edge of the beach.

The design was developed in great detail and revived many of the themes Bawa had incorporated into the Batujimbar project some fifteen years earlier. It stemmed from an idea that had first surfaced at the Blue Lagoon Hotel (1965) and had been developed in the 1970s by Bawa's former assistants Pherooze Choksy and Ismeth Raheem in their design for the Habarane Lodge Hotel, whereby a series of pavilions was arranged in clusters in a formal orthogonal manner reminiscent of Buddhist monasteries. The various clusters contained pavilions of different sizes and degrees of luxury, from semi-detached villas to a moated presidential suite, and the overall effect would have been that of a vast Balinese palace beside the sea.

The project was abandoned following the imposition of new building restrictions in Bali and the site remains fallow to this day. As an unbuilt idea it had a considerable influence on the next generation of Asian hotels, however, and there can be little doubt that its impact as a finished building would have been enormous.

A further Indonesian project came into the office in 1991 when Banyan Tree Resorts commissioned Bawa to design a hotel on the island of Bintan. The site was a hilly promontory that separated two long stretches of beach. Bawa envisaged a low-density development of villa clusters straddling a trio of hills around a central agora. The clusters were connected by a system of narrow lanes and guests were to be provided with electric buggies. In the end a more modest scheme was adopted for a smaller site and another architect was appointed, though the built scheme bore the hallmarks of Bawa's initial involvement.

Bawa worked on the Larry Gordon House on Fiji from 1989 to 1991. The house could be thought of as an unbuilt design, because what was eventually built bore only a passing resemblance to the original drawings. Bawa met the Gordons when he was invited to Fiji to advise on an extension to the Fiji Suva Hotel, and they asked him to help them build a house on a cliff overlooking the Koro Sea. Bawa made a single visit to the site and was excited by its potential. During the following year he and Sumangala produced at least three separate schemes, developing the idea of a cluster of timber-framed pavilions under steep hipped roofs of straw thatch. Bawa's designs only reached their full potential when he was able to develop a design and supervise its construction on site, but Fiji was too far away for regular site visits. In the event the project was completed by local architects, who changed the layout and altered the roofs, while the interiors were redesigned by Bali-based decorator Linda Garland. When the house was eventually featured in *Architectural Digest*

(Viladas 1994) its architecture was attributed to Geoffrey Bawa, though he had little to do with its execution. Garland was credited as the interior designer. Bawa, of course, believed implicitly that outside and inside were indivisible, that architecture involved a dialogue between interior and landscape, and he maintained that no self-respecting architect would ever employ an interior designer.

In 1992 Bawa was asked to design a house on the outskirts of Ahmadabad for the Sarabhai family, collectors of architecture who owned a house by Le Corbusier. A scheme for a large courtyard house was developed but never built.

In the same year Bawa was persuaded to design a large house in Delhi for a wealthy businessman, Lalith Modi, and his wife, Minal. He travelled to Delhi to meet the client and see the site and during the journey he fantasized about an elegant woman in her expensive sari greeting guests in a columnated hall, leading them past courtyards to a panoramic lounge with loggias overlooking a beautiful garden: the seeds of the design had been sown. The scheme that evolved after the visit consisted of a core pavilion with two large internal courtyards – one of them 'a fire court for dining on chilly winter evenings' – and splayed wings that defined outer terraces. A sketch sent in October 1992 included a note to the clients that ended: 'I haven't written down the detailed description of the materials to be used, but in general they would be limited to stone, timber and plastered walls – simple yet grand in their simplicity. The spaces are what count and the movement through them.' Bawa arranged for the Delhi architect Ashok Lal to act as his local executive architect and for the first and only time one of his designs was drawn up in CAD (computer-

aided design). The client failed to obtain planning permission, however, and the project was abandoned.

Another couple from India travelled down to Colombo in 1994 with the sole purpose of persuading Bawa to build a house for them. The Poddars had become the owners of Chickajhalla Fort, some 20 kilometres north of Bangalore and wanted to convert it into a house. The fort was contained within an elliptical walled enclosure and boasted a beautiful stepped well and a Hindu temple dedicated to Hanuman. Bawa was intrigued. He sped to Bangalore to see the fort for himself and produced a sketch design on the spot. However, the Poddars had bought the fort from an ageing courtesan, the mistress of a local *zemindar* (landlord), and she was later stabbed to death in a dispute with her children over the division of the proceeds of the sale, and the project was sadly cancelled.

This period was important for Bawa, enabling him to clear his mind of the baggage of the past thirty years and to work out a new set of design priorities. It came to an end when reality returned in the shape of a real commission from Aitken Spence to design a new hotel, the Kandalama, in Sri Lanka's Dry Zone (1991; p.200).

Dilshan Ferdinando, who had acted as a friend and travelling companion as well as a colleague, left the office at the end of 1991 to pursue his family-business interests in Singapore and was replaced by a young architect called Channa Daswatte, who had studied at Moratuwa and worked in Anjalendran's office before finishing his studies at University College London. He worked initially on the Kandalama Hotel but soon graduated to become Bawa's main associate and was involved in all subsequent projects.

Top: 'More Hotels', a cartoon by Sumangala
Middle: 'Mr Bawa at work' by Sumangala
Bottom: Bawa on site at Kandalama with Milroy Perera

Middle left: Christoph Bon
at Lunuganga
Bottom left: Bawa at Stowe
during a visit to Britain
Bottom right: Bawa with Jean
Chamberlin on the western
terrace at Lunuganga

The Lunuganga book

The idea to make a book specifically about the garden at Lunuganga came originally from Jean Chamberlin and Christoph Bon and it was they who funded the project. Work started in 1988 and continued over two years. The photographs, taken mainly by Christoph with help from Dominic Sansoni, were shot in black and white in order to capture the monochromatic quality of the landscape. Christoph would prowl the garden, his cigar stub between his teeth, waiting for the light to change. He used a hand-held Leica with three fixed lenses. These photographs were complemented by a set of beautifully evocative and often witty drawings made by Sumangala. The images were assembled in London and the book was published in 1990. *Lunuganga* stands as a remarkable record of a garden at a particular moment in its evolution and succeeds in capturing the magical qualities of the place.

Bawa dedicated the book to his brother Bevis 'whose love of gardens helped me to start and maintain my own'. Bevis died two years later in September 1992 at the age of eighty-three after a long illness that had left him bedridden and almost blind. The two brothers had lived in their respective gardens on either side of the Bentota River for almost half a century, but they seldom met. They had a difficult relationship, conditioned in part by the difference in their ages and in part by their relations with their parents. In his unpublished memoirs Bevis said of his brother:

It was only natural that we were more or less strangers after his years abroad, I Eastern in my outlook, and Geoffrey, British…His whole life is tied up with arts, beauty, culture…He avoids anything that could be depressing, such as sickness and sorrow, misery and squalor. Things he would far rather avoid he faces up to with a stiff upper lip like the typical stoic Britisher of old.

And so it was that Bawa avoided his brother during his final illness just as he had avoided their mother during her last year, but was heartbroken when he died.

Bawa continued to travel, making regular visits to Australia to visit his old friend and client Chris Raffel, and to England to spend time with Jean Chamberlin and Christoph Bon. In October 1995 he was invited to Brazil for the opening of an exhibition of his work in Sao Paulo and stopped off in London for what would be his last visit to South Edwardes Square. However, when Jean and Christoph visited Colombo the following July, Bawa treated them with inexplicable disdain and they departed for the last time under a cloud of bitter resentment.

Jean Chamberlin died in September 1997 and Christoph Bon in October 1999. Their relationship with Bawa had lasted for twenty years and during that time they had been constant travelling companions and close friends. They were the prime movers in organizing the *Mimar* book – which, in its acknowledgments, refers to them as 'architect friends in London who insist they remain anonymous' – as well as the later book on Lunuganga. There can be no doubt that Bawa loved them dearly but in the end they broke one of his unwritten rules when they began to move from one compartment of his life to another. He felt threatened when they became close to his other friends, particularly Ena de Silva and Sunethra Bandaranaike, and may even have resented their popularity. Bawa had a great capacity for friendship and could be warm

and generous, witty and gregarious, but he also had an inbuilt recoil mechanism that caused him to repel people that got too close. And after the deed was done he would be inconsolable.

Failing health

Bawa had never been physically very active and was a heavy smoker. During the 1990s he became progressively less mobile and relied more and more on a wheelchair to get about. In 1994 he suffered a serious fall that left him unable to walk without the aid of a stick or a helper. A second fall at Lunuganga in 1997 considerably shook him and he finally gave up smoking. He continued to work, however, and during 1997 developed designs for the President's House (p.227) and supervised the building of the Lighthouse (1995; p.212) and Blue Water (1996; p.216) hotels. He also set out on his last foreign journey, travelling with Channa Daswatte to South Africa in September to judge a competition for a new constitutional court building.

In October 1997 Bawa finally formalized the dissolution of his partnership with Poologasundram and agreed to buy his

partner's share of the Alfred House Road office. He paid a final visit to the office and was taken in his wheelchair to the first courtyard, where he presided over a massive clear-out of old drawings and files. Tubes and drawers full of drawings were brought down from the attic above the gatehouse and passed in front of him in what became a bonfire of the vanities. Some of these dated back to the 1920s and 1930s. Many had been eaten by ants or mildew, but a number of the older drawings were on linen and were still in good condition. At Bawa's bidding huge quantities of the drawings were loaded onto a trailer and taken away to be burnt. Only a few survived to be thrown in a heap in the garage of 33rd Lane, where they continued to rot until the following summer, when some attempt was finally made to conserve and catalogue them.

Bawa was now worried about his health and fearful of the possibility that, like his mother and brother, he would face a long lingering illness. The old office lay on the edge of the burgeoning Galle Road business district and was now a valuable property. Renting it out would help to pay for the

upkeep of his household at 33rd Lane if he were to fall seriously ill. In December he agreed to let the building to a young businessman called Shanth Fernando, who proposed to run it as a restaurant and gallery. Fernando already ran a chain of design shops and offered a substantial rent. A long-standing admirer of Bawa, he also gave assurances that he would restore the old building with care.

On 30 December 1997 Bawa made what was to be his last working site visit. A house that he had been designing in Mirissa (1997; p.223) was now finished and its owners were staying there over the Christmas period. Bawa drove down from Lunuganga with Channa Daswatte to have tea with the family and give them the benefit of his 'after-sales' advice. He left after sunset feeling very pleased with the way the house was 'being lived in', but soon after returning to Lunuganga, at the end of a long and enjoyable but tiring day, he suffered his first stroke.

The stroke did not appear to be serious and he recovered quickly. Within a couple of weeks he was back at work, supervising the redesign of the President's House and

Top right: The Gallery Restaurant in the old Alfred House Road office
Middle right: The rear courtyard of the Gallery Restaurant
Bottom left: Bawa with Michael Ondaatje in the Bajaj at Lunuganga
Bottom right: Bawa with Channa Daswatte at 'Number Eighty-Seven' in 1997

worrying about various jobs still under
construction. In January 1998 his old
friend Dr Raffel came from Australia to
see him, counselling him to take things
easy and helping him to draw up a will.
A board of trustees had already been
formed to look after Lunuganga in
the event of Bawa's death and its
responsibilities were now widened.

A royal visit

The year 1998 marked the fiftieth
anniversary of Sri Lanka's independence
and a muted celebration was planned
to take place in Colombo on 4 February.
Britain was represented by Prince Charles,
but last-minute concerns for his safety
meant that he only attended the first
part of the public ceremonies. A long-
time admirer of Bawa's architecture, he
asked if he could use his free afternoon to
visit the garden in Lunuganga. The request
was passed to the President's office and
reached 33rd Lane mid-morning. Bawa
rushed down to Bentota with Channa
Daswatte, stopping at hotels to buy the
ingredients for a royal tea. Although
Prince Charles was accompanied by
security personnel, the visit was a relaxed
and impromptu occasion. The Prince was
met by Bawa in his wheelchair and shown
around the garden by Daswatte. Tea was
taken on the south terrace and the Prince
dutifully signed the visitors' book. This
whole episode gave Bawa an enormous
thrill but it also added to his growing
state of exhaustion.

A world collapsing

Soon after the Prince's visit, news reached
Colombo of the death of Piyasena, the head
gardener at Lunuganga and husband of
Leela the housekeeper. When Bawa went to
see Leela at Lunuganga she announced that
she was leaving his service to return to her

family's village and ceremoniously
handed over her keys. Bawa was
devastated. He had a growing sense
that his world was collapsing, that his
life was slipping away from him. As a
result of his own stubbornness he had
lost some of his closest friends and now
his household was falling apart.

It is difficult today to appreciate the
bonds that existed between someone in
Bawa's position and his domestic staff.
Leela's mother, Ensa, had been Bawa's
childhood nurse and was buried under
the moonamal tree at Lunuganga a few
feet from the spot he had earmarked for
his own burial. To a man who had no
close relatives, these people were his
family. Leela's departure came as a
bitter blow. Then, on 1 March, he
suffered the massive second stroke
that left him almost totally paralysed.

Henceforth Bawa needed – and
continues to need – constant nursing,
and his bedroom in 33rd Lane was
converted into a care unit. At first it
seemed that every vital spark of this
extraordinary man had been extinguished,
though friends slowly realized that a part
of him had survived deep inside his wasted
body and found ways to reach him. On the
other side of his bedroom wall the life of
the office went on under the direction
of Channa Daswatte who, as one of Bawa's
trustees, also took on an important role in
managing Bawa's affairs. Work continued
in fits and starts on the President's House,
and a number of private houses were taken
towards completion – the Spencer House in
Colombo, the Jacobson House in Tangalla
and the Mehta House in Mumbai.

Bawa's health improved slowly during
1999, though he has remained paralysed
and has never recovered the power of
speech. Now, on good days, he can be
moved around the house in his wheel-

chair and he is taken down the long white
corridor to the office to be shown the latest
designs on the drawing boards. When the
doctors give their consent, he travels down
to Bentota in the company of an entourage
of nurses to spend a few precious days in
his beloved garden at Lunuganga.

Towards the end of his career, Bawa
received honours in his own land: in 1985
President Jayewardene conferred on him
the title ' Vidya Jothi' or 'Light of Science',
and in 1993 President Premadasa made
him 'Deshamanya' or 'Pride of the Nation'.
But in 2001 he finally received international
recognition of his achievements. This came
not from Britain, the country in which he
received his education, nor from the Royal
Institute of British Architects, of which he
had been a member for over forty years, but
from the Aga Khan Award for Architecture.
These awards are presented every three
years to celebrate buildings, mainly in
the developing world, judged by an international jury to be of particular merit.
Exceptionally, the chairman's special award
can be presented to an individual architect
in recognition of the whole body of his
work, though in eight cycles stretching
over twenty-four years this honour has
only been bestowed on three occasions: to
Hassan Fathy in 1980, to Rifat Chardirji in
1986 and to Geoffrey Bawa in 2001. Bawa
was too ill to attend the award ceremony
in Aleppo in Syria, but the award was
accepted on his behalf by Channa Daswatte.

The Singapore Cloud Centre, 1988

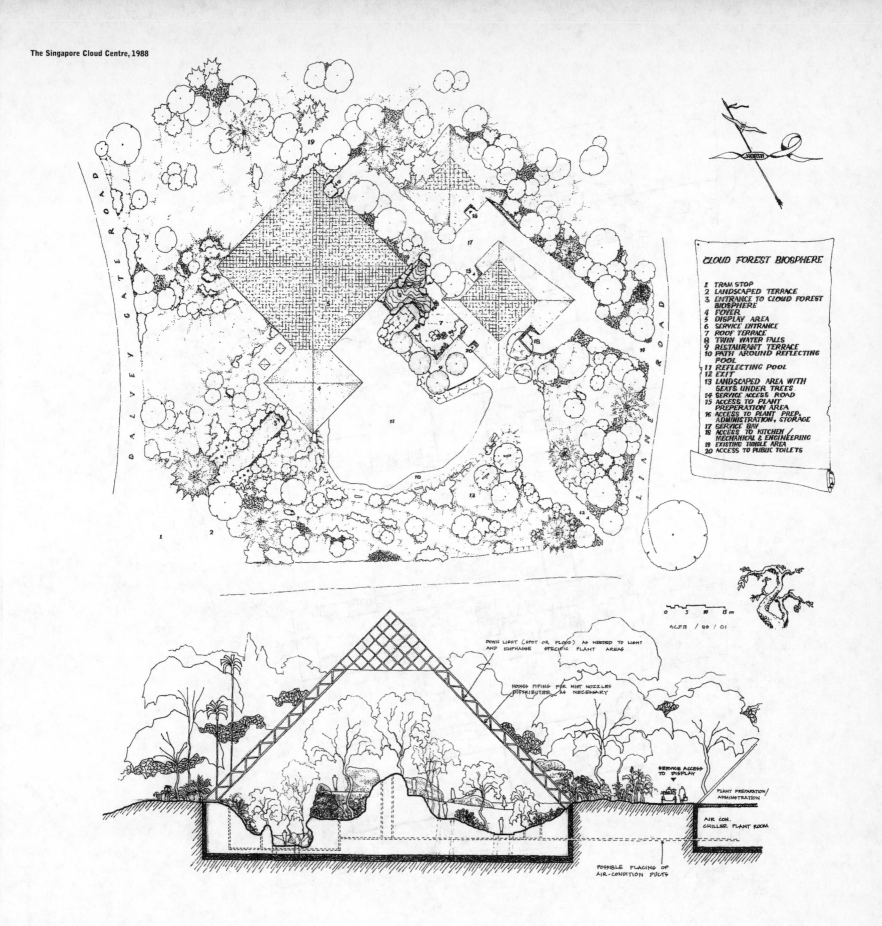

CLOUD FOREST BIOSPHERE

1 TRAM STOP
2 LANDSCAPED TERRACE
3 ENTRANCE TO CLOUD FOREST
   BIOSPHERE
4 FOYER
5 DISPLAY AREA
6 SERVICE ENTRANCE
7 ROOF TERRACE
8 TWIN WATER FALLS
9 RESTAURANT TERRACE
10 PATH AROUND REFLECTING
   POOL
11 REFLECTING POOL
12 EXIT
13 LANDSCAPED AREA WITH
   SEATS UNDER TREES
14 SERVICE ACCESS ROAD
15 ACCESS TO PLANT
   PREPARATION AREA
16 ACCESS TO PLANT PREP,
   ADMINISTRATION, STORAGE
17 SERVICE BAY
18 ACCESS TO KITCHEN
   MECHANICAL & ENGINEERING
19 EXISTING JUNGLE AREA
20 ACCESS TO PUBLIC TOILETS

SCFB / 89 / 01

DOWN LIGHT (SPOT OR FLOOD) AS NEEDED TO LIGHT
AND EMPHASISE SPECIFIC PLANT AREAS

HOUSES PIPING FOR MIST NOZZLES
DISTRIBUTED AS NECESSARY

SERVICE ACCESS
TO DISPLAY

PLANT PREPARATION /
ADMINISTRATION

AIR CON.
CHILLER PLANT ROOM

POSSIBLE PLACING OF
AIR-CONDITION DUCTS

SECTION A·A - THROUGH MAIN DISPLAY
SCALE 1:200

0 1 2 3 4 5   10 METRES

SCFB / 89 / 07

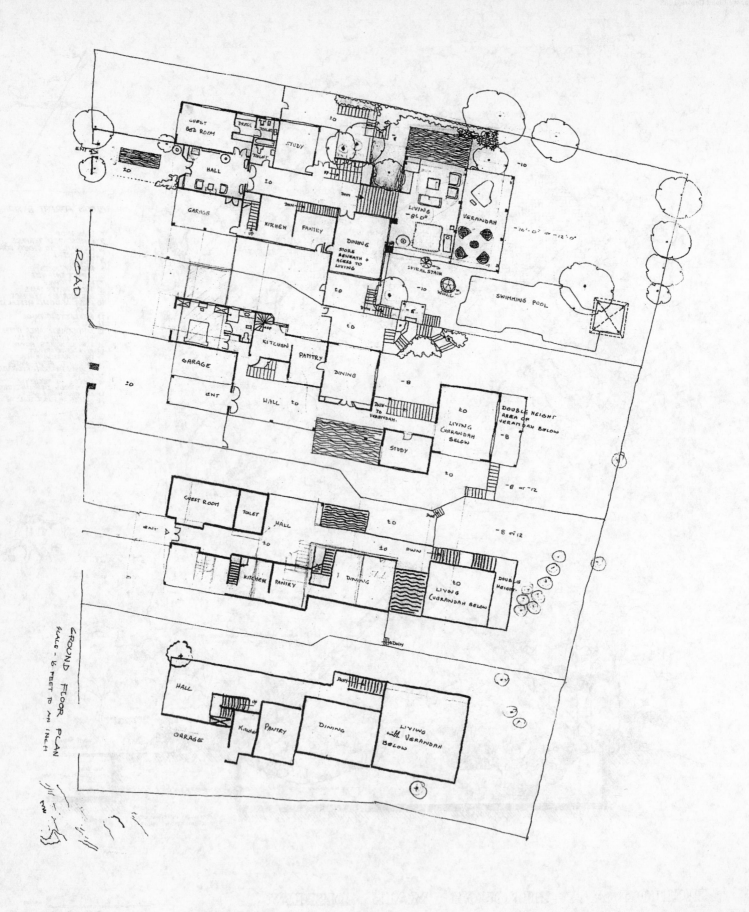

GROUND FLOOR PLAN
SCALE - 16 FEET TO AN INCH

ROAD

ENT

GUEST BED ROOM
DRESS
TOILET
STUDY
TO

HALL
TOILET
TO

GARAGE
KITCHEN
PANTRY
UP
DWN

DINING
STORE BENEATH & ACCESS TO LIVING

LIVING -8'6"
VERANDAH

SPIRAL STAIR

WALL

SWIMMING POOL

GARAGE
KITCHEN
PANTRY
DINING
-8
DWN TO VERANDAH

ENT
HALL
TO
LIVING (VERANDAH BELOW)
DOUBLE HEIGHT AREA OF VERANDAH BELOW
-8

STUDY
-8 or -12

GUEST ROOM
TOILET
HALL
TO
DWN
-8 or 12

ENT
KITCHEN
PANTRY
DINING
LIVING (VERANDAH BELOW)
DOUBLE HEIGHT

HALL
GARAGE
KITCHEN
PANTRY
UP
DINING
LIVING with VERANDAH BELOW

DWN

The Albert Teo Houses, Singapore, 1989

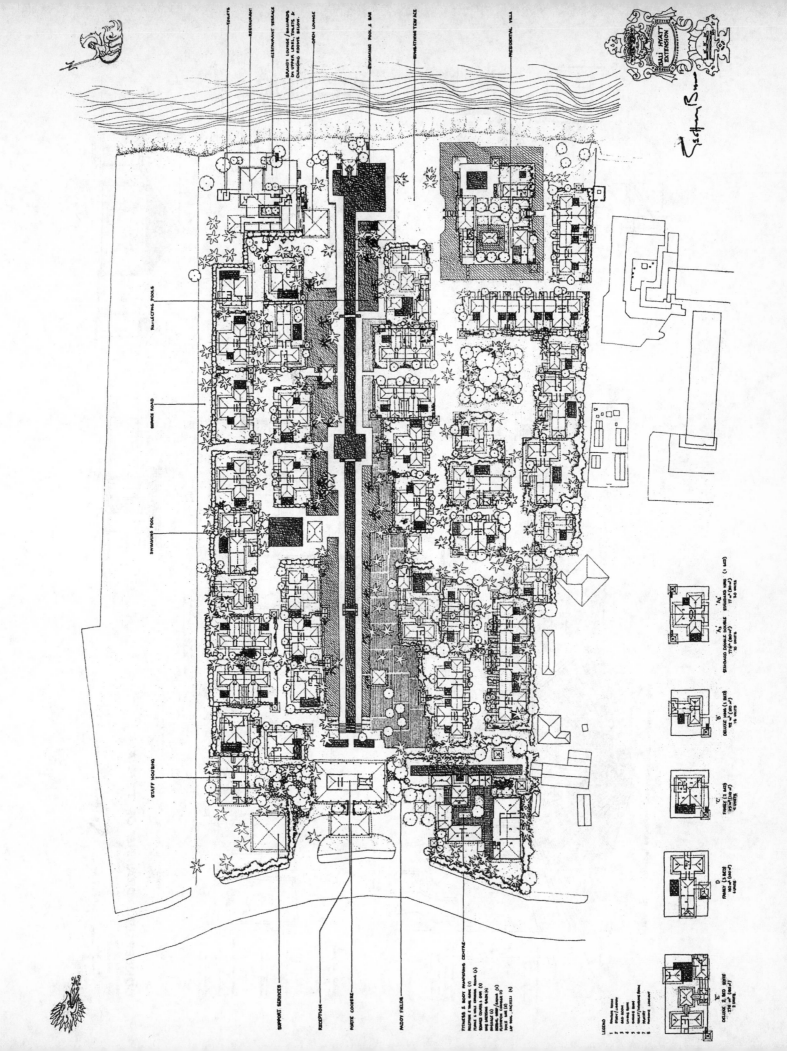

Layout of the Bali Hyatt Extension, 1989

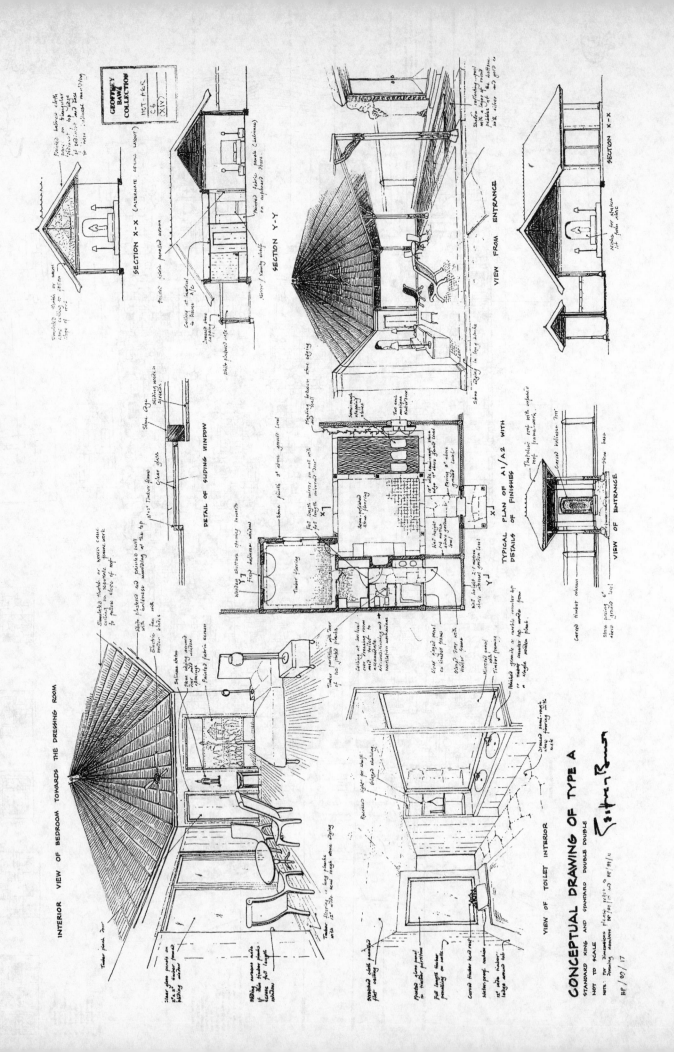

Details of the Bali Hyatt Extension, 1989

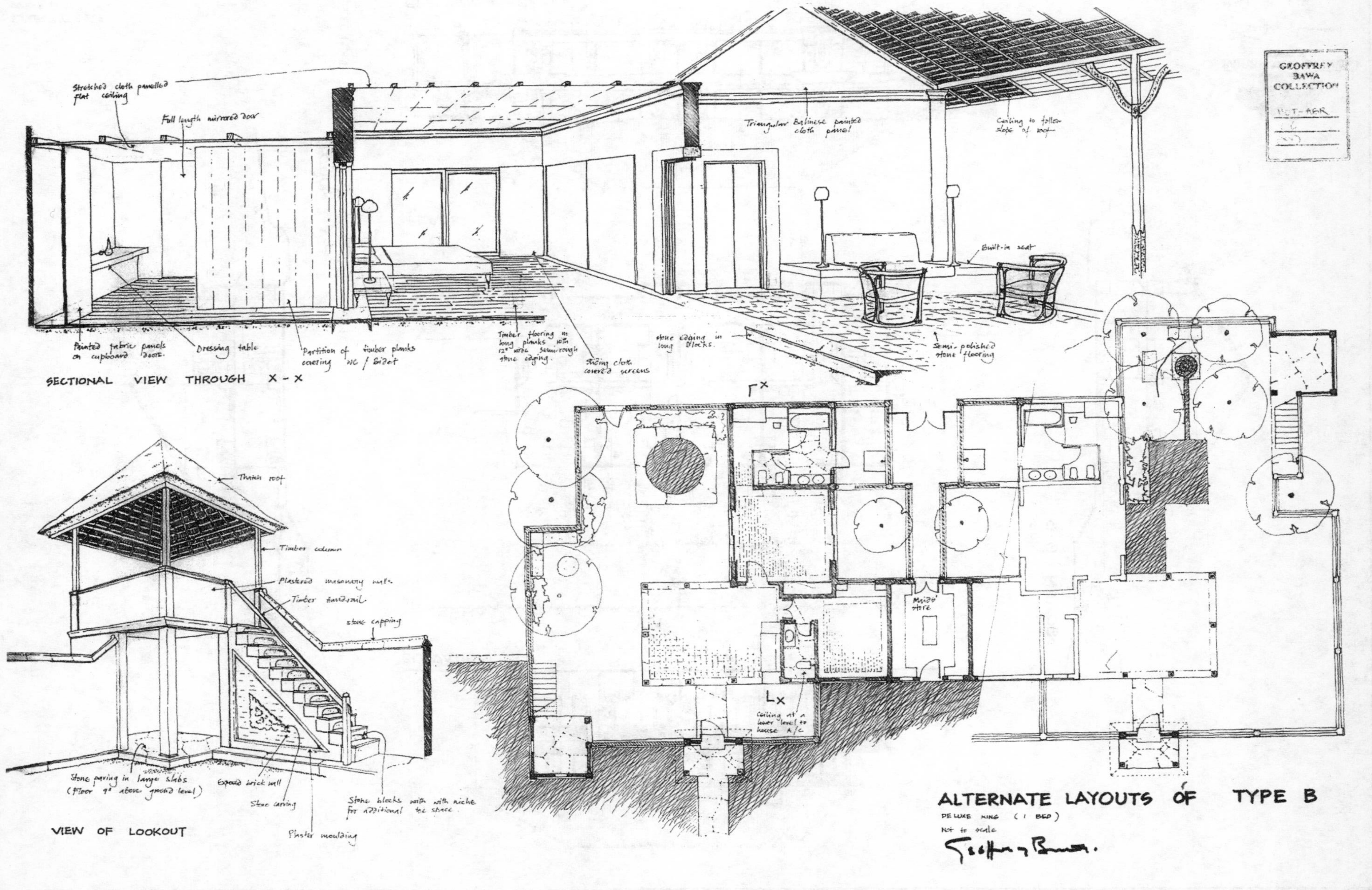

GEOFFREY
BAWA
COLLECTION

ALTERNATE LAYOUTS OF TYPE B

DE LUXE KING (1 BED)

not to scale

Geoffrey Bawa.

Stretched cloth panelled flat ceiling

Ceiling to follow slope of roof

Full length mirrored door

Triangular latticed painted cloth panel

Built-in seat

Semi-polished stone flooring

Dressing table

Painted fabric panels on cupboard doors

Portion of timber planks coating WC / toilet

Stone cladding in long blocks

Timber flooring in long planks, 12" wide. Showing close. Covered? screens

SECTIONAL VIEW THROUGH X - X

Thatch roof

Timber column

Plastered surrounding wall

Timber handrail

Stone capping

Stone blocks with with niches for additional tiled stones

Stone coving

Stone paving in large slabs (Floor at above ground level)

Partly insulating

VIEW OF LOOKOUT

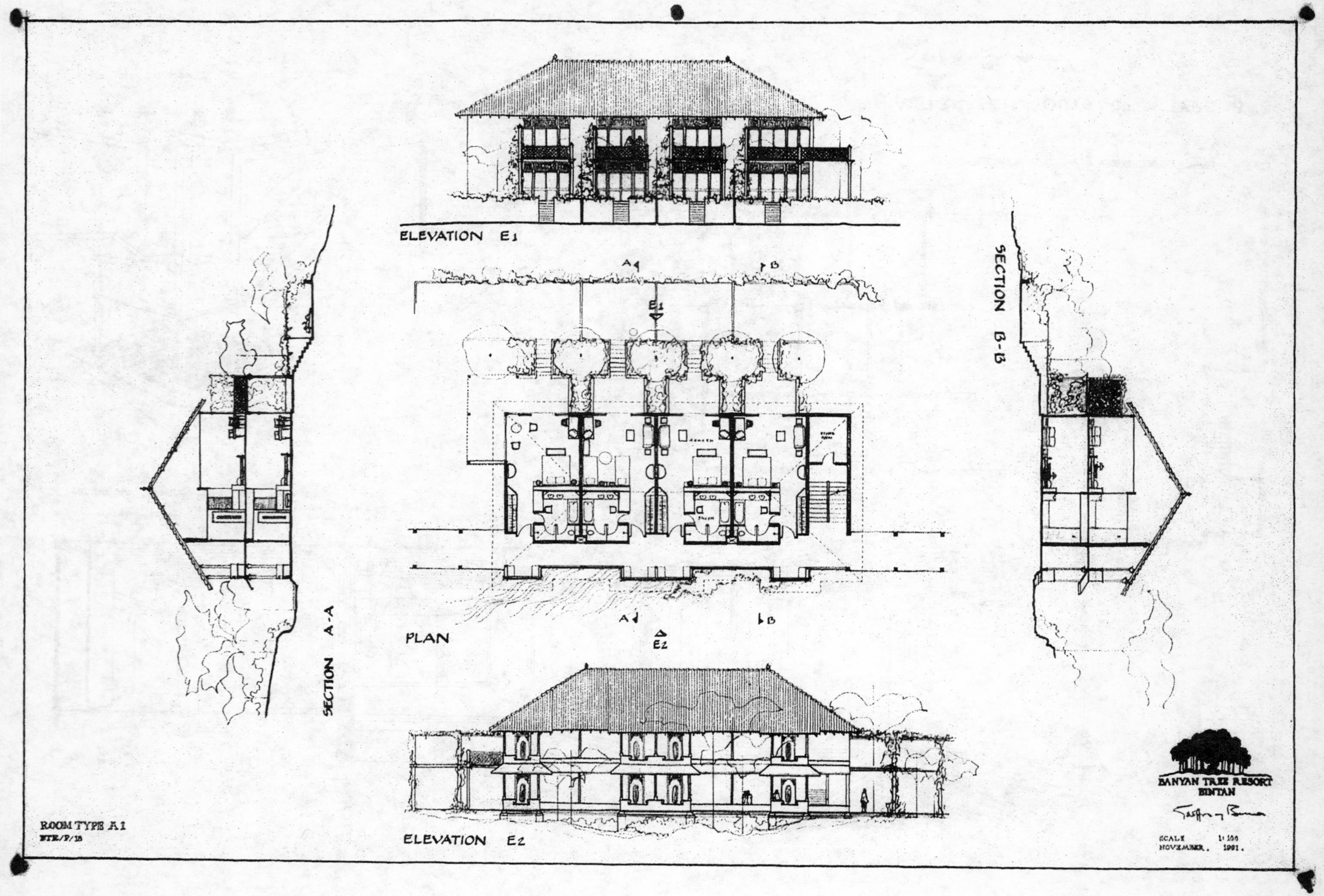
ELEVATION E1
A1
B
E1
SECTION B-B
SECTION A-A
PLAN
A1
E2
B
ELEVATION E2
ROOM TYPE A1
BTE/P/15
BANYAN TREE RESORT
BINTAN
SCALE 1:100
NOVEMBER. 1991.

Details of the Banyan Resort Hotel, Bintan, 1991

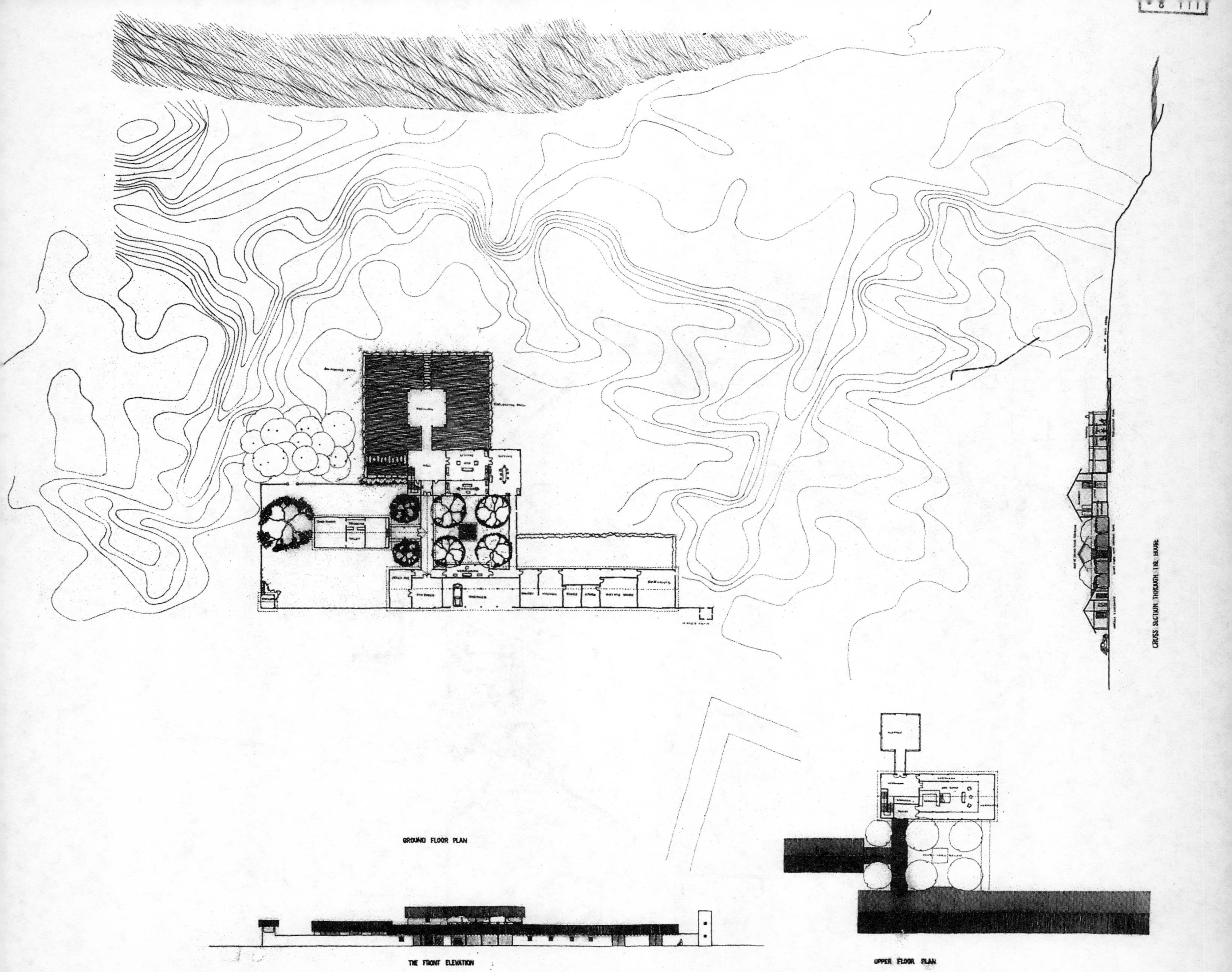

CROSS SECTION THROUGH THE HOUSE

UPPER FLOOR PLAN

GROUND FLOOR PLAN

THE FRONT ELEVATION

The Sarabhai House, Ahmadabad, 1992

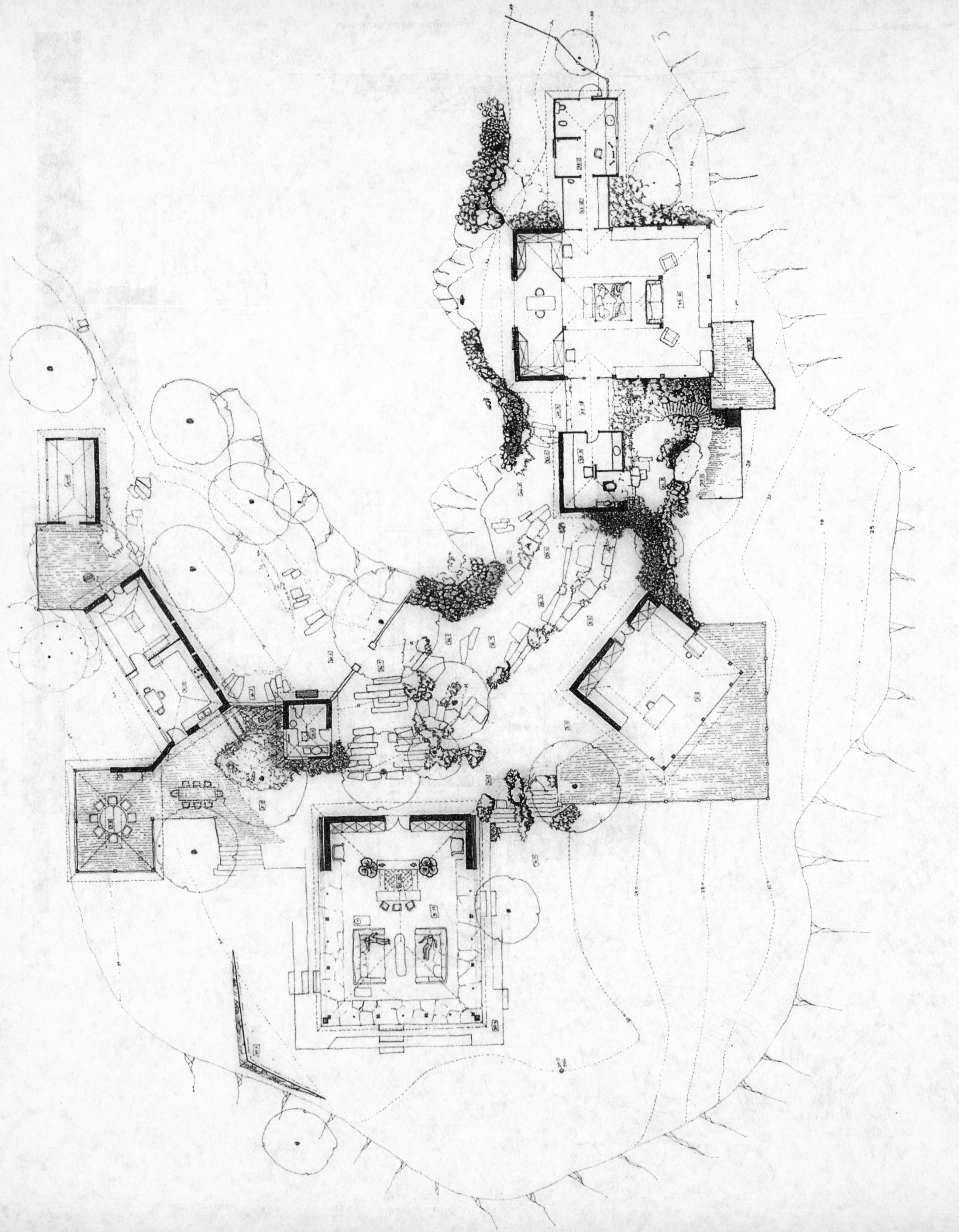

The Larry Gordon House, Fiji, 1989

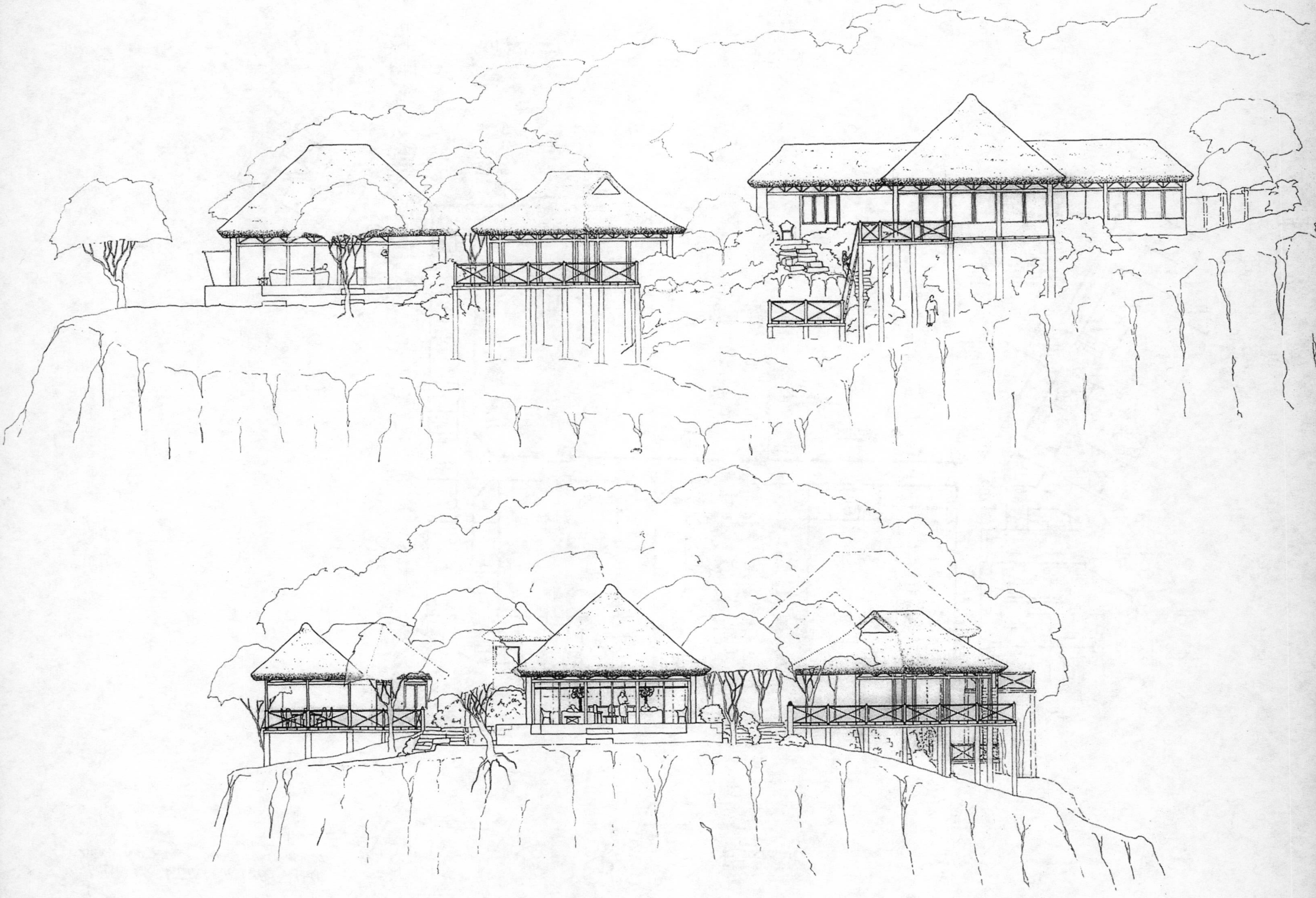

The Larry Gordon House, Fiji, 1989

The Modi House, Delhi, 1992

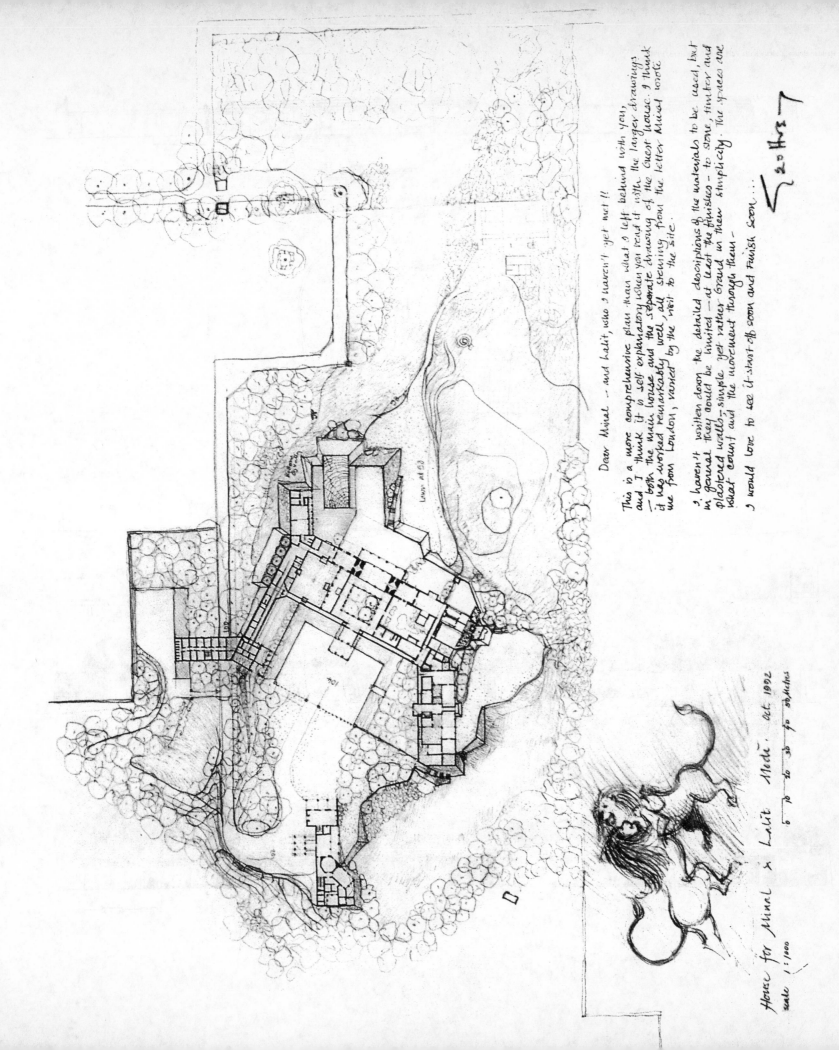

Dear Mrinal — and Lalit, who I haven't yet met!!

This is a more comprehensive plan than what I left behind with you, and I think it is self explanatory when you read it with the larger drawings — both the main house and the separate drawing of the Guest House. I think it has worked remarkably well, all stemming from the letter Mrinal wrote me from London, varied by the visit to the site.

I haven't written down the detailed descriptions of the materials to be used, but in general they would be limited — at least the finishes — to stone, timber and plastered walls; simple yet rather Grand in their simplicity. The spaces are what count and the movement through them —

I would love to see it start-off soon and finish soon ...

House for Mrinal & Lalit Modi. Oct. 1992
scale 1:1000

The Modi House, Delhi, 1992

The Poddar House, Chickajhalla Fort, near Bangalore, 1994

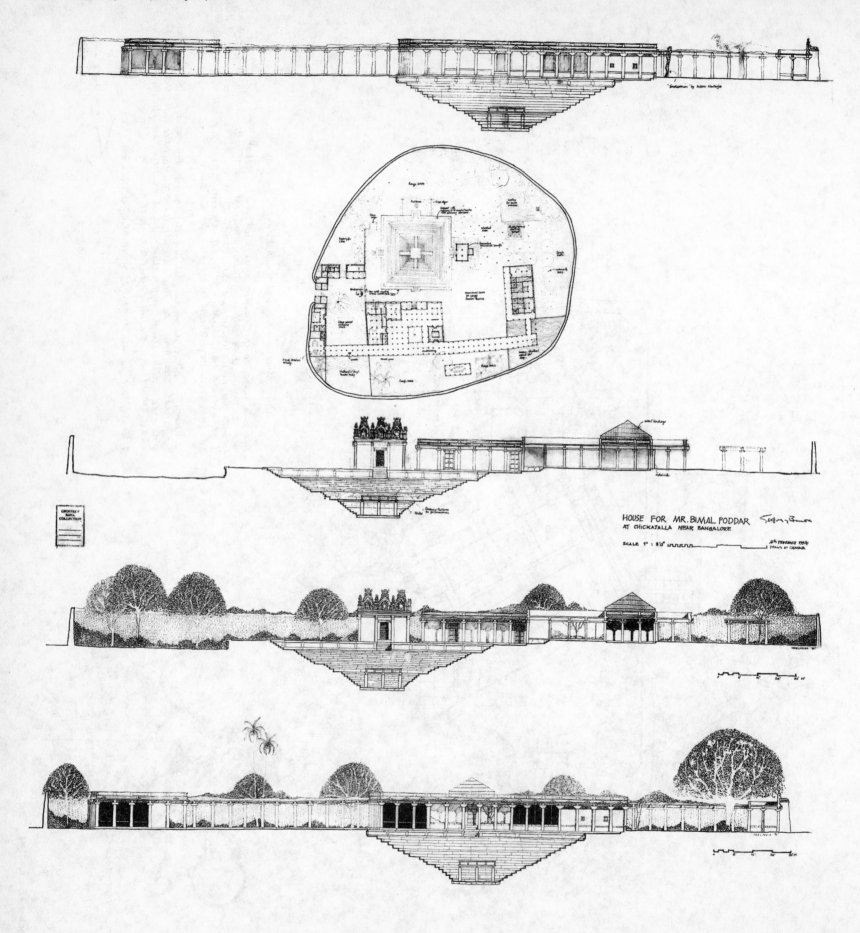

'When one delights as much as I do in planning a building and having it built, I find it impossible to describe the exact steps in an analytical or dogmatic way... I have a very strong conviction that it is impossible to explain architecture in words... I have always enjoyed seeing buildings but seldom enjoyed reading explanations about them... architecture cannot be totally explained but must be experienced.'

the projects 1988–

kandalama hotel

DAMBULLA 1991–94

The crushing of the JVP in 1989 brought a lull to Sri Lanka's spiralling violence, encouraging a resurgence of tourism. Package tour operators started to offer a week at the beach on Sri Lanka's south-west coast combined with a week visiting the ancient cities in the 'Cultural Triangle' of the Dry Zone, and hotel developers found that they needed to have a 'foot in both camps'. Aitken Spence decided in 1991 to build a hotel in the Dry Zone to complement their popular Triton Hotel at Ahungalla and asked Bawa to be their architect. The company had an option on a site at Sigiriya not far from the foot of the ancient rock where King Kasyapa had made his fortress in the fifth century, and early in 1991 a party of directors travelled with Bawa to inspect it. Bawa rejected the site out of hand but suggested that the directors should look at 'a beautiful tank a short way away to the south-west' that would serve them better. The party set off in a convoy of cars along a country track that led them for about 10 kilometres through a landscape of huge rocky outcrops to the bund of the ancient Kandalama Tank. Bawa pointed dramatically with his stick towards his proposed site for the new hotel. Was this a spontaneous suggestion based on a vague memory of some long-forgotten trip in the Rolls, or was it a premeditated piece of theatre based on 'inside knowledge' gleaned from the old British 'One-Inch' maps or from his friend Laki Senanayake, who had a farm a few kilometres away to the south? For Bawa the original site lacked any sense of surprise or drama – the Sigiriya Rock was simply there, 'in your face'. What he wanted was a site that would offer mystery and suspense: visitors would be forced to make a long trek through the jungle to arrive at the edge of a tank, across which they would finally see Sigiriya in the distance.

He persuaded the clients to go along with his suggestion and a few days later the group flew over the site by helicopter, viewing an island at the centre of the tank and, behind it, a long ridge terminating near the edge in a rocky outcrop. Ridge or island? For a few days Bawa sketched ideas for both possibilities. Meanwhile Milroy Perera managed to reach the ridge by jeep and came back with stories of a long cliff face with an old cave hermitage, of thick jungle rich in wildlife, of superb views across the tank toward Sigiriya. Bawa was carried up to the ridge

in a makeshift palanquin. The whole story of the hotel now formed itself in his mind: visitors would arrive through the jungle from Dambulla, a few kilometres to the west, and would encounter a huge and seemingly impenetrable ridge; the hotel entrance would be formed like a cave mouth near the top of the ridge, reached by a huge ramp; a cave-like corridor would lead from the entrance through the ridge to reveal the hotel's main terraces and a view across the tank towards Sigiriya; four floors of rooms situated below the main reception level would then snake away around the face of the cliff towards the east.

Aitken Spence, to their credit, seem to have taken all of this in their stride. The government released the land and the project received the public backing of President Premadasa. Bawa worked on the scheme from 33rd Lane with his small in-house team, while Milroy Perera and his engineer partner Deepal Wickramasinghe were appointed by the client as executive architects. The building contract was awarded to a local firm called Link Engineering.

In the first designs the residential wing was given pitched roofs and kept close to the cliff face but in later developments flat roofs were adopted and the rooms were moved away from the cliff face to create a wider angle of vision. The design was developed during 1991 and work started on site in 1992. Only then did the project encounter any real opposition – the monks of the Dambulla Temple objected to the bedroom wing's encroachment onto an old monastic precinct and environmentalists protested that the buildings would threaten the catchment area of the tank. Both of these concerns were groundless but a barrage of publicity forced Bawa to change the design and half the rooms were relocated in a new wing to the west of the ridge above the approach road. Bawa was stung by the public

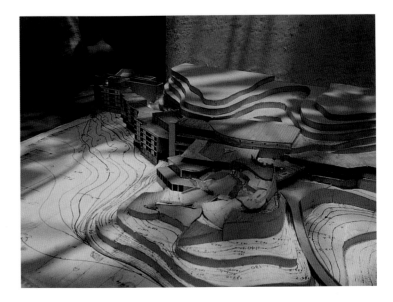

protests and saddened by the changes, which threatened to dilute the impact of his original vision. Much of that concept has survived, however. The new 'Dambulla' wing is screened by vegetation and the ramped ascent to the cave-like entrance and through the rock to the first lounge is still full of drama.

The use of flat roofs and a starkly expressed concrete frame mark a radical departure from Bawa's earlier work, and yet both are ideally suited to the site and to the Dry Zone climate. The snaking form makes it possible for the two residential wings to echo the shape of the ridge, so that the journey to the rooms runs alongside the overhanging cliff face, the structure burrowing into the ridge in some places, in others standing proud and allowing the rocky landscape to run beneath. The concrete frame carries an outer skin of timber sun-breakers, which in turn support a screen of vegetation, while the flat roof has been turned into a garden. As a result the hotel under its cloak of foliage melts into the jungle to such a degree that from the opposite shore of the tank it is almost invisible. Its environmental impact on its surroundings has also been minimized: water is drawn from wells, sewage is carefully treated and all waste is removed from the site.

The architecture is stark and understated, emphasizing the idea that this is not a building to look at, but a building to look from, like a giant belvedere. If they really try, guests can escape onto terra firma, though neither the architect nor the management ever intended that they should do so. They are marooned in a huge ocean liner with decks above and cabins below that has come to rest like Noah's Ark on some faraway mountainside. The only obvious contact with the ground is at entrance level, where the lounge opens towards the main swimming pool, which seems to hang like a shelf on the edge of the cliff.

The materials used in the public spaces are cool and hard and work with the large expanses of naked rock to convey an appropriate feeling of austerity that contrasts with the lushness of the encroaching vegetation: one might be inside an evocation of King Kasyapa's Palace. The ample rooms, dwarfed by the generous corridors, function as cells that look out across the tank towards the horizon; even the bathrooms share the view. The Kandalama Hotel offers a unique experience to its guests and stands as the remarkable achievement of a seventy-five-year-old architect and his team of youthful assistants.

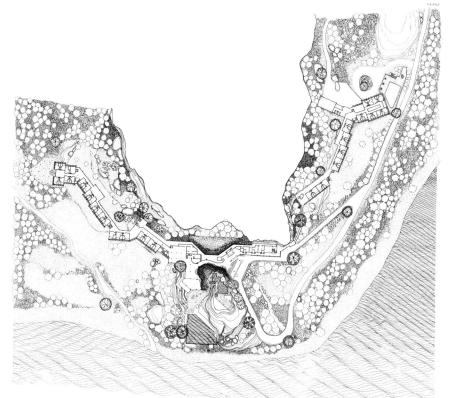

Opposite
Top: View of the Kandalama Hotel from across the Kandalama Tank

Middle: A design model of the Kandalama Hotel

Bottom: Sectional elevation through the Kandalama Hotel showing the relationship of the building to the cliff

This page
Top: Aerial view

Bottom: Plan at the main entrance level

This page: **The main entrance**

Opposite: **The entrance tunnel**

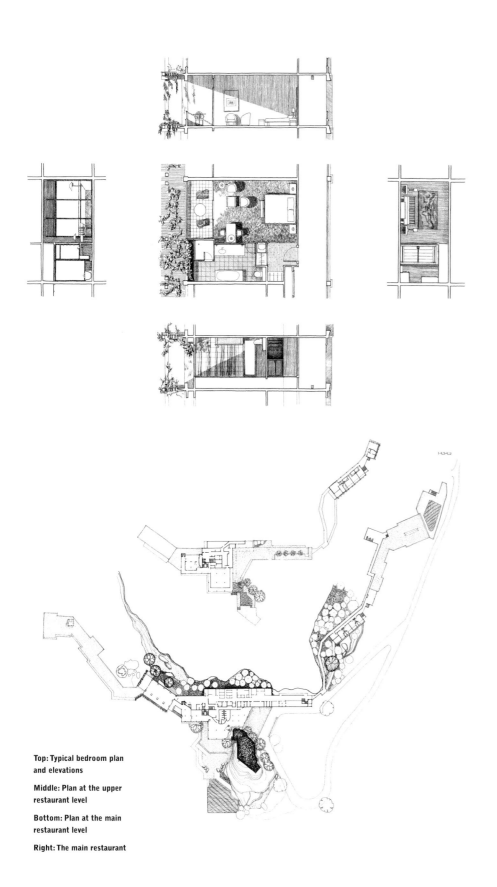

Top: Typical bedroom plan
and elevations

Middle: Plan at the upper
restaurant level

Bottom: Plan at the main
restaurant level

Right: The main restaurant

Left: A flying owl sculpted
by Laki Senanayake

Opposite
Top: A sitting room

Bottom: The link to
the Dambulla Wing

sinbad garden hotel

KALUTARA 1994–96

In the 1990s tourism in Sri Lanka continued to grow and two further hotel commissions appeared in 1994. The Orion Hotel was planned for Aitken Spence at Ahungalla to duplicate the earlier Triton Hotel. Its layout resembled the Triton, though the bedroom wings were splayed at angles from the core in order to define an amphitheatre of space.

The Sinbad Garden Hotel at Kalutara was planned to complement the Sinbad Hotel, occupying the end of a spit between a lagoon and the sea at the mouth of the Kalu Ganga River and dating from the 1970s. In 1990 its owner, Asker Moosajee, commissioned Bawa's friend Rico Tarawella, a Swiss furniture maker, to supervise a refurbishment of the old hotel. Bawa tried to muscle in and the hotel's manager, Bawa's old friend S. M. A. Hameed, had to draw a line in the sand – Rico would be responsible for the bedroom wings and Bawa for the main reception areas.

Bawa was then asked to design a new hotel to the south, again on a site spanning the sea and the lagoon but divided by the older hotel's access road. Channa Daswatte recalls that Bawa sketched a number of sub-Triton ideas but then one day, recalling the Villa Hadrian, switched to a concept based on two monumental spine walls. These served as combined service tracts and corridors, crossing the site at right angles, one running north–south from the kitchens to the bar and the other east–west above the road from the sea to the lagoon. The spines became the Cartesian coordinates for the scheme as well as providing the main axes of circulation. Conventional hotel rooms were lined up within a coconut grove at the edge of the sea, while a more picturesque group of villa apartments was scattered among the mangroves beside the lagoon. The main public rooms were placed on either side of the northern spine under huge lean-to roofs.

In January 1996 a massive terrorist bomb damaged a large area of Colombo's central business district and precipitated an immediate collapse of the tourist industry. As a result the Orion Hotel was cancelled, while the Sinbad project was put on hold and the empty shells of its buildings, by this time 70 per cent complete, were abandoned.

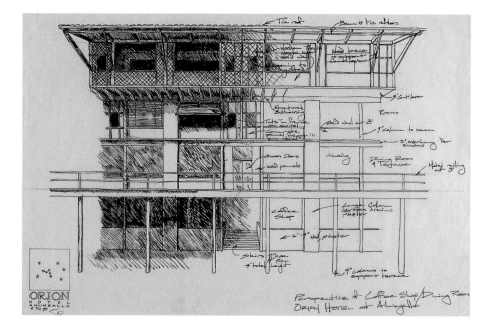

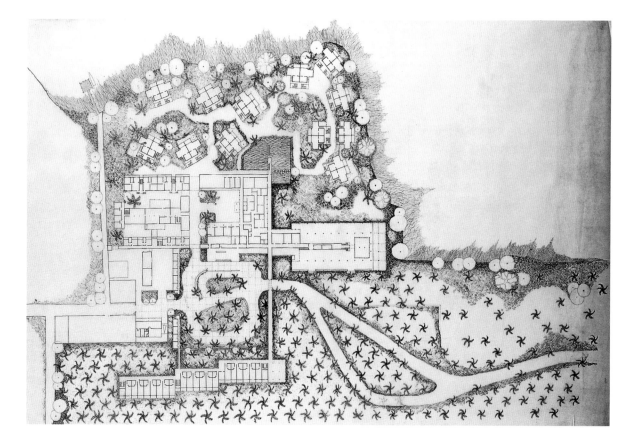

Top: Elevation study for the Orion Hotel

Bottom: Plan of the Sinbad Hotel

Top: Entrance to
the Sinbad Hotel

Bottom left: The entrance
pool in the Sinbad Hotel

Bottom right: The abandoned
Sinbad Garden Hotel

lighthouse hotel

GALLE 1995–97

In spite of the downturn in tourism, the Lighthouse Hotel was commissioned by Herbert Cooray in 1995 for his travel company Jetwings. Cooray's father had been the contractor for the Carmen Gunasekera House in 1958, and the Coorays had built a number of Bawa's projects before becoming successful developers and hoteliers in their own right.

The hotel is sited on a rocky promontory once occupied by a magistrates' circuit bungalow, and sits tightly between the main road and the sea about a mile to the north of Galle. The sea is inhospitable but the views are stunning. The main entrance and reception buildings of the hotel hug the southern tip of the ridge and offer views towards the Galle fort, the entrance and service points being housed within rubble retaining walls that enclose the lower slopes of the rock.

A massive *porte cochère* leads past the reception desk to a vertical drum enclosing the main stair, which spirals upwards to the upper terraces and restaurants. The staircase itself was designed by Bawa's old friend Laki Senanayake and is conceived as a swirling mass of Dutch and Sinhalese warriors re-enacting the Battle of Randeniya. The lounges and restaurants carry memories of old rest houses and planters' clubs, while the furnishing of the terraces and verandahs is solid and rugged to withstand the buffetings of the south-west monsoon. The first floor is finished in samara-coloured render and the upper floor is recessed behind a delicate colonnade. A three-storey range of hotel rooms runs along the edge of the shore northwards from the main reception areas, a parallel service block behind forming a tranquil courtyard of clipped grass and bare rock. A second range of hotel rooms steps back towards the road to create an open terrace with a bar and pool looking out to the ocean.

The strategy is to both confront the relentless crashing of the waves and provide contrasting areas of shelter and tranquillity. No single space is self-contained or complete: each is in part the consequence of a previous space and the anticipation of a subsequent one; each retains links with its neighbours and with the outside so that the eye is continually invited to explore. The architecture itself is muted, but offers subtle memories of Moorish palaces, ocean liners, ancient manor houses and colonial villas.

Top: Cross-section through the Lighthouse Hotel from east to west looking south

Middle right: View of the hotel from the sea's edge

Bottom left: The north wing

Bottom right: Aerial view from the north

Opposite
Middle left: View of the hotel from the south

Bottom left: Plan at the main terrace level

Right: Plan at entry level

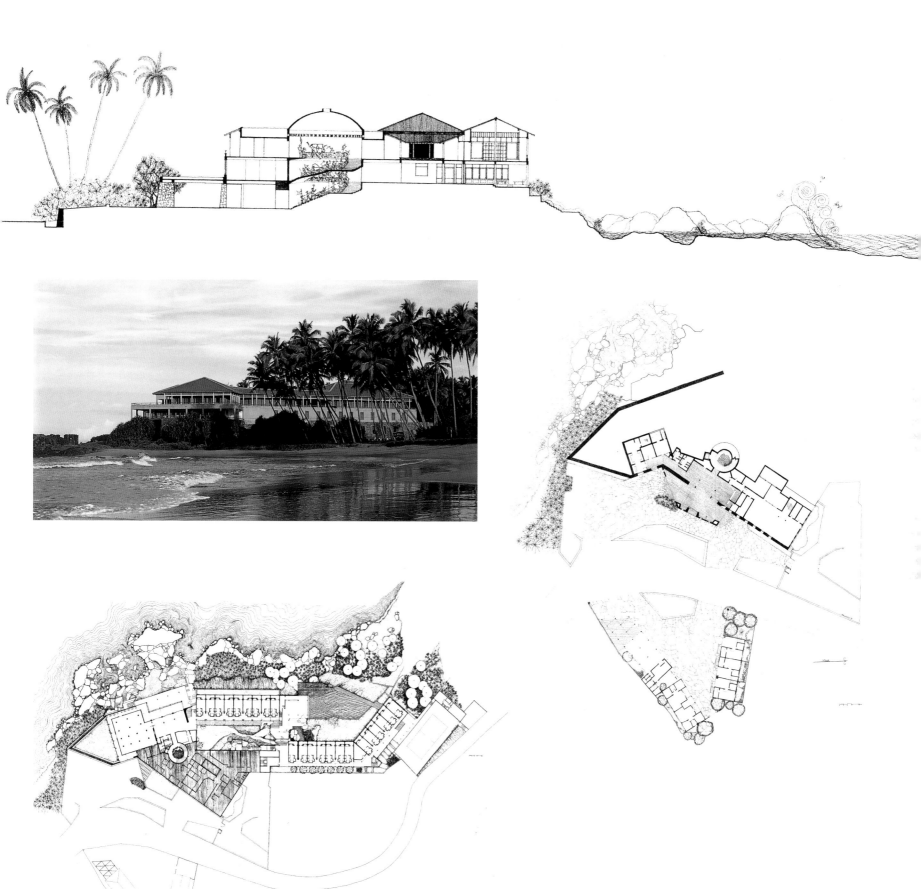

Top left: The *porte cochère*

Top right: The foot of
the main staircase

Bottom left: The main
staircase with sculpted
handrail by Laki Senanayake

Bottom right: The main terrace

Opposite
Top: The upper pool court

Bottom left: The main
garden court

Bottom right: The bed-
room wing with its samara-
coloured render

blue water hotel

Although Bawa never did manage to build
a hotel in the heart of Colombo, his last hotel
was located at the southern edge of the metro-
politan area at Wadduwa and was conceived as
a vast urban palazzo. The developer was Ajit
Wijesekera, a garment manufacturer who
was new to the hotel business but 'hell-bent
on getting Geoffrey Bawa' as his architect. The
site had little to commend it: a few hectares of
coconut plantation stuck between a featureless
stretch of beach and the coastal railway line in
the dreary ribbon of suburban sprawl stretching
down the coast from Moratuwa to Kalutara.

Bawa trawled through his memory of unbuilt
schemes and resurrected ideas that had first
surfaced in his plan of the Fiji Suva Hotel.
He also went back to a room mock-up made
for the Orion Hotel in which the bed faced the
window in front of a partially glazed bathroom.
The design was developed and the result is a
cool and palatial version of the simple rest-house
prototype first used in the Serendib Hotel back
in 1967. A lofty porch indicates a main entrance
in an enclosing wall that screens the hotel from
the railway. Doors swing open to reveal a long
axial arcade running across a large garden court,
past the hotel lobby and out through the coconut grove towards the sea and the horizon. The
sequence of spaces is formal and controlled;
the materials highly polished, light in tone and
muted in colour; the architecture restrained but
monumental – the perfect setting for ceremonies
and celebrations.

Bottom left: Bawa on site with
Sumangala, 1997

Bottom centre: Plan

Right: View across the main
garden court towards the entrance

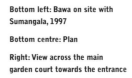

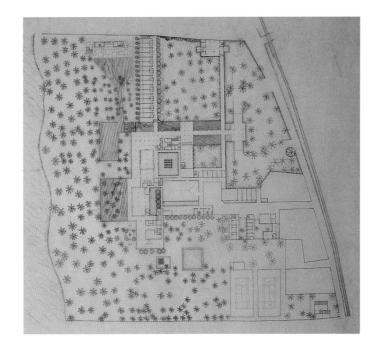

Left: The meeting of the axes

Top right: View from the main
court towards the sea

Bottom right: The dining
room terrace

Top: View from the beach

Bottom: View towards the sea

jayakody house

COLOMBO 1991–96

Here we meet the architect in his prime, designing with certainty to create a civilized retreat within a hostile environment. The client, Rohan Jayakody, was married to President Premadasa's daughter, Dulanjalee, and it was Mrs Premadasa who persuaded Bawa to take on the project. The house is built on an odd-shaped plot of 450 square metres (18 perches) in a cul-de-sac lane on the edge of the Union Place business district.

Generically the design can be described as tower–courtyard hybrid. The blank street façade is perforated by a pair of garage doors and a relatively understated entrance, leading into a small court with the main hall beyond. The ground-floor reception rooms, opening into small garden courts, have an almost subterranean quality, the dining room being partly lit by a blue-painted light shaft that acts as a ventilation stack. On the first floor the principal bedrooms each have their own private courtyards, while above, half of the second floor is given over to a large terrace partially sheltered by a high loggia. On the third floor there is a small swimming pool with an open terrace giving views across the neighbouring roofs towards Colombo's main park.

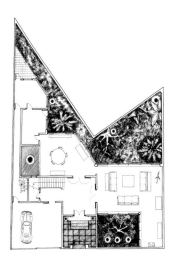

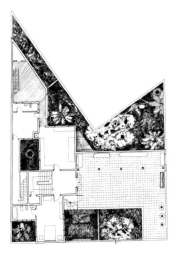

Top left: The entrance in Park Street

Middle right: The second-floor loggia

Bottom left: Elevation

Bottom centre and right: Ground and second-floor plans

Overleaf: View of the sitting room

pradeep jayewardene house

MIRISSA 1997–98

Until their home was totally destroyed by fire at the end of the 1980s, the Jayewardene family enjoyed the use of an old coconut estate bungalow perched high on the red cliffs that frame the eastern side of Weligama Bay on the south coast of Sri Lanka. In 1997 Bawa was asked by J. R. Jayewardene's grandson, Pradeep, to design a replacement. The site lies at the end of a steep track off the main Galle-to-Matara road. After a short climb, the noise of the traffic is left far behind and a final twist in the track reveals a breathtaking view westwards across the bay and a grove of coconut palms, silhouetted against the sky. On closer inspection a platoon of black columns can be discerned among the coconut trunks, a thin horizontal roof floating amongst their fronds: a simple pleasure pavilion stands on a stepped plinth. The roof is a galvanized steel deck sloping gently southwards and supported on three rows of six concrete-encased columns: there are no walls, no doors, no windows, no shutters. Part of the plinth is raised to accommodate a lower bedroom level and this raised area creates a place for sitting, while the lower floor is dominated by a huge dining table that rests on an old electricity generator, a remnant from the original bungalow. An enclosed stairway leads down to a half-buried space containing service areas and bedrooms that open onto a lower courtyard.

The house is separated in time from the A. S. H. de Silva House by almost forty years, but they are two points on the same journey. Both consist in essence of a roof inserted into a landscape to exclude sun and rain while admitting cooling currents of air. It may be that one house is simply a distillation of the other or that it takes forty years to gain the confidence to strip things down to their bare essentials.

Soon after the house was completed, the following poem was written by Michael Ondaatje, the uncle of Pradeep Jayewardene's wife:

House on a Red Cliff, 26 January 1998

There is no mirror in Mirissa
the sea is in the leaves
the waves are in the palms
old language in the arms of the casurina pine
parampara, parampara
from generation to generation

The flamboyant a grandfather planted
having lived through fire
lifts itself over the roof
unframed
the house an open net
where night concentrates on a breath
on a step
a thing or gesture we
cannot be attached to

just the long, the short,
the difficult minutes
of night's phenomena

where even in darkness
there is no horizon without a tree

just a boat's light in the leaves
A last footstep before formlessness
(Ondaatje 1998)

Top right: Plan

Middle right: Cross-section through the cliff

Bottom left: Bawa with Pradeep Jayewardene on site

Bottom right: View from the approach

Overleaf: Longitudinal view

Top left: The lower courtyard

Top right: The stair tower

Bottom left: View from the upper platform

Bottom right: The main sitting area

official residence of the president

KOTTE 1997–

The establishment of a presidential system of government in Sri Lanka in 1978 created the need for new presidential offices. In 1983 the old Parliament buildings, left empty by the opening of the new Parliament in Kotte, were converted by Bawa into a presidential secretariat. Successive presidents lived in what had been the residence of the British governors inside the Fort, while prime ministers continued to live at Temple Trees in the Galle Road.

In 1996 it was decided to build a new presidential complex at Kotte on a site overlooking the Parliament at the north-eastern corner of the lake. It would consist of four principal elements: a secretariat, a banquet suite, a residence and a service block. Bawa was designated as the main designer and Suren Wickremasinghe and Associates were appointed executive architects.

Bawa worked on an initial design during the early part of 1997 and President Kumaratunga attended a private view of his proposals at Lunuganga in March. The four elements were to be arranged in linear fashion along a low ridge and connected by a system of covered loggias, with an architectural language and vocabulary of materials and details developed from the earlier design for the Parliament. The project provoked fierce criticism in the press because its location necessitated the re-routing of a public road and because a section of the site was still in private ownership. In the face of mounting opposition, it was finally decided at the end of the year to shift the scheme to an alternative site on the south-western bank of the lake. The change was announced shortly before Bawa's first stroke in December, but he still managed to make a number of visits to the new site with Channa Daswatte in January 1998 and together they sketched out the alternative scheme that would form the basis of all later development. The original linear scheme was cranked through ninety degrees to create an L-shape with the banquet hall at its elbow and a large formal entry court enclosed between its arms.

After Bawa's second stroke, Daswatte continued to work on the revised scheme, but at the end of 1998 the project was put on hold. It was revived in late 2000 and work actually started on site, only to be halted indefinitely in mid-2001.

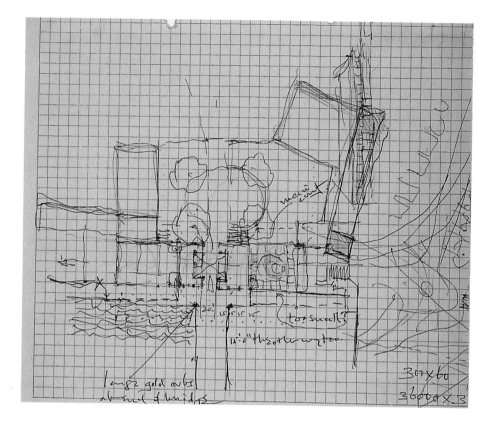

Top: A 1997 Bawa sketch for the President's House

Bottom: Working model

III

'For years the garden had grown gradually into a place of many moods, the result of many imaginings, offering me a retreat to be alone or to fellow-feel with friends. An added pleasure is to observe the reactions to this place, from puzzlement to the silence of contentment, from the remarkable comment of the friend of a friend – "This would be a lovely place to have a garden!" – to the lorry driver who walked around the garden whilst his bricks were being unloaded and then said to me: "But this is a very blessed place!"'

[chapter 8] **court and garden** 1948–98

33rd lane

In 1959, two years after his return from London, Bawa rented the third in a row of four tiny bungalows in a narrow cul-de-sac at the end of 33rd Lane off Colombo's Bagatelle Road and converted it into a small *pied-à-terre* with a sitting room, a minute kitchen, a bedroom and a room for his manservant Miguel. Soon after moving in Bawa persuaded his landlord, Harold Pieris, to sell him the whole row as and when the individual units became free. The fourth house in the row was occupied by a journalist called Sooti Banda and was used for meetings of the inner cabinet of the communist LSSP Party. In 1961, Bawa managed to prise out Mr Banda and annexed the fourth house to the third to create a dining room, exhibition space and garage. Bawa obtained possession of the two remaining bungalows in 1968 and embarked on a major remodelling of the whole group. The third bungalow was knocked through to the second to enlarge the main bedroom and create a guest suite. The first bungalow was then demolished to make way for a four-storey structure incorporating a car port at ground-floor level, a first-floor library, a second-floor loggia and a third-floor roof terrace. The original side lane, now redundant, was transformed into a long entrance passage lit by a series of tiny courtyards.

Over a period of forty years the houses were subjected to continual change and the identities of the original bungalows are now all but lost. Although the plan form of the whole might at each stage have been thought to be simply the result of an arbitrary process of stripping away and adding, any accidental or picturesque quality has always been tempered by a strong sense of order and composition. It was here that Bawa developed his interest in architectural *bricolage*: elements salvaged from old buildings in Sri Lanka and South India were artfully incorporated into the evolving composition. The final result is an introspective labyrinth of rooms and garden courts that together create the illusion of endless space on what is, in reality, a tiny suburban plot. Words like inside and outside lose all meaning: here are rooms without roofs and roofs without walls, all connected by a complex matrix of axes and internal vistas.

Entering from the street you first encounter a darkened car port where a pair of beautifully polished cars sit forever on their chocks like two pieces of automotive sculpture. A long white corridor draws you past a set of doors decorated by Donald Friend towards a distant lightwell framed by a pair of antique Chettinad columns, where a horse's head nudges you onto a cross-axis and another courtyard lures you to the very heart of the labyrinth, where the central unifying axis runs from the main bedroom towards the furthermost garden court.

If the main part of the house is an evocation of a lost world of verandahs and courtyards assembled from a rich collection of traditional devices and plundered artefacts, the tower that Bawa created above the car port is nothing less than a reworking of Le Corbusier's Maison Citrohan – a skilfully manipulated succession of volumes formed by plain abstract surfaces and connected by a winding staircase leading to an upper roof terrace. The tower forms a periscope rising from a cool, shady netherworld to give views across treetops and neighbouring roofs towards the ocean. Architectures ancient and modern, Asian and European coexist as complementary parts of the same whole: the earthbound complexities of the labyrinth are

Top right: The entrance seen from 33rd Lane

Bottom: East–west cross-section through the main corridor

Opposite
Top: The main corridor seen from the car port

Bottom: Plans at ground, first and second-floor level

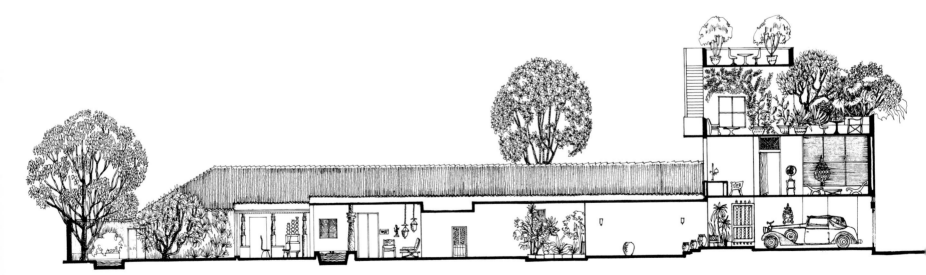

subtly enhanced by the cool infinities of the Cubist pavilion.

The various stages in the evolution of 33rd Lane correspond to key developments in Bawa's house designs for other clients. His first essays, typified by the A. S. H. de Silva House in Galle (1959), were characterized by a desire to break up the traditional colonial bungalow into its component parts and reassemble them in an apparently informal composition of pavilions and court-gardens, unfettered by a defining boundary. As Colombo became more congested, Bawa went on to produce designs that packed the component elements within delineating limits. Thus the Ena de Silva House (1960) is totally introspective and consists of a chequer-board arrangement of linked pavilions and small courts all contained within a walled enclosure. This spawned a number of variants, such as the de Saram Row Houses (1970), which are all by-products of his experiments at 33rd Lane. As plot sizes shrank even further, Bawa developed the concept of a tower house that would reach up towards the sky like a tree. The tower at 33rd Lane is contemporary with Peter Keuneman's tower house (1967) and spawned the Martenstyn, de Soysa, Jayakody and Spencer houses.

After 1988 the guest suite on the ground floor of 33rd Lane next to the car port was converted into an office and, as Bawa became less mobile, a lift was installed to carry him up to the roof terrace. When in 1998 he suffered his second stroke his bedroom was transformed into a care unit.

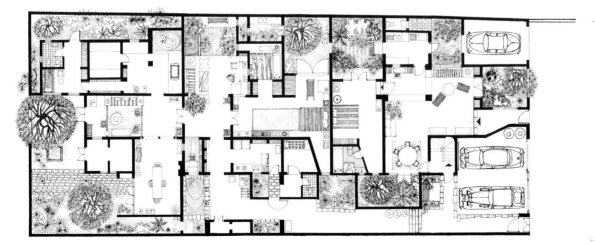

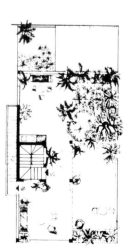

Top left: The main corridor with a Donald Friend sculpture on the wall

Top right: The pool court with doors by Donald Friend

Bottom left: A lightwell

Bottom right: Inlaid door by Ismeth Raheem on the staircase

Opposite:
Top left: The main verandah

Top right: The first-floor sitting room

Bottom left: The sitting room

Bottom right: The roof terrace with chairs by Rico Tarawella

Overleaf
Left: The dining room

Right: View from the dining room towards the sitting room with doors by Donald Friend

lunuganga

1948–98

The Colombo house, as the main residence and generally the first port of call for visitors, offers a contrasting prelude to Bawa's country estate at Lunuganga, and together they reflect Andrea Palladio's advice to the citizens of Vicenza in his *Quattro Libri dell'Architettura*:

A city house is certainly of great splendour and conveniency to a gentleman who is to reside there all the time he shall require for directing his own affairs and those of the state. But perhaps he will not reap much less utility and consolation from a country house, where the remaining part of his time will be passed in the art of agriculture and improving his estate, where exercise will preserve the health and strength of his body and where his mind, fatigued by the agitations of the city, will be greatly restored and comforted so that he can devote himself to literature and contemplation. Thus the ancients commonly used to retire to such like places, where being oftentimes visited by their virtuous friends, having pavilions, gardens, fountains and such pleasant places, they could easily aspire to as much happiness as can be attained here below. (Palladio 1738, 2, ch.12, p.46)

The journey to Lunuganga begins on the doorstep of the house in 33rd Lane, whence the car sets out on the harrowing journey along the coast road to Galle. After 60 kilometres the road crosses the Bentota River over the old Dorman Long Bridge, providing glimpses of the Bentota Beach Hotel, Bawa's lost masterpiece, and the sea beyond. On the left a narrow, bumpy road snakes through a dense hinterland of small villages to a causeway that crosses the neck between the Bentota River and the Dedduwa Lake, offering the first distant view of Lunuganga's northern terraces. But, like William Kent's scenario for the great eighteenth-century English garden at Stowe, the road now leads off in a circle so that the final approach to the house is from the other side. At last a laterite track leads through a paddy field and towards a thickly wooded hill where an overgrown portal announces the boundary of Lunuganga and a steep driveway swings up through the trees to arrive at the foot of a cascade of steps that climb to the bungalow's southern terrace. The view from the entrance terrace towards Cinnamon Hill and a distant temple comes as a complete surprise. It is as if, having been spun around in a game of blindman's buff, the blindfold has suddenly been removed to reveal the centre of a magic kingdom. The bungalow lies at the hub of the composition

and it is the only point from which all of the garden's separate elements can be comprehended.

The estate sits astride two low hills on a promontory jutting into the Dedduwa Lake, a brackish lagoon fed by an estuary of the Bentota River. A mile away to the west, the waves of the Indian Ocean roll in over coral reefs to break onto a white beach fringed with coconut palms. To the east, beyond serried ranks of rubber-tree-covered hills and rice-carpeted valleys, lies the mysterious Sinharaja Forest, Sri Lanka's last surviving area of primeval rainforest. The area around Lunuganga is the wettest and most fertile region of the island, a vast hothouse of exotic trees and plants. But, like so much of Sri Lanka's landscape, Lunuganga is a man-made creation, which in its previous incarnations has been a Dutch cinnamon garden and a British rubber estate.

In 1948 there was nothing more here than an undistinguished bungalow surrounded by 25 acres of rubber trees, enjoying only limited views northwards across the Dedduwa Lake. Since then hills have been moved, terraces cut, woods replanted, new vistas opened up and the old estate road has been buried within a ha-ha. The house itself has been turned inside out, but the original shell survives within a cocoon of new verandahs, courtyards and loggias.

Conceptually the garden at Bentota owes more to the gardens of Renaissance Italy and eighteenth-century England than it does to King Kasyapa's vast water garden at Sigiriya or the great Mogul gardens of India. One is constantly reminded of Pope's advice to the young Lord Burlington:

To build, to plant, whatever you intend,
To rear the Column or the Arch to bend,
To swell the terrace or to sink the Grot,
In all, let Nature never be forgot,
But treat the Goddess like a modest fair,
Nor overdress, nor leave her wholly bare,
Let not each beauty everywhere be spy'd
Where half the skill is decently to hide,
He gains all points who pleasingly confounds,
Surprises, varies and conceals the Bounds.
(Pope 1985)

It is tempting to see Bawa as a latter-day Burlington, and Lunuganga as his Chiswick Villa. Here he held court, drawing together a circle of painters, designers and architects and plotting with them to write a new chapter in the history of Sri Lankan art and architecture. Here also he developed and honed new ways to set buildings into their site, to create enclosed and semi-

enclosed outdoor spaces, to link interior with exterior. The garden may well have been inspired by the gardens of the Villa Orsini or Stourhead, but it is still fresh and vital, while they are now the conjectural remains of something formerly great. It is today what they once were: a place for private enjoyment, for contemplation, for gatherings of friends.

Bawa never kept a systematic record of the evolution of the garden and its chronology is now hard to unravel. One fascinating diary of events is provided by a large leather-bound visitors' book containing a plethora of photographs and sketches as well as signatures and greetings: in 1965 Ulrik Plesner reflects on the problems of the Hilton project; in 1966 Ismeth Raheem records having seen over forty species of bird during one afternoon; in 1973 Donald Friend leaves a doodle of his museum on Bali; in 1997 President Kumaratunga approves the designs of her new Official Residence; and in 1998 Prince Charles drops in for tea. Perhaps the most memorable visit of all, however, was on 3 January 1988 when a friend called Ray Wijewardene flew down from Colombo in a microlight and, misjudging his landing, crashed into the main roof of the bungalow.

During the early 1950s Bawa was still feeling his way into his garden project and lacked the money to pay for ambitious designs. He turned the house around, moving the main entrance to the southern terrace and converting the old west porch into a glazed verandah, so that cars were excluded from the immediate vicinity of the house and were hidden in the trees below the steps. He also levelled the northern terrace and began clearing the Cinnamon Hill vista. Work was interrupted, however, when he left to pursue his architectural studies in Britain in 1953.

After 1958 the Cinnamon Hill vista was completed and the cliff below the northern terrace was excavated to create the 'Scala Danese'. The enthusiasm of this period was recorded by Ulrik Plesner in an article for a Danish magazine (Plesner 1959a), later translated for the White Book:

Recently, whilst the hill was being excavated and the staircases were being finished off and ferns were being planted and one was debating whether to lower or raise the level of the paddy fields or whether to build a series of pyramids...suddenly it was realized that there was a hidden view lying behind 200 metres of trees and plants. The chairs were turned, all other work was abandoned, and in a few hours trees were felled, undergrowth

Opposite: Cross-section through Cinnamon Hill showing the north front of the main house

removed, branches cut, snakes killed and a whole new view – and garden – was made. (Taylor 1986, p.44)

During the late 1960s and early 1970s Bawa was busy with various projects in and around Bentota and found it convenient to bring part of his office down to Lunuganga. A covered bridge was thrown over the ha-ha and next to it a small house was built to accommodate office staff who came down to work over the weekend. Sometime in the mid-1970s, Bawa added a tiny square pavilion to the eastern terrace and called it the 'hen house'. This simple, elegant structure – four brick piers infilled with timber lattice on three sides and with a door on the fourth, supporting a square hipped roof of Portuguese tile – established in one stroke the entire grammar and vocabulary for the Seema Malaka and the Parliament building in Kotte. Soon after, a guest house was built in the form of a portal to separate the entrance terrace from the eastern terrace beyond.

In 1983 the 'Garden Room' or 'Sandella' was built along the southern edge of the eastern terrace. This exquisitely proportioned pavilion forms an edge to the terrace and resolves the various axes that cross it: here Bawa could sit and work, perched in his eyrie above the drive, keeping half an eye on the entrance terrace, looking out through the trees towards the causeway on the lake, seeing without being seen. Next, beyond the Sandella he built the ochre-coloured Gothic Court that ends the axis from the entrance steps and leads into the sequence of sculpture galleries that terminate at the eastern tip of the hill.

The fame of the garden finally reached the ears of the priest of the Katakuliya temple that, with its white *stupa*, forms the focus of the Cinnamon Hill vista. He suggested that, as Mr Bawa derived so much pleasure from contemplating the *stupa*, he should donate the money needed to pay for its repainting. Bawa considered this request for a moment and then suggested that, as he could see only half the *stupa* from Lunuganga and had little interest in its reverse side, he would happily make a donation, but only for half the cost.

Over the years Bawa was unsuccessful in his attempts to extend the estate by acquiring the lower half of the promontory on which it was set, but he did manage to acquire two neighbouring islands. During the 1970s the Bandaranaike government introduced laws limiting the size of private estates and the larger island was officially registered as a wildlife sanctuary to prevent its being confiscated.

During the 1980s, pressure of work in Colombo produced a period of relative stasis at Lunuganga. Bawa retreated to his garden not to work but to recover from the travails of the week. He still had ambitions to buy out his neighbour and extend his domain westwards beyond the 'Field of Jars' but the owner could not be budged. And so Bawa built a new pool court and loggia on the west side of his bedroom, framing the view towards his neighbour's land, and added the Black Pavilion and Sundial to the lily ponds at the eastern end of the Broad Walk.

The view southwards from the main entrance terrace is now framed by a corridor of trees: in the middle distance a lone moonamal tree leans over a large pot on the summit of Cinnamon Hill, pointing to the white *dagoba* of the distant Buddhist temple beyond a thin sliver of water, so that the eye runs down and up through a cone of space, leaping from the pot – the 'hand of man' – towards the temple and the sky. The area to the east of the bungalow has been transformed into a series of interconnected terraces that step down towards the lake's edge and are framed by kitchens, outhouses, servants' quarters, the guest house, the office pavilion and the sculpture gallery. To the north a lawn runs from the foot of a spreading aralia tree towards the undulating parapet of a steep cliff, offering views northwards and westwards across the lake. Below the parapet

a narrow pathway snakes along the face of the cliff between the rock face and the undergrowth, connecting to a series of stairways. At the foot of the cliff a broad swathe of swamp has been transformed into a water meadow divided into rice paddy squares leading to the lake's edge. To the west of the bungalow, lawns slope towards a fringe of shady terraces that drop down into the Field of Jars and the valley of rice paddy that runs towards the lake.

A garden is not a static object: it is a moving spectacle, a series of scenographic images that change with the season, the point of view, the time of day, the mood. And so Lunuganga has been conceived as a series of separate contained spaces, to be moved through at leisure or to be occupied at certain times of the day. From the house it is possible to set out in any direction and combine the different parts of the garden into any one of an infinite number of possible spatial sequences. All of this has been achieved on a piece of land measuring 500 metres from north to south across the peninsula and 300 metres from east to west along the Broad Walk. The limits of the whole garden can be inspected by a brisk walker in fifteen minutes, though to experience it in all its parts would take the better part of a day.

Over the years the original rubber trees have been replaced progressively by a rich variety of trees and plants, and the hill has been liberally sprinkled with pavilions, walls and statues. The result is a civilized wilderness, not a garden of flowers and fountains; it is a composition in monochrome, green on green, an ever-changing play of light and shade, a succession of hidden surprises and sudden vistas, a landscape of memories and ideas. Here is no orgy of topiary and bric-à-brac. Works of art are carefully placed to form objects for contemplation, punctuation marks on routes, pointers or distant beacons: a leopard lies in the dappled shade beside the lake,

guarding the watergate; a young boy beckons on the edge of the cliff; a grotesque Pan grins up from the edge of the paddy.

Christoph Bon's beautiful black-and-white photographs for the book that records the garden for all time capture perfectly the monochromatic quality of the planting and the constant dappling of the light. Bawa wrote in the book's epilogue:

For years the garden had grown gradually into a place of many moods, the result of many imaginings, offering me a retreat to be alone or to fellow-feel with friends. An added pleasure is to observe the reactions to this place, from puzzlement to the silence of contentment, from the remarkable comment of the friend of a friend – 'This would be a lovely place to have a garden!' – to the lorry driver who walked around the garden whilst his bricks were being unloaded and then said to me: 'But this is a very blessed place!' (Bawa et al. 1990, p.219)

In 1992 Bawa made his last substantial addition to the garden. On the far side of Cinnamon Hill on the edge of the trees lay the ruins of the former workshops of the metalwork craftsman Bellic Baas. These were removed to make way for another guest house – the 'Cinnamon Hill House', a simple structure of four roofed pavilions – two bedrooms with open-to-the-sky bathrooms, an open loggia and a servant's room – connected by flat roofed links. But it is a house that is full of echoes. The entrance is formed by the splay of the bedrooms and the servant's room, and is a miniature version of the entrance to the Kandalama Hotel. The visitor arrives through the woods from the ha-ha and is funnelled into the 'mouth of the cave' to discover the loggia and the views out across the tank towards the Katakuliya temple. And the loggia itself contains a memory of the church in Bandarawela: a blank wall to the right, an open screen with cruciform columns to the left, and an 'altar table' on the axis. Bawa, whose work was always enlivened by quotations from other architects, now quotes himself.

After his stroke in 1998 Bawa was exiled from his garden for over a year, being confined to his Minotaur's lair at 33rd Lane. But in 2000 his health improved sufficiently for him to start visiting Lunuganga again and he is now able to stay there for weeks at a time. Although he is still paralysed and unable to speak, his general health has improved and he clearly derives great benefits from these visits. The garden is now managed by two young architects, Michael and Aasha, who are employed by the Lunuganga

Trust. Each morning Bawa is wheeled out onto one or other of the terraces to meet them, and together they plan the day's cutting and pruning: Michael points towards a clump of trees, Aasha whispers in his ear and Bawa gestures with his good left hand. In this way, although trapped within a corporeal prison, Bawa can still communicate with the garden he has been crafting for more than half a century.

Today the garden seems so natural, so established, that it is hard to appreciate just how much effort has gone into its creation. Vast quantities of earth have been shifted, trees and shrubs have been planted and transplanted, branches have been weighed down with stones to train their shape: nothing exists now that has not been introduced into the composition or consciously allowed to remain. The various buildings constructed down the years appear simply to have grown out of the ground, carefully restored remnants of some earlier period of occupation, messages on a palimpsest. Nor is it apparent how much work is needed to maintain such careful casualness. Ignore the garden for a week and the paths and staircases will clog up with leaves; ignore it for a month and the lawns will run wild; ignore it for a year and the terraces will start to crumble; after two or three years the jungle will return and the garden will be lost for ever.

In 1948 as Sri Lanka was shaking off the shackles of empire, a young man dreamt of making a garden. Today the garden is in its prime but, after the passage of over fifty monsoons, Sri Lanka has lost its innocence and the young man has grown old. As he sits in his wheelchair on the terrace and watches the sun setting across the lake it may be that he reflects on his achievement. Perhaps the garden had simply been waiting there for him to discover it beneath a canopy of jungle?

But this is a work of art, not of nature: it is the contrivance of a single mind and a hundred pairs of hands working together with nature to produce something that is 'supernatural'. What should become of this magic world? Ought it to be frozen or preserved? Ought it to become a national monument maintained by bureaucrats and trampled over by thousands of souvenir-hunting tourists? Better by far to let the jungle swallow it up than to see it turned into a travesty of its former self.

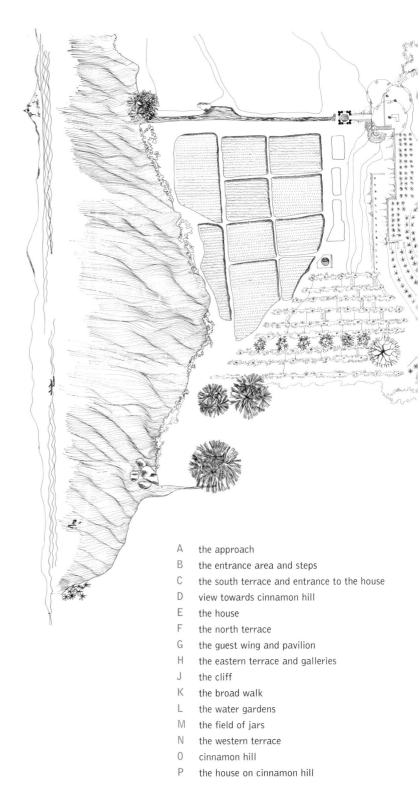

A   the approach
B   the entrance area and steps
C   the south terrace and entrance to the house
D   view towards cinnamon hill
E   the house
F   the north terrace
G   the guest wing and pavilion
H   the eastern terrace and galleries
J   the cliff
K   the broad walk
L   the water gardens
M   the field of jars
N   the western terrace
O   cinnamon hill
P   the house on cinnamon hill

Previous pages: View of the south
front of the house (C) from the
ha ha

This page: The south terrace
of the house (C)

Opposite: View across Cinnamon
Hill towards the Katakuliya
Temple (O)

Opposite: The main sitting area, formerly the entrance porch of the original bungalow (E)

This page: The main sitting area with the lamp 'copied' from Poul Henningsen's 'pine-cone' design (E)

Opposite: The north terrace (F)

This page: The edge of the cliff (J)

Overleaf
Top left: View through the porch under the guest wing (G) towards the Garden Room (H)

Top right: The interior of the Garden Room (H)

Bottom left and right: Views into the Garden Room from the eastern terrace (H)

Previous page: View from the Garden
Room (H) towards the guest wing (G)

This page: The Hen House (H)

Opposite
Top left: The Gothic Court below the
eastern terrace (H)

Top right: Looking from the Art
Gallery towards the Gothic Court (H)

Bottom: Drawing by Sumangala

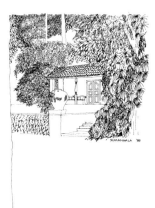

**Left: Stairs descending
the cliff (J)**

**Right: Below the north-west
corner of the cliff (J)**

Left: The Broad Walk looking
towards the Black Pavilion (K)

Right: The Field of Jars (M)

Opposite: Looking along
the western terrace (N)

This page:
Left: The corner of the
north lawn (F)

Right: The south terraces
of Cinnamon Hill (O)

Left: The verandah of the
Cinnamon Hill House (P)

Opposite: The northern terrace (F)

[chapter 9] an asian guru

Geoffrey Bawa's life has spanned many divides, while his family embraces many strands of Sri Lanka's ethnic weave, and throughout his career this provided him with unique insights into his times and added extra dimensions to his architecture. His background gave him a chameleon-like quality, enabling him to fit into almost any milieu, and he could be European or Asian when it suited him. He was also addicted to travel and after 1948, when he returned and settled permanently in Ceylon, not a year passed without his embarking on at least one foreign journey, filling his mind with a rich store of images – quadrangles in Cambridge, gardens in Italy, courtyards in the Alhambra, cascading roofs on Keralan palaces…He would sometimes pretend that his formal education had done little to prepare him for his later career, though his legal training had honed his ability to think logically, while his Cambridge engineering tutor had equipped him with a clear grasp of structural design principles and his years at the AA School in London had introduced him to contemporary architectural debates.

Bawa came to be known primarily as a designer of hotels and private houses. Indeed he designed around seventy houses, of which about fifty were built, and a total of thirty-five hotels, of which he built twenty. His portfolio of work, however, covers a broad variety of building types, including social buildings, housing, office and industrial buildings, educational buildings, religious buildings and public buildings and for many of these he succeeded in establishing a new canon of prototypes within the context of a modernizing Sri Lanka.

An intuitive designer, he had a strongly developed spatial sense and was able to conceive fully fledged ideas in his head before committing them to paper. He was also an incisive judge and an uncompromising critic who knew when a design wasn't working or when it had arrived at its optimum state. As a man

of few practical skills – he could hardly draw, had only an intuitive grasp of building construction and knew little about the horticultural aspects of gardening – he recognized the need to surround himself with people who were good at doing those things he was unable to do himself.

In the office he operated always at the centre of the team, directing, encouraging, cajoling and inspiring great loyalty. He would develop the main concept for a project, suggest a line of development and then act as critic and arbiter until a satisfactory outcome had been achieved. While he would scarcely have been able to function without his team of collaborators and assistants, it was he who brought them together, who inspired them and directed them and who was always the leading spirit. And it was he who drove projects on site, demanding the highest standards from the builders and craftsmen; with his last-minute adjustments he was the one person who could breathe the final magic into a design.

He remained mistrustful of theory and was always reluctant to provide justifications or explanations for his work, insisting that architecture had to be experienced directly and that it could be understood only in its own terms. For him the ultimate test of a building's design was to put it to use – if other people understood and enjoyed his buildings then nothing more needed to be said. He doubted that buildings could be ascribed specific meanings; their true significance would be established in the minds of their users and would develop through time. It may be that this reluctance to probe stemmed from his desire to protect his privacy and keep his thoughts to himself. It is also possible that it resulted from a deep-seated lack of confidence. It may be that his lawyer's training had left him suspicious of the humbug that permeates so much of what passes for architectural discourse.

Bawa supervising tree-cutting at Lunuganga in 1989

Spanning the second half of the twentieth century, his career coincided with the final stages of the Modern Movement in architecture and the early stages of Sri Lanka's development as an independent country in a rapidly modernizing and globalizing world. Having heard the arguments of some of the main protagonists in the Modernist debate during his sojourn at the AA, Bawa found that, back in Sri Lanka, he was cut off from the main centres of architectural discourse and he came to rely on trips abroad and discussions with occasional visitors to test his emerging ideas. Working instinctively to apply Modernist methods within a localized context, he seems to have anticipated many of the emerging responses to the Post-modern or late-modern condition and his ideas can be linked to a number of the 'isms' of the day, though he rarely applied labels to his work or acknowledged their validity.

Insofar as he was wedded to the idea that a design must originate from a clear statement of functional requirements, Bawa always remained a Modernist at heart. But, if the core idea for a building evolved from its functional programme, its conception took place only when the core idea was introduced into a context. For Bawa, the word context embraced site, climate, people, tradition, history – everything that together contributed to what Alexander Pope once described in his epistle to Lord Burlington as 'The Genius of the Place in all' (Pope 1985), and he would proceed from a careful analysis of the site towards a resolution that both respected and enhanced its unique qualities.

This belief that design must begin with an appraisal of context made Bawa a 'regionalist' long before the term came into common use. Even his earliest projects embodied most, if not all, of the criteria set out by Kenneth Frampton in his definitive essay on 'Critical Regionalism' of 1983. Indeed Frampton later felt it necessary to extend his 'Critical History' of 1980 precisely because of its failure to accommodate regionalist Modernists such as Bawa (Frampton 1985).

When the Malaysian architect Jimmy Lim asked him about regionalism in a rare interview in 1989, Bawa replied:

I have begun to think that regionalism is what happens automatically, coming out from the needs of the place…

If you take local materials and the general feel of the place into account, the resultant building automatically becomes regional. I do not make it regional and I do not take regionalism as a creed. I just build what I am asked to build…What frightens me is that regionalism is thought to be a lessening of civilization. It is not! Philip Johnson's house in Connecticut is as regional as a mud hut. (Lim 1990)

Bawa was, by instinct, a bioclimatic designer, concerned always to achieve optimum levels of human comfort with the minimum expenditure of energy. His early work predated the widespread use of air-conditioning and he set out to create environments that were cooled naturally by stack- and cross-ventilation and protected from direct solar gain and heavy monsoon rain. This led him to experiment with courtyards and verandahs, pergolas and overhanging eaves. He also used materials that increased the thermal mass of his buildings and provided insulation against solar gain, or that encouraged ventilation and transpiration: his pioneering use of half-round clay tiles laid on corrugated cement sheeting offered a roofing system that was cool, waterproof, structurally efficient and aesthetically pleasing, while his boxed-out lattice windows – inspired by the windows of old Muslim town houses, themselves the descendants of Arabian *mashrabiya* – provided effective rain-screens and enabled ventilation. Although a couple of rooms in his 33rd Lane house were eventually fitted with air-conditioners for use during periods of extreme humidity, the office in Alfred House Road and the house at Lunuganga were both naturally ventilated throughout, as were many of the houses he built for private clients. His early hotels were all designed to function without air-conditioning, and it was only later, when tour operators came to demand artificial cooling in hotels, that Bawa bowed to the inevitable and incorporated air-conditioning in dining rooms and bedrooms.

His architecture embraced the concept of sustainability, though this was not a word he ever used. Where possible he used locally produced materials and local technologies. It could be argued that during the 1960s and 1970s, when imports were restricted, he had little choice, but he exploited these restrictions to develop a rich architectural vocabulary based largely on the use of timber, clay products and plaster. The Bentota Beach Hotel (1967), for example, was built entirely from local materials, its ironmongery, furniture, light fittings and soft furnishings all being produced nearby, and only the lift was imported, though its beautiful doors were made by Bellic Baas in the workshops at Lunuganga to designs by Anura Ratnavibushana. Bawa applied the same tenets when working outside Sri Lanka: at the Madurai Club (1971) he used locally napped stone for the structural columns and rubble for the walls, while the ceilings were lined with locally produced cotton and the floors paved with recycled stone slabs from the cotton mills.

In the same way Bawa always took care to disturb as little as possible of a site's existing vegetation and added new planting as a matter of course. Thus the Institute for Integral Education at Piliyandela (1978) was insinuated into an existing rubber plantation; the Kandalama Hotel (1991) was built with minimum disturbance to the existing topography; and the Ena de Silva (1960), Martenstyn (1977) and de Soysa (1985) houses were all carefully designed around existing trees. His hotel projects often relied on groundwater and used on-site sewerage systems to ensure that only treated effluent was released into the surroundings.

During much of his career Bawa avoided gratuitous ornament or applied decoration. His early buildings used the white abstract cubic forms associated with Tropical Modernism and in his later projects he adopted a stripped-down minimalism that exploited the colours and textures of natural materials and anticipated the patinas of ageing. He was keen, however, to incorporate works of art in his buildings and to encourage local artists and craftsmen who, like Laki Senanayake, Barbara Sansoni and Ena de Silva benefited from his encouragement and made significant contributions to his buildings.

His interest in *bricolage*, first developed when he was modifying his own homes and later used to good effect at the Madurai Club and the Lidia Gunasekera House (1978), lay not in the decorative quality of the artefacts but in their ability to create a sense of continuity with the past and to accentuate the simplicity of his own design. Much as he enjoyed contrasting the old and the new, however, he had little time for 'building conservation'. For him buildings were things to be used and reused and to be removed or replaced when necessary. In this he remained totally consistent, expressing little surprise or emotion when his own buildings were altered or demolished.

For Bawa, like Le Corbusier, the 'plan was the generator' but, once the main elements of the plan were established, he focused on how these would relate to each other spatially and volumetrically. A design evolved from a careful assessment of a building's functions, often developing as a formal assemblage of rectangular elements on an orthogonal grid. Any obvious symmetries in the plan, however, would soon be lost as it responded to the particularities of the programme or the vagaries of the site. This approach – evident in early houses such as that for Ena de Silva, and in the elegant planning of the Madurai Club and the Agrarian Research and Training Institute – may have resulted from his Modernist training, orthogonal planning being a characteristic of functional Modernism. But it could also be that he was responding instinctively to Sinhalese classical architecture as demonstrated in the plans of the monasteries of Anuradhapura.

In essence Bawa was a playful designer. He derived enormous enjoyment from making buildings, particularly for people he liked or with whom he could empathize, and he sought always to give pleasure through architecture, to amuse and to delight. In this respect he functioned much like a stage designer or scenographer: architecture had to be experienced dynamically by moving through it and a design was conceived as a series of interconnected tableaux. The plan was manipulated to control the sequence of discovery, so that each space would contain within it the anticipation of other spaces. Views would be hidden or partially revealed, as at the Club Villa (1978), or held in reserve, as at Kandalama. His games with symmetry arose in part from a desire to set up expectations and then to confound them. His aim was initially to confuse, then to arouse and finally to reveal. This method was used in his own home in 33rd Lane, where the whole sequence from the front door to the sitting area is a piece of theatre, bringing the visitor to the very heart of the plan in a state of mounting anticipation. It was also used on a larger scale at the Bentota Beach Hotel and at Lunuganga, where the induced movement followed a clockwise spiral towards the centre and the final denouement.

His sense of theatre also revealed itself in his approach to lighting, both natural and artificial, and in this he may have been influenced by his early studies of Baroque architecture in Italy and southern Germany. He made due allowance for the fierceness of the tropical sun and introduced light sparingly, often indirectly. His use of narrow courtyards and thin slit roof openings, as at Ruhunu University (1980), allowed him to bounce light off internal wall surfaces, and he loved to play with the chiaroscuro effects of the moving shadows cast by sunlight shining through waving foliage.

Bawa broke down the barriers between interior and exterior space, between a building and its site, showing that architecture and landscape could be united in a single continuum of space. As inside and outside became one, so walls took on the role of planes that simply defined spaces or divided one space from another. The landscape was free to invade the interior and a building could colonize its surroundings, taking in pools, boulders and even whole trees.

In the final analysis Geoffrey Bawa should be seen as an Asian architect and his work viewed in the context of a country in flux, whose population has more than quadrupled during his lifetime and whose communities have been fractured by bitter political and ethnic disputes. In today's Sri Lanka, fast cars vie with bullock carts on narrow roads, young girls in saris sew designer jeans for Western retail chains, farmers gather in the evening under the village tree to watch Western soaps on *rupavaheeni* – 'the picture from heaven' – and soldiers armed with the most up-to-date military hardware fight the latest battles in a conflict that is as old as time.

Although it might be thought that his buildings have had almost no impact on the lives of ordinary people, Bawa has made a very real contribution to the emerging culture of a newly independent country. His designs have inspired succeeding generations of architects in his native Sri Lanka and his ideas have been carried to the four corners of the earth like seeds in the wind. In celebrating the island's rich history and cultural diversity he has developed a new architectural language, truly of its place, but his commitment to Modernist ideals has enabled him to find new ways to resolve the contradictions inherent in the dialogue between the local and the global.

partners and associates

Ulrik Plesner was born in Italy in 1930, the son of a Danish painter, Johan Plesner, and his Scottish wife, Kathleen Risk. Plesner studied at the Royal Danish Academy from 1950 to 1955 and worked in London and Copenhagen, before travelling to Ceylon in January 1958 to work with Minette de Silva in Kandy, switching to E. R. & B. in January 1959. He became a close friend of Bawa, operating as his *de facto* partner from 1960 until the end of 1966. At the same time he designed a series of innovative houses under his own name, playing an important role in establishing the school of architecture at Kattubede, and, with Barbara Sansoni, was instrumental in gathering together a group of enthusiasts to photograph and measure Sri Lanka's old buildings.

Plesner's marriage to Tamar Liebes early in 1966 affected the equilibrium of his friendships with Bawa and Sansoni and he also became irritated by Bawa's failure to acknowledge his contribution to their joint work. After the Hilton Hotel débâcle in 1967 he quit the practice. He and Bawa agreed to a 'division of the spoils' under which each would be given exclusive credit for certain projects. The Strathspey Bungalow, Bandarawela Chapel and Polontalawa Bungalow were attributed to Plesner, while both de Silva houses were attributed to Bawa. This compromise distorted the reality of their collaboration and obscured the fact that they worked together. In various perceptive articles about Ceylon and the work of the practice, Plesner gave joint credit to himself and Bawa for the Sansoni, Peiris and Perera houses (Plesner 1971), and claimed Polontalawa as his own (Plesner 1969, 1986). Bawa for his part effectively expunged Plesner from the record in the 'White Book' (Taylor 1986).

Plesner was undoubtedly the most important of Bawa's architectural collaborators and made an enormous contribution to the development of the practice, bringing a commitment to pragmatic Modernism, a respect for craftsmanship and tradition, an appreciation of detailing and a belief in professionalism. He was also the only colleague whom Bawa accepted as a friend on equal terms. After quitting E. R. & B. he returned to London, where he worked for Arup Associates, before moving to Jerusalem in 1972 with his Israeli wife and setting up his own practice. Between 1982 and 1987 he worked as an occasional consultant to the Mahaweli Architecture Unit and was responsible for designing a number of new settlements. He now lives in Tel Aviv.

Dr K. Poologasundram, known affectionately as 'Poologs' or 'the Doctor', was born in Jaffna in 1932, the son of a Tamil Hindu landowner. He studied at Jaffna College from 1937 to 1950 and in 1950 won a place in the newly established engineering faculty of the University of Ceylon, Colombo. In 1955 he joined the PWD Architects' Department in Colombo, and worked on the design of Peradeniya University,

before studying at Imperial College London in 1956, gaining his PhD in 1959. After working for a year as site engineer on New Zealand House, one of London's first 'skyscraper' office buildings, he returned to Ceylon and became a senior design engineer in the State Cement Corporation, moonlighting for several years during the early 1960s as Bawa's structural engineer, before finally joining E. R. & B. as a full partner and office manager in 1966.

Poologasundram had the instincts of a businessman. He admired Bawa – 'One of the cleverest men I've met' – and was confident that together they would succeed. Bawa for his part recognized that he needed a partner who would take care of the day-to-day running of the practice, and who would look after the business side of things. Poologs also had a creative grasp of structural design and was an expert in reinforced-concrete construction.

His biggest triumph was the Parliament project, which he managed from the outset and brought in on time and under budget. After 1983, however, his world started to fall apart: anti-Tamil rioting led him to question his future in Sri Lanka and he was angered – justifiably – by his exclusion from books and exhibitions about the practice's work. When Bawa withdrew from E. R. & B. after 1990 Poologasundram was happy to follow suit.

Poologasundram was a key figure in the practice. Without him Bawa would never have been able to tackle the more complex projects such as Parliament or Ruhunu. He had a quick brain that enabled him to think on his feet and he could work out quantities and complex estimates on the back of the proverbial envelope with incredible accuracy. He was a skilled engineer and made an important contribution to the structural clarity and elegance that characterized the practice's work.

Channa Daswatte was born in 1965. He studied architecture at the University of Moratuwa from 1985 to 1987 and worked briefly with Anjalendran before completing his studies at University College London. He joined Geoffrey Bawa in 1991 and worked initially on the Kandalama Hotel. After 1993 he became Bawa's principal assistant, as well as a close friend and travelling companion, and he later became an associate of Bawa's practice, working as job architect on the Lighthouse and Sinbad hotel projects. After Bawa's stroke at the beginning of 1998 Daswatte took on the role of principal in the office and developed the designs for the President's House. As a member of the Geoffrey Bawa Trust he has been responsible for running Bawa's household during his long illness and has done much to improve Bawa's quality of life. He has written many perceptive articles on Bawa's work and worked as studio teacher in the Colombo and Moratuwa schools. In 1999 he opened his own practice with Murad Ismail.

Valentine Gunasekera studied alongside Bawa at the Architectural Association in London and returned to Colombo in the same year, 1957, when the two were

both offered jobs at E. R. & B. as '10 per cent partners'. However, they were never close friends: Gunasekera was a devout Catholic with a serious nature, and their architectural temperaments were also different, Gunasekera having worked with Eero Saarinen and tending more towards Expressionism in comparison to Bawa's functionalism. Although the two managed the practice together, they always worked on separate projects with separate teams. Over the years these divisions became more and more marked, leading in 1968 to Gunasekera's departure from E. R. & B.

He continued to practise in Colombo and built the Bambalapitiya Jesuit Chapel (1969) and the much-admired Tangalla Bay Hotel on the south coast (1970). After 1970 he failed to find new clients and moved to Nigeria, before emigrating with his family in 1986 to the United States. His career may well have suffered because he wore his political allegiances on his sleeve and was always overshadowed by Bawa. However, he made an important contribution to the development of architecture in post-independence Sri Lanka.

office staff

Bawa managed to gather about him a team of excellent designers and technicians and he relied on them to execute his ideas. The following brief notes describe some of the more significant people who worked with him during his forty years in practice.

Nihal Amarasinghe joined E. R. & B. as a draughtsman in 1956 and worked with Bawa on the Deraniyagala and Gunasekera houses. He left for England in 1959 to study at the Architectural Association, qualifying in 1964, and rejoined E. R. & B. in 1965, working on the Bentota Beach and Serendib hotels, an office building in Matara and the Pallakelle Industrial Estate. In 1971 he moved to Mauritius and worked for six years with Abbas and Zulphi Currimjee, two friends from his time at the AA, as well as acting as Bawa's executive architect on the Peter White House. He returned to Sri Lanka in 1978 and, after practising briefly with Turner Wickramasinghe and Chris de Saram, opened his own small office.

C. Anjalendran was born in Colombo in 1951, the grandson of a famous Tamil politician called Sundaralingam. After initially training to be a dancer he studied architecture at the University of Moratuwa and at University College London, qualifying in 1977. Although he worked at E. R. & B. for only a brief period at the end of the 1970s, he became Bawa's close friend and confidante and during the 1980s acted as his unpaid assistant and amanuensis, establishing an archive of Bawa's drawings and photographs. He also played an important role in assembling material for the White Book (Taylor 1986) and the RIBA exhibition of 1986.

Anjalendran is one of the few architects close to Bawa who managed to 'break out from under the umbrella' and develop new ideas. He started his own practice in 1982 and worked for several years from his mother's verandah with a single assistant. He has built a series of remarkable children's homes for the Austrian charity 'SOS Children's Villages' (Robson 1992), as well as a number of inventive private houses (Powell 1996, 1998) and his work is now widely admired throughout Asia. He is the author of a number of articles on Sri Lankan architecture and is a highly respected teacher.

Nihal Bodhinayake studied architecture at the universities of Belgrade and New South Wales, qualifying in 1979. He first met Bawa at a dinner party in Sydney and accepted an invitation to return to Colombo and work in his office. Bodhinayake became the job architect for Ruhunu University and single-handedly produced almost all of the working drawings. He had an uneasy relationship with Bawa and failed to win the recognition he deserved. After the closure of E. R. & B. in 1990, he worked briefly in south India and Vietnam before returning to open his own office in Colombo, from which he designed the much celebrated Tea Factory Hotel near Nuwara Eliya. In 1998 he was responsible for the unfortunate refurbishment of the Bentota Beach Hotel.

Pherooze Choksy was the son of the Parsee judge N. K. Choksy. He studied architecture at Katubedde from 1961 to 1964 before going to Copenhagen on a Danish government scholarship and qualifying in 1968. He worked at E. R. & B. from 1969 to 1976, specializing in interiors and furniture design, and was involved with the Serendib Hotel and the Agrarian Research and Training Institute. In 1976 he set up a practice with Ismeth Raheem, with whom he has built a number of interesting houses, hotels and commercial projects.

Dilshan Ferdinando worked as a draughtsman with Surath Wickramasinghe from 1978 until 1983, when he opened his own small construction company. In 1987 he joined the part-time architecture course of the Sri Lanka Institute of Architects and started working for Bawa in 33rd Lane. He became Bawa's main assistant in the fledgling office and worked on almost all the $10,000 Projects, as well as helping to manage Bawa's property and accompanying him on a number of foreign trips. In 1992 he left the office to work in Singapore. He never completed his studies and now works in his family import company.

Vasantha Jacobsen (née Chandraratne) studied at the school of architecture at Katubedde from 1961 to 1964 and in 1966 was one of four students selected to study in Copenhagen. It was there that she met and married a Danish designer called Jacob Jacobsen. She joined E. R. & B. in 1969 and after 1980 acted as Bawa's senior assistant. Jacobsen took a leading role in designing the National Institute of

Management Studies, the Ladies' College Vocational Training Centre and the Anuradhapura Pilgrim's Rest House and was the project architect for Parliament. The latter project took its toll and soon after it was completed she and her husband disposed of all their possessions and each retired to separate Buddhist monasteries. Vasantha Jacobsen's achievements have never been fully documented and she deserves to be remembered alongside Minette de Silva as one of Sri Lanka's first woman architects.

Sumangala Jayatilleke studied at Moratuwa and worked intermittently at E. R. & B. from 1986 until 1993, when he went to Cambridge to read for an MSc. He was the first assistant based exclusively in 33rd Lane and worked on the $10,000 Projects, as well as producing the drawings for the de Soysa House and acting as a key member of the team that designed the Kandalama Hotel. He is remembered for his witty cartoons and greetings cards.

Milroy Perera played an important supporting role in Bawa's later career, though he only worked in the office as a consultant for short periods during the 1980s. Perera studied at the Colombo School of Architecture and subsequently at North London Polytechnic, where he qualified in 1975. In the late 1970s and early 1980s he divided his time between a consultancy job in London and a small practice in Colombo. It was during this period that Perera became Bawa's unofficial agent in London, helping him during his frequent visits to Europe. He was also a key member of the team that prepared material for the 1986 White Book and RIBA exhibition. At the same time he 'helped out' in the Colombo office and was involved with Parliament and Ruhunu University. During the 1990s he worked in a consultancy practice with the engineer Deepal Wickramasinghe and acted as the executive architect for the Kandalama and Blue Water hotels and the Jayakody House. Having been involved in politics from his student days, he was elected treasurer of the UNP in 1997.

Stanley Perera was an architectural technician who studied at the Maradana Technical College. He joined E. R. & B. in 1946, before Bawa's arrival, and was still there when Bawa left in 1990. He was a cousin and close associate of Dr N. M. Perera, the SLFP politician who became minister of finance in the Bandaranaike government of 1970–77 and his political connections not only helped him to ensure that E. R. & B. projects were given the necessary statutory consents, but also brought into the practice a number of key projects such as the Vidyodaya University Campus and the State Mortgage Bank Office Tower.

Mahaname Prematilake joined E. R. & B. in 1973 after studying for two years in Copenhagen and worked on the 'foreign projects' of the 1970s: the Madurai Club, the Peter White House and the Batujimbar Pavilions. He was also entrusted with the initial design of the Seema Malaka Temple. Prematilake was an excellent draughtsman, and when Bawa decided to sell some of his Donald Friend paintings and sculptures he employed Prematilake to produce copies. He started his own office in 1982.

Ismeth Raheem was born in Hultsdorf in 1941, the son of a Jaffna Muslim lawyer, and was educated at Royal College, Colombo. He worked intermittently for a number of architects, including E. R. & B., and helped Laki Senanayake to found the Young Artists' Group. In 1961 he joined the first batch of students to study architecture at Katubedde, where he came under the spell of Ulrik Plesner and through him met Donald Friend, who had a considerable influence on his painting and drawing techniques. In 1966 he was one of a quartet of students who went to study in Copenhagen and between 1969 and 1976 he worked mainly with Bawa, and was involved with the Bentota Beach and Serendib hotels, the Connemara Hotel, the YWCA in Colpetty and Agrarian Research and Training Institute. In 1976 he joined with Pherooze Choksy in establishing the practice of Choksy & Raheem and built the much-admired Habarane Lodge Hotel.

Anura Ratnavibushana was born in Galle in 1940 and studied at Kingswood College, Kandy. He was a member of the first batch of architecture students at Katubedde in 1961 and the only one who qualified in three years. He joined E. R. & B. in 1963 and designed the exhibition tower for the Steel Corporation stand in the Colombo Industrial Exhibition. In 1966 he was offered a place to study in London but was refused entry into Britain and so joined Raheem, Choksy and Chandraratne in Copenhagen. Back in Colombo he became Bawa's favourite assistant, working closely with him on a number of projects including the Yahapath Endera Farm School and the Osaka Expo Pavilion.

After 1971 Ratnavibushana began to moonlight as a partner in a young practice called DG5 and although he continued to be employed by E. R. & B. he also worked independently, often on projects passed to him by Bawa or Poologasundram. During this period he designed the Ceylon Mercantile Union (CMU) offices in Colpetty and the Jaffna College Library and built his own magical courtyard house at Lunava (Powell 1996). He worked for a brief spell in Nigeria in 1979 before becoming a director of Mahindu Keerthiratne Associates, designing the Mahaweli Museum and the Low-Lying Lands Reclamation Board Offices. In 1997 he established his own office.

Laki Senanayake was born in Colombo in 1937 and was educated at Royal College. He trained briefly as an artist and helped to found the Young Artists' Group with Ismeth Raheem. In 1959 he joined E. R. & B. as an architectural technician and worked on a number of important early projects such as the A. S. H. de Silva House, the Ena de Silva House, and Bishop's College. Through Ulrik Plesner he got to know Donald Friend, who helped him to develop new techniques in painting and sculpture and Senanayake was largely responsible for developing the particular style of architectural drawing that later became the hallmark of Bawa's office.

Senanayake was more an artist than an architect and in 1964 he quit E. R. & B. to join Ena de Silva in her new batik business. Over the years he has worked as an occasional architect and landscape designer but has always returned to painting and sculpture. In 1979 he designed a beautiful set of banknotes based on drawings of Sri Lankan flora and fauna, and he has continued to produce artwork for Bawa, making the great silver chandelier in the parliamentary debating chamber at Kotte and the metal staircase at the Lighthouse Hotel.

Turner Wickramasinghe studied at Regent Street Polytechnic in London and worked with Bawa during the late 1960s and early 1970s. He was part of the team that built the Bentota Beach and Serendib hotels and was job architect for Pallakelle Industrial Estate and Vidyodaya University. After a brief spell in practice with Nihal Amarasinghe he joined the State Engineering Corporation, where he applied Bawa's philosophy to a number of major public projects, including Seeduwa New Town and the Summit Flats in Bauddalokah Mawatha.

other staff

Among the many others who worked in Bawa's office were: Balasubramaniam, Tim Beecher, Quaid Doongarwallah, Alex Ellenberger, Augustus Fernando, Lal Fernando, Philip Fowler, Ashley Gibson, Waruna Gomis, Edward Hollis, E. Isaac, Murad Ismail, Jesudasan, Janet Kanageswaran, Pradeep Kodikara, Simon Laird, Jamie de Lapena, Amila de Mel, Vipula Munasinghe, S. Narasingham, Vernon Nonis, Sinan Onais, Senake Pieris, Buddhin Perera, Aquila Pieris, Ranjan Ponniah, David Roberts, Rupert Scott, Eric Tallender, Ashley de Vos, Neelanga Weerasekera.

collaborators

Bawa sat at the hub of a circle of friends, several of whom who also operated in their different ways as collaborators or advisers. These included his English friends Jean Chamberlin and Christoph Bon; the Swiss furniture maker Rico Tarawella, who was his neighbour at Lunuganga; the hotelier S. M. A. Hameed, who managed the Serendib and Club Villa hotels; and the designers Ena de Silva and Barbara Sansoni.

Ena de Silva Ena de Silva was the daughter of Sir Richard Aluvihara, a member of the Kandyan Goyagama elite who became inspector general of police. In 1938 she caused a great scandal when, at the age of sixteen, she was married 'out of caste' to Osmund de Silva, one of her father's assistants. A great beauty, she was chosen to represent the 'Spirit of Lanka' in the pageant marking Sri Lanka's independence in 1948. In 1960 she and her husband commissioned Geoffrey Bawa to design their house in Colombo and as a result they became close friends. Her son, Anil, was a promising artist, who worked with Bawa on the sculpted panels for St. Thomas's Prep School, but his career was nipped in the bud by a tragic car accident. After this Ena turned her house into a batik studio and worked with Laki Senanayake to produce designs of great originality. After 1980 she moved her studio to her family home above Matale and started a craft cooperative with local villagers. Bawa used her work in a number of his projects and often asked her advice. She produced the batik ceiling above the reception in the Bentota Beach Hotel and the great *korale* flags hung in front of Parliament on important occasions.

Barbara Sansoni (née Daniels) was the daughter of a senior civil servant and was distantly related to Bawa. Her father's work took him to various parts of Sri Lanka and she lived in a series of interesting houses, including the villa next to the Bawa's family home in Darley Road. A devout Catholic, she became involved with the nuns of the Good Shepherd Convent, with whom she helped set up handloom cooperatives. This inspired her to study textile design and production and she developed Barefoot, a successful business designing and marketing clothes and soft furnishings.

Her close friendship with Bawa began in 1959 when she and her first husband, Hilden Sansoni, commissioned E. R. & B. to design an annexe to their Anderson Road home. The house was designed by Ulrik Plesner, who became its first tenant. Sansoni and Plesner then began to take an interest in the traditional architecture of Sri Lanka and embarked on an ambitious project to record and preserve old buildings. It was through Sansoni that Bawa received his first commissions from the Catholic Church, and she was part of the team that designed Bandarawela Chapel. Bawa used Barefoot products extensively, particularly in his hotel designs, and often used Barbara Sansoni as a colour consultant.

After Hilden Sansoni's death, Barbara married Ronald Lewcock, the eminent architectural historian, and they collaborated to produce a book that brought together her years of careful research on the old buildings of Sri Lanka (Lewcock et al., 1998). Her son, Dominic, is an acclaimed photographer and now runs the Barefoot business.

The practices with which Bawa was associated went through
a number of phases of development between 1923 and 1998:

1923–52
Edwards, Reid and Booth, later Edwards, Reid and Begg
Booty & Edwards was founded in 1923, later becoming Edwards,
Reid and Booth and finally Edwards, Reid and Begg. Bawa worked
with H. H. Reid as an assistant for a short period in 1951.

1952–57
Edwards, Reid and Begg under Nilgiria
Jimmy Nilgiria took over the practice after the death of Reid
in 1952 and operated as sole partner with Morris Russell as
his associate until 1957.

1957–67
Edwards, Reid and Begg under Nilgiria, Bawa and Gunasekera
Geoffrey Bawa and Valentine Gunasekera joined the practice
in late 1957 as '10 per cent partners'. They managed their own
portfolios of work from the outset, while Nilgiria took a back seat.
Between 1959 and 1966 Bawa worked closely with Ulrik Plesner,
who he treated as a *de facto* partner, and in 1966 Poologasundram
became a full partner. Nilgiria was bought out in 1966; Plesner
quit in 1967; and Gunasekera moved out in 1968.

1967–88
Edwards, Reid and Begg under Bawa and Poologasundram
After 1967 the practice was run by Bawa and Poologasundram,
who acted as structural engineer and office manager.

1988–97
Geoffrey Bawa Associates operating from 33rd Lane
In 1988 Bawa began to withdraw from E. R. & B. and started
to work alone from his home in 33rd Lane. After 1993 Channa
Daswatte acted as his principal associate.

1998–
Geoffrey Bawa Associates under Daswatte
Bawa suffered a stroke in March 1998. Various projects already
started were continued under the direction of Channa Daswatte.

The following list takes into account the fact that, of the many
projects that passed through E. R. & B. between 1957 and 1988,
there were several with which Bawa had little or no involvement
or from which he later chose to disassociate himself. The task of
drawing up a definitive list has been complicated by a number of
factors:
Employees were allowed to work on their own projects in the
office, and sometimes used the office name when submitting
schemes for municipal consent.
Bawa would 'farm out' those jobs he considered to be boring,
particularly if he didn't like the client.
Many projects designed in the office were never actually built,
and records of these are often vague.
Office records were not always complete, drawings not always
numbered and dated, and drawing schedules not comprehensive.

notes
The right-hand column indicates the condition of the project at the end of 2000.

chapter 2   pre-1957

1937–38	25 Torrington Avenue, Colombo	much altered
1951–52	Illangakoon House, Charles Circus, Colombo 3	much altered

chapter 4   1957–70

1951–59	Deraniyagala House, 26 Guildford Crescent, Colombo 7 **(p. 62)**	good condition
1957–64	Classrooms for St. Thomas's Preparatory School, Galle Road, Colombo 3 **(p.66)**	much altered, poor condition
1958–59	Carmen Gunasekera House, Dharmapala Maw., Colombo 3 **(p.63)**	good condition
1959	The Shell Ideal Home prototype, St. Bridget's Convent, Colombo 7	demolished
1959	Tennis Club, Ratnapura	poor condition
1959	Wimal Fernando House, Colombo **(p.64)**	unbuilt
1959	Housing scheme at Hendela for Claude Perera	unbuilt
1959	Housing scheme in Hill Street for low-to-middle-income families	unbuilt
1959–60	House for Dr. A. S. H. de Silva, Elliot Road, Woodward Mawatha, Galle **(p.71)**	fair condition
1959–60	Ekala Industrial Estate, 2km north-east of Jaela **(p.70)**	poor condition
1959–60	Estate Bungalow at Upcot on the Strathspey Estate **(p.73)**	fair condition, alterations
1959–60	Offices for the Automobile Association, Sir Marcan Markar Maw., Colombo 3	much altered
1959–61	Aelian Kanangara House, 42/1 Horton Place, Colombo 7 **(p.64)**	good condition
1959–63	Warehouse and Offices for Baur & Co, Jethawana Road, Colombo 14	poor condition
1959–64	Upali Wijewardene House, 36 Thurston Road, Colombo 3 **(p.65)**	much altered, poor condition
1960	House for Mrs A. F. Wijemanne, Ananda Coomaraswamy Maw., Colombo 7	unbuilt
1960	Leather factory, Mathakuliya Church Road, Colombo 15	unbuilt
1960	Offices for the Port Cargo Corporation, Colombo	unbuilt
1960	Remodelling of Rest House, Ella	unbuilt
1960–61	Staff bungalow for Shell, Harischandra Road, Anuradhapura New Town	much altered
1960–61	Shanmurganathan House, 9/5 Independence Avenue, Colombo 7	much altered
1960–61	Sammy Dias Bandaranayake Flats, Mahanuge Gardens, Colombo 3	much altered
1960–61	Flats for D. Perera, 18th Lane, Galle Road, Colombo 3	much altered
1960–62	House for Ena and Osmund de Silva, Alfred Place, Colombo 3 **(p.74)**	fair condition
1960–62	Muthukumarana House, Jawatta Road, Colombo 5	much altered
1960–63	Classrooms or Bishop's College, Boyd Place, Colombo 3 **(p.67)**	poor condition, much altered
1961	First Hilton Hotel project, Hotel Colombo, Galle Face Green, Colombo 3	unbuilt
1961	House in Brasilia for the Brazilian Ambassador to Ceylon	unbuilt
1961	Jayawardene House, Ananda Coomaraswamy Maw., Colombo 7	poor condition
1961–62	Chapel for the Good Shepherd Convent, Bandarawela **(p.88)**	fair condition
1961–62	Flats for Mrs A. F. Wijemanne, Ananda Coomaraswamy Maw., Colombo 7	much altered, poor condition
1961–62	Flats for Lancelot Fernando, Galle Face Terrace, Colombo 3	much altered
1961–63	House for Dr Bartholomeusz, 2 Alfred House Road, Colombo 3 **(p.84)**	good condition, altered
1961–64	House for Chris Abeyawardene, Rosmead Pl. and Kannangara Maw., Colombo 7	altered, fair condition
1962	Club House for the Colombo Rugby and Football Club, Colombo	unbuilt
1962	Offices and flats for Messrs Tucker Ltd, Union Place, Colombo 2	unbuilt
1962–64	House for Chris and Carmel Raffel, 57 Ward Place, Colombo 7	good condition
1963	Muthukumarana House, Kynsey Road, Colombo 7	altered
1963–64	Montessori School, St. Bridget's Convent, Maitland Crescent, Colombo 7 **(p.68)**	fair condition, altered
1963–64	Pin and Pam Fernando House, 47/1A Kannangara Maw., Colombo 7	fair condition
1963–64	Interiors for Chartered Bank, Janadhipathi Maw., Colombo Fort	altered
1963–65	Boys' Town, Diagala, 2km north of Ragama, for the de la Salle Brothers	altered, poor condition
1963–65	Leela Dias Bandaranayake House, Hotel Road, Mount Lavinia	good condition
1963–65	Polontalawa Estate Bungalow, 10km west of Nikarawetiya **(p.93)**	fair condition, altered
1963–66	Two houses for the Chartered Bank, Queen's Road/Duplication Road	fair condition
1964	House for Miss Wickremasinghe, location unknown	unbuilt
1964	Nayakanda Convent	unbuilt
1964–65	Cement Corporation Pavilion, Agriculture and Industry Exhibition, Colombo	demolished
1964–65	House for Dr Panditaratne, 31 Guildford Crescent	altered
1964–66	House for Chandra Corea, Alfred House Road	altered
1965	Second Hilton Hotel project, Galle Road (Oberoi site), Colombo 3	unbuilt
1965–66	Classrooms for Ladies' College, Ernest de Silva Maw., Colombo 7	good condition

1965–66	Blue Lagoon Hotel, Talahena, south of Negombo	poor condition
1965–66	YWCA Building, Rotunda Gardens, Colombo 3	fair condition
1965–66	Office interior for UTA, Prince Building, Sir Baron Jayatilleke Maw., Fort, Colombo	demolished
1965–67	Boys' Town, Nagamalai, Madurai, India for the de la Salle Brothers **(p.92)**	unfinished, fair condition
1965–67	Extensions to the Coral Gardens Hotel, Hikkaduwa for the Hotels Corporation	demolished
1965–71	Yahapath Endera Farm School, Halgasena, 4km south-east of Hanwella **(p.89)**	poor condition, altered
1966	Extensions to Grand Hotel, Nuwara Eliya	unbuilt
1966	TV Station, Torrington Avenue, Colombo	unbuilt
1966	Transport Museum at Moragahahena Estate, Yahalakelle Group, Horana	unbuilt
1966	BOAC Hotel at Pegasus Reef, Hendala	unbuilt
1966	Tourist Board offices, Colombo	unbuilt
1966–67	Third Hilton Hotel project, Galle Road (Oberoi site), Colombo 3	unbuilt
1966–69	Alterations to Taprobane Hotel, York Street, Colombo Fort	demolished
1966–69	Offices and housing for the Steel Corporation at Oruwela, near Aturugiriya **(p.106)**	fair condition, alterations
1967	Estate Bungalow at Beruwana 10km south of Avissawela on the Ratnapura Road	unbuilt, drawings exist
1967	Hotel at Mahakanda, 5km south of Peradeniya	unbuilt
1967	Remodelling of Lionel Wendt Theatre, Guildford Crescent, Colombo	fair condition
1967–69	House for Peter Keuneman, 27th Lane, Inner Flower Road, Colombo 3 **(p.95)**	good condition
1967–69	Bentota Beach Resort, Bentota, master plan for Ceylon Hotels Corporation	fair condition, alterations
1967–69	Bentota Beach Hotel, Bentota **(p.96)**	disastrously altered
1967–70	Serendib Hotel, Bentota **(p.102)**	fair condition, altered
1968	Yala Resort Hotel, Yala	unbuilt, drawings exist
1968	St. Joseph's Church, Pamunuvila	unbuilt
1968	Offices for the Ceylon Tourist Board, Colombo	unbuilt
1968	Post Office at Ratnapura	unbuilt
1968–69	Interior of Grindley's Bank, York Street, Colombo Fort	destroyed
1969	Nochchiyaduwa Tourist Resort tourist cottages, north of Chilaw	unbuilt
1969	Rasanayagam House, Norris Canal Road, Colombo 10	unbuilt
1969	Coconut Research Buildings and Museum, Wenapuwa	poor condition
1969–70	Ceylon Pavilion for World Fair in Osaka, Japan, built by Mitsui **(p.107)**	demolished
1969–70	Public Library, Kalutara	poor condition
1969–70	Offices on the seafront at Matara	poor condition
1969–73	Silk Farm at Mahahalpe, above the Peradeniya–Galaha road,	poor condition

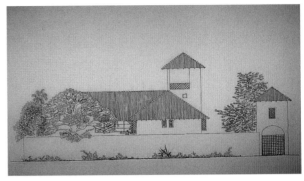

1962–64 The Raffel House, Ward Place, Colombo

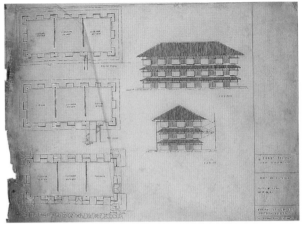

1965–66 Classrooms for Ladies' College, Colombo

chapter 5   1970–77

1970	Next Door Club, Galle Road, Colombo, behind the Green Cabin	demolished, no visual records
1970	Cheshire Home, Thoppur, Tamil Nadu, India	unbuilt
1970–71	Swissair Ticket Office, Baur's Building, Fort, Colombo	demolished
1970–71	Gem Corporation Shop and Office, Fort Colombo	demolished
1970–71	Pallakelle Industrial Estate, 10km east of Kandy near Digana **(p.131)**	altered, poor condition
1970–71	Convent for the nuns of the Good Shepherd, Church Road, Wattala	fair condition
1970–72	Science Faculty, University of Vidyodaya, Soratha Mawatha, Nugeguda	poor condition
1970–73	4 Row Houses for P. C. de Saram, 5th Lane, Colombo 3 **(p.117)**	fair condition, altered
1971	Hotel at Karukkuponai, close to mouth of Dedura Oya, north of Chilaw	unbuilt
1971	First Mount Lavinia Hotel project with Wimberley, Whisen, Allison, Tong & Goo	unbuilt
1971–72	Stanley de Saram House, Cambridge Place, Colombo 7 **(p.117)**	fair condition, altered
1971–74	Madurai Club for the Madurai Mills, outskirts of Madurai, India **(p.119)**	fair condition
1971–75	Remodelling of Connemara Hotel, Mount Road, Madras, India	much altered, little remains
1972	Hotel and Visitor Centre at Kadagannawa for the Obeysekeras	unbuilt
1972	Monks' dormitory and refectory for the Kelaniya Temple	unbuilt
1972	Club Mediterranée at Nilaveli, north of Trincomalee	unbuilt
1972	St. Joseph's Industrial School and Boys' Home, Tindivanam, India	unbuilt
1972	West End Hotel, Bangalore, India, for the Connemara Group	unbuilt
1972–75	Herbert and Norma Tennakoon House, 33rd Lane, Bagatelle Road, Colombo 3	good condition
1972–75	Batujimbar Pavilions, Bali, Indonesia for Donald Friend **(p.123)**	incomplete, much altered
1973	Offices for Air Ceylon, Prince Building, Sir Baron Jayatilleke Maw., Fort, Colombo	demolished
1973–74	Peter White House, Pereybere, Grand Bay, Mauritius **(p.127)**	much altered
1973–76	Neptune Hotel, Beruwela **(p.129)**	good condition
1974	Proposals for new Parliament, Colombo	unbuilt

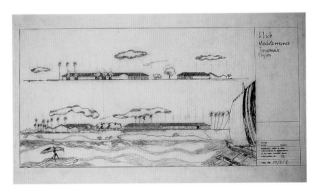

1972 Club Mediteranée, Trincomalee

1974–76	Agrarian Research and Training Institute, Wijerama Maw., Colombo 7 **(p.132)**	good condition
1975	School for children with special needs, Chitra Lane, Colombo 5	unbuilt
1975	Staff houses for Madurai Mills, Ambasamudrum	no records
1975	Kumaraja M. A. M. Muttiah Hospital at Adyar near Madras, India	unbuilt
1975	House for Mrs Meena Muttiah, Madras, India	unbuilt
1975	Hotel at Amaduwa, Yala for Brown's Beach Hotels	unbuilt
1975	Hotel at Pondicherry, India for the India Tourism Development Corporation	unbuilt
1975	2nd Mount Lavinia Hotel extension project for Hyatt International	unbuilt
1975	House for Mr Ravi Narayanam, Madras, India	unbuilt
1975–76	National Institute of Management Studies, Vidya Maw., Colombo	altered, poor condition
1975–78	State Insurance Corporation offices, Chittampalam Gardiner Maw., Colombo 2	much altered, disowned
1976	Hotel at Panama, Arugam Bay, south of Pottuvil on the east coast	unbuilt
1976	Offices for Aitken Spence, Vauxhall Street, Colombo 2	unbuilt
1976	Motor Car Museum, Guildford Crescent, Colombo 7, for Mr H. C. Peiris	unbuilt
1976–78	Seema Malaka, Beira Lake, Colombo **(p.136)**	fair condition, alterations
1976–78	Offices for the State Mortgage Bank, Hyde Park, Darley Road, Colombo 10 **(p.134)**	poor condition, much altered
1976–78	Hotel at Passikudah, north of Batticaloa	unbuilt
1976–79	Offices and staff quarters for the State Fertilizer Corporation at Sapugaskanda	poor condition, much altered
1977	Extension to Central Bank, Janadhipathi Maw., Fort, Colombo	unbuilt
1977	Candoline Hotel, Goa, India, for Indian Tourism Development Corporation	unbuilt
1977	Classrooms for the Overseas Children's School, Muttiah Road, Colombo	demolished

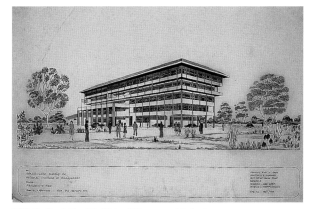

1974–76 The National Institute of Management, Colombo

chapter 6   1977–88

1977–79	Martenstyn House, 47/1B Kannangara Maw., Colombo 7 **(p.168)**	fair condition
1977–79	Ratnasivaratnam House, 410/6 Bauddhaloka Maw., Colombo 7	good condition
1978	Urban design proposals for Galle Face Green, Colombo	unbuilt
1978	New residence for the Canadian High Commission, Colombo	unbuilt
1978–79	Tourist Police Station, Galle Road, Beruwela	fair condition
1978–79	House for Gamini Dissanayake, Colombo	demolished
1978–79	Office for Greater Colombo Economic Commission, Prince Building, Colombo Fort	much altered
1978–79	Office refurbishment for the Prime Minister, Ernest de Silva Maw., Colombo 3	much altered
1978–79	French Ambassador's Residence, Alfred Place/Duplication Road, Colombo 3	fair condition
1978–80	House for Lidia Gunesekera, 87 Galle Road, Bentota	good condition, alterations
1978–80	House for Anura Bandaranaike, Rosmead Place, Colombo 7	fair condition
1978–80	Housing to the east of the BMICH in Bauddhaloka Maw., Colombo 7	fair condition
1978–81	Hameed Beach Villas and Club Villa Hotel, Bentota	good condition, alterations
1978–81	Institute for Integral Education, Piliyandela, overlooking the Bolgoda Lake **(p.156)**	fair condition
1979	New residence and chancery for the Australian High Commission, Colombo	unbuilt
1979	Auditorium for the Good Shepherd Convent, Nuwara Eliya	unbuilt
1979	Interior for the Indo-Suez Bank, Janadhipathi Maw., Colombo Fort	destroyed by bomb in 1996
1979–80	Remodelling of house at 10 Edward Road, Bangalore for Mr and Mrs Martin Henry	fair condition
1979–80	Bank of Ceylon Building, Devinuwara	altered
1979–81	Triton Hotel, Ahungalla near Ambalangoda **(p.164)**	good condition, some changes
1979–82	New Parliament Buildings, Sri Jayawardhanapura, Kotte **(p.146)**	good condition
1980–81	Offices and Library for the British Council, Duplication Road, Colombo 3	much altered
1980–88	Ruhunu University Campus, east of Matara **(p.156)**	good condition
1981–82	Offices for Cargo Boat Development Company, Janadhipathi Maw., Colombo Fort	destroyed by bomb in 1996
1982–83	Vocational Training Centre for Ladies' College, 27th Lane, Inner Flower Road	fair condition
1982–83	Pilgrim's Rest House, Jayanthi Maw., Anuradhapura New Town	fair condition
1982–83	Offices for H. T. L. Thompson Ltd., Joseph Frazer Road, Colombo 5	demolished
1982–84	Presidential Secretariat, Lotus Road, Colombo 1	much altered
1984	Galadari Hotel, Islamabad, Pakistan	unbuilt
1984	International Winged Bean Institute, Kandy	unbuilt
1984–86	House for Sunethra Bandaranaike, Horagolla **(p.172)**	good condition
1984–87	Royal Oceanic Hotel and Blue Oceani Hotel, Negombo	fair condition
1985	UN Headquarters at Mali in the Maldive Islands	unbuilt
1985	Offices for the Indo-Suez Bank, Galle Road, Colpetty, Colombo	much altered
1985	Tajuddin House, Karachi, Pakistan	unbuilt
1985–86	House for Richard Fitzherbert, 10km west of Tangalla **(p.174)**	good condition, some additions
1985–86	House for L. R. P. Dossa, Kotte	damaged by fire
1985–91	House for Cecil and Chloé de Soysa, Wijerama Maw., Colombo **(p.176)**	good condition

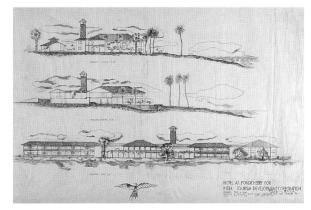

1975 Hotel in Pondicherry, India

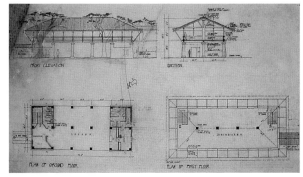

1982–83 Pilgrims' Rest House, Anuradhapura

1986–94	House for Bashir and Najma Currimjee, Floréal, Curipipe, Mauritius **(p.178)**	good condition
1987	House for Mrs Pam Lache, Mauritius	unbuilt
1987	Mangapwani Beach Hotel, Zanzibar, project for the Aga Khan	unbuilt
1987–90	The City Dispensary, Union Place, Colombo 2	fair condition
1987–94	De Saram Houses, Ward Place, Colombo 7	good condition

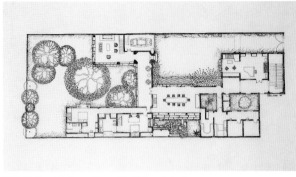

1987–94 Druvi de Saram House, Ward Place, Colombo

chapter 7   1988–98

1988	Exhibition stand for the Ceylon Tourist Board, London	demolished
1988	Fiji Suva Hotel	unbuilt
1988	Singapore Cloud Centre	unbuilt
1989	Extension to the Hyatt Hotel, Bali, Indonesia	unbuilt
1989	Row Houses for Albert Teo, Singapore	unbuilt
1989	Diamond Bay Development, Penang, Malaysia	unbuilt
1989–91	House for Larry Gordon, Wakaya, Fiji, 1992	good condition, some alterations
1990–92	Extension to the Sinbad Hotel, Kalutara	good condition
1991	Hotel on the Island of Bintan, Indonesia for Banyan Tree Resorts (Ho Brothers)	unbuilt
1991–94	Kandalama Hotel, 10km east of Dambulla, south of Sigiriya **(p.200)**	good condition
1991–96	House for Rohan and Dulanjalee Jayakody, Park Street, Colombo 2 **(p.221)**	good condition
1992	House for Suhrid Sarabhai, Ahmadabad, India	unbuilt
1992	House for Lalith and Minal Modi, Dehra Mandi Village, Delhi, India	unbuilt
1994	Poddar House, Chickajhalla Fort, near Bangalore, India	unbuilt
1994	Mowbray Country Club, Kandy	unbuilt
1994	Orion Hotel, Ahungalla for Aitken Spence	unbuilt
1994–96	Sinbad Garden Hotel, Kalutara **(p.210)**	unfinished
1995–97	Lighthouse Hotel, 2km north of Galle **(p.212)**	good condition
1996	House for Jay Mehta, Alabaug, Mumbai, India	incomplete
1996–97	Ward Beling House, Hokandare, east of Talawatugoda	good condition
1996–98	Blue Water Hotel, Wadduwa **(p.216)**	good condition
1997	Official Residence and Secretariat for the President, Kotte **(p.227)**	unbuilt
1997–98	House for Pradeep Jayewardene at Mirissa, near Weligama **(p.223)**	good condition
1997–98	House for David Spencer (de Saram), Rosmead Place, Colombo 7	good condition
1997–2002	Jacobson House, Tangalla, Bawa sketch design, built without his supervision	good condition

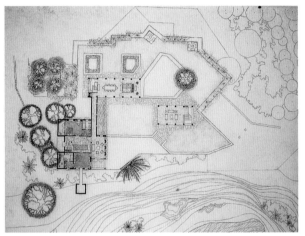

1996 The Mehta House, Mumbai, India

chapter 8   Lunuganga and 33rd Lane

1948	Geoffrey Bawa's own garden at Lunuganga, Bentota **(p.238)**	fair condition
1960	Geoffrey Bawa's Colombo home, 11 33rd Lane, Bagatelle Road, Colombo 3 **(p.232)**	fair condition

E. R. & B. buildings attributed to Ulrik Plesner

1957–60	Offices and Factory for Lever Bros., Lukmanjee Square, Grand Pass, Colombo 14	much altered
1959	Pavilions at Bandaranaike Memorial, Horagolla	unbuilt
1959–60	House for N. U. Jayawardena, Cambridge Place, Colombo 3	good condition
1960–64	Annexe to Sansoni House, Anderson Road, Colombo 5	poor condition
1960–65	House for Soli Captain, 8 Clifford Avenue, Colombo 3	much altered
1962–63	Pieris House, Barnes Place, Colombo 7	good condition
1962–63	House for Maurice and Malcanthie Perera, Alfred House Gardens, Colombo 3	good condition
1965–66	House for Gertrude de Soysa, Bolgoda Lake, Moratuwa	altered
1965–67	Offices and factory for ARPICO, High Level Road, Nawinna, Maharagama	altered
1966	House on an island in the Bolgoda Lake, Moratuwa (Ulrik's Island)	demolished
1966–67	House for Shelton de Silva at Bolgoda, Moratuwa	unbuilt

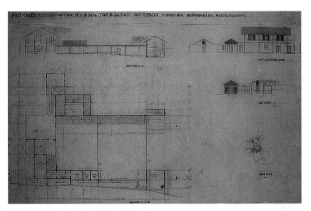

1997–2002 The Jacobson House, Tangalla

E. R. & B. buildings attributed to Anura Ratnavibushana

1963–65	Steel Tower, Agriculture and Industry Exhibition, Racecourse, Colombo	demolished
1965–66	Twin houses for Mrs G. Seniveratne, Guildford Crescent, Colombo 7	fair condition
1969–71	CMU Building, 22nd Lane, Galle Road, Colombo	fair condition
1972	Library and Reading Room at Chunnakkam, north of Jaffna	unbuilt
1973–74	Library and Research Centre for Jaffna College	may still exist
1977–78	Hotel in Jaffna	destroyed in the war
1977–79	National Institute of Chartered Accountants, Malalasekera Maw., Colombo 7	fair condition

Aluwihara, R. C., and D. B. Navaratne, *British Period Architecture in Sri Lanka,* Colombo: Aitken Spence, 1992.

American Institute of Architects, 'Quietly Monumental Parliament in the New Capital City', *Architecture,* USA, September 1984.

American Institute of Architects, 'Gracefully Horizontal University Buildings Overlooking the Sea', *Architecture,* USA, September 1988.

Anjalendran, C., 'Offices for Milk Board, Narahenpita', *Mimar,* no. 20, April–June 1986.

Anjalendran, C., 'The Hermann-Gmeiner School, Piliyandela', *Mimar,* no. 34, March 1990.

Anjalendran, C., 'Current Architecture in Sri Lanka', *Mimar,* no. 42, March 1992.

Anjalendran, C., and Channa Daswatte, 'Recent Architecture in Sri Lanka: 1991–93', *Architecture + Design,* vol. 11, no. 4, July–August 1994.

Anjalendran, C., and Rajiv Wanasundera, 'Trends and Transitions – A Review of Styles and Influences on the Built Form in Sri Lanka, 1940–1990', *Architecture + Design,* vol. 7, no. 2, March–April 1990a.

Anthonisz, R. G., *The Dutch in Ceylon,* Colombo, 1929.

Aung-Thwin, M., 'Soon All Roads will Lead to Kotte', *Serendib,* Sri Lanka, vol. 3, no. 2, April–July 1984.

Baldaeus, Phillipus, 'A True and Exact Description of the Great Island of Ceylon', trans. P. Brohier, Colombo: Saman Press, 1960.

Baldwin, Jan, *Colombo Heritage,* Oxford: Gresham, 1984.

Bandaranayake, Senake, 'Sinhalese Monastic Architecture', in *Studies in South Asian Culture,* vol. 4, ed. Van Lohuizen-De Leeuw, Leiden: E. J. Brill, 1974.

Bandaranayake, Senake et al. (eds), *Sri Lanka and the Silk Road of the Sea,* Colombo, 1990.

Bawa, Bevis, *Briefly by Bevis,* Colombo: Sapumal Foundation, 1985.

Bawa, Geoffrey, 'A Way of Building', *Times of Ceylon Annual,* Colombo, 1968.

Bawa, Geoffrey, 'Ceylon: a Philosophy for Building', *Architects' Journal,* 15 October 1969.

Bawa, Geoffrey, *Batujimbar Bali,* Colombo: Edwards, Reid and Begg, 1976.

Bawa, Geoffrey, 'My Architecture', *ARCASIA Forum Conference, Bali, 24 October 1987,* Hong Kong: Architect Asia Publications, 1988.

Bawa, Geoffrey, 'The Eighties', *Architecture and Design,* vol. 7, no. 2, March–April 1990.

Bawa, Geoffrey, and Ulrik Plesner, 'Gamle Bygninger pa Ceylon', *Arkitekten,* no. 16, 1965a.

Bawa, Geoffrey, and Ulrik Plesner, 'Arbejder pa Ceylon', *Arkitekten,* no. 17, 1965b.

Bawa, Geoffrey, and Ulrik Plesner, 'Ceylon – Seven New Buildings', *Architectural Review,* February 1966a.

Bawa, Geoffrey, and Ulrik Plesner, 'The Traditional Architecture of Ceylon', *Architectural Review,* February 1966b.

Bawa, Geoffrey, Christoph Bon and Dominic Sansoni, *Lunuganga,* Singapore: Times Editions, 1990.

Bingham, P. M., *History of the Public Works Department: Ceylon 1796–1913,* Colombo: Ceylon Government Printer, 1921–23.

Boisselier, Jean, *Ceylon – Archaeologia Mundi,* Geneva: Nagel, 1979.

Boyd, Andrew, 'Houses by the Road', *Ceylon Observer Pictorial,* Colombo, 1939.

Boyd, Andrew, 'A House at Colombo', *Architectural Review,* July 1940.

Boyd, Andrew, 'A People's Tradition', *MARG,* vol. 1, no. 2., Bombay, January 1947a.

Boyd, Andrew, 'A House in Kandy', *Architectural Review,* March 1947b.

Brawne, Michael, 'The Work of Geoffrey Bawa', *Architectural Review,* April 1978.

Brawne, Michael, 'The University of Ruhunu', *Architectural Review,* November 1986.

Brawne, Michael, *From Idea to Building,* London: Butterworth Heinemann, 1992.

Brawne, Michael, 'Paradise Found', *Architectural Review,* December 1995.

Brohier, R. L., and J. H. O. Paulusz, *Land Maps and Surveys,* 2 vols., Colombo: Survey Department, 1951.

Brohier, R. L., *Furniture of the Dutch Period in Ceylon,* Colombo: National Museums of Ceylon, 1969.

Brohier, R. L., *Changing Face of Colombo,* Colombo: Lake House, 1984.

Bryant, Lynne, 'House in Colombo Sri Lanka', *Architectural Review,* London, May 1983.

Bryant, Lynne, 'Sub-Tropical Retreat', *Belle,* Australia, May–June 1984.

Bryant, Lynne, 'Colombo – Bagatelle Road', *Interior Architecture,* January 1991.

Carswell, J., 'China and Islam', *Transactions of the Oriental Ceramic Society,* vol. 42, London, 1977–78.

Cave, H. W., *The Ruined Cities of Ceylon,* London: Sampson Low, Marston & Co., 1897.

Cave, H. W., *The Book of Ceylon,* London: Cassel & Co., 1908.

Coomaraswamy, Ananda, *Medieval Sinhalese Art,* London: Essex House Press, 1908. Facsimile ed., New York: Pantheon, 1956

Curtis, William J., *Modern Architecture Since 1900,* 3rd edition, London: Phaidon, 1996.

Daswatte, Channa, 'In the Urban Tradition', *The Sri Lanka Architect,* vol. 101, no. 14, September–November 1995.

Daswatte, Channa, 'The Architecture of Paradise', *The Sri Lanka Architect,* vol. 101, no. 20, December–February 1997–98.

Daswatte, Channa, 'Perceptions of Paradise', *The Sri Lanka Architect,* vol. 101, no. 20. December–February, 1997–98.

Daswatte, Channa, 'At Kandalama: an Environmentally Friendly Architecture?', *The Sri Lanka Architect,* vol. 101, no. 15, December 1995.

Daswatte, Channa, 'Bawa on Bawa', in Tan Kok Meng, *Asian Architects 2,* Singapore: Select Publishing, 2001.

Davies, Philip, *Splendours of the Raj,* London: John Murray, 1985.

Davy, John, *An Account of the Interior of Ceylon,* London: Longman, 1821; facsimile ed. Colombo: Praksakayo Ltd., 1969.

De Silva, K. M., *A History of Sri Lanka,* Delhi: OUP, 1981.

De Silva, Minette, 'A House in Kandy', *MARG,* vol. 6, no. 3, Bombay, June 1953.

De Silva, Minette, 'Experiments in Modern Regional Architecture in Ceylon', *Journal of the Ceylon Institute of Architects,* 1965–66.

De Silva, Minette, 'Minette de Silva', *Architecture + Design,* vol. 11, no. 4, Delhi, July–August 1994.

De Silva, Minette, *The Life and Work of an Asian Woman Architect,* vol. 1, Colombo: Smart Productions, 1998.

De Silva, Nimal, *Landscape Traditions of Sri Lanka,* Colombo: Deveco, 1996.

De Silva, R. K., and W. G. M. Beumer, *Illustrations and Views of Dutch Ceylon 1602–1796,* Leiden, 1986.

Dissanayake, Ellen, 'Minette de Silva – Pioneer of Modern Architecture in Ceylon', *Orientations,* Hong Kong, August 1982.

Edwards, Reid and Begg, *Parliamentary Complex at Sri Jayawardenepura,* Colombo: Edwards, Reid and Begg office brochure, 1983.

Fergusson, J., *A History of Indian and Eastern Architecture,* London: Burgess & Spires, 1910.

Fernando, Bonnie, 'The Man who made a Dream a Reality', *Daily News,* Colombo, 29 April 1982.

Fernando, P. G. K., 'SLIA Gold Medal Citation', *SLIA Silver Jubilee Souvenir,* Colombo: SLIA, 1983.

Fletcher, Sir Bannister, *History of Architecture,* 19th edition, ed. John Musgrove, London: Butterworth, 1987.

Fonseka, Michelle, Romesh Fonseka and Dilshan Ferdinando, 'A Garden Called Brief', *Architecture and Design,* vol. 7, no. 2, Delhi, March–April 1990.

Frampton, Kenneth, 'Prospects for a Critical Regionalism', *Perspecta,* no. 20, 1983, pp.147–62.

Frampton, Kenneth, *Modern Architecture – A Critical History,* London: Thames & Hudson, revised edition, 1985.

Friend, Donald, *The Cosmic Turtle,* Perth: Carroll's Pty Ltd., 1976.

Geiger, W., trans., *The Mahavamsa,* Colombo: Ceylon Government Information Department, 1950.

Geiger, W., trans., *The Culavamsa,* Colombo: Ceylon Government Information Department, 1953.

Ghirardo, Diane, *Architecture After Modernism,* London: Thames & Hudson, 1996.

Goldschmid, M., 'Baur Building', *MARG,* vol. 5, no. 3, Bombay, 1952.

Gooneratne, R., 'Gallery Cafe', *The Sri Lanka Architect,* vol. 102, no. 3, July–August 2000.

Hill, Kerry, 'The Pleasure of Architecture', *Monument,* no. 16, Sydney, 1996.

Hocart, A. M., *Memoirs of the Archaeological Survey of Ceylon,* 6 vols., Colombo: Government Printer, 1924; reprinted Delhi: AES, 1996.

Hockings, John, 'Geoffrey Bawa', *Architecture Australia,* vol. 85, no. 6, Sydney, 1996.

Hollamby, Ted, 'Andrew Boyd, His Life and Work', *Keystone,* vol. 36, no. 3, London: Association of Building Technicians, 1962.

Hulugalle, A. J., *Colombo: A Centenary Volume – 100 Years of Municipal Government 1865–1965,* Colombo: Municipal Council, 1965.

Hulugalle, H. A. J., *Ceylon of the Early Travellers,* Colombo: Multi-Packs Ltd., 1965.

Jayewardene, Shanti, 'The Work of Geoffrey Bawa – Towards an Historical Understanding', MSc dissertation, University College London, 1984.

Jayewardene, Shanti, 'Bawa – A Contribution to Cultural Regeneration', *Mimar,* no. 19, January–March, 1986a.

Jayewardene, Shanti, 'Jewel of the Orient', *Building Design,* 14 March 1986b.

Jellicoe, Sir Geoffrey, and Susan Jellicoe, *The Landscape of Man,* London: Thames & Hudson, 1987.

Johnson, B. L. C., and M. Scrivenor, *Sri Lanka: Land, People and Economy,* London: Heinemann, 1981.

Keniger, Michael, *Bawa: Recent Projects 1987–95,* Brisbane: Queensland Chapter of the RAIA, 1996.

Khan, Hassan-Udin, *Contemporary Asian Architects,* Cologne: Taschen, 1995.

Killick, John, 'The Decaying Neighbourhood', *Architectural Design,* October 1956.

Knox, Robert, *An Historical Relation of Ceylon,* London, 1681; reprinted Colombo: Tisara Prakasakayo, 1958.

Kuruppu, Indrajith, and Gamini Wijesuriya, 'The Conservation of the Galle Fort and its Environs', *Journal of the Department of Archaeology,* no. 15, Colombo: Director General of Archaeology, 1992.

Laird, Simon, 'Geoffrey Bawa and the Architecture of Sri Lanka', *Mackintosh School of Architecture Journal,* Mac 11, Glasgow, 1984.

Lal, Ashok, 'The Architecture of Geoffrey Bawa – An Intimacy of Experience and Expression', *Architecture and Design,* vol. 7, no. 2, March–April 1990.

Lewcock, Ronald, 'Bawa – Arcadia in Sri Lanka', *RIBA Journal,* February 1986.

Lewcock, Ronald, Suha Ozkan and David Robson, 'Bawa', *Arredemento Dekorasyon,* Istanbul, June 1992.

Lewcock, Ronald, Barbara Sansoni and Laki Senanayake, *The Architecture of an Island,* Colombo: Barefoot, 1998.

Lewis, J. P., 'Dutch Architecture in Ceylon', *Architectural Review,* London, September 1902 and January 1904.

Lewis, J. P., 'Kandyan Architecture', *The Book of Ceylon,* London: Cave, Cassel & Co., 1908.

Lewis, J. P., 'The Portuguese Dutch Churches of Jaffna', *Ceylon Antquary ,* vol. 2, part 1, Colombo, July 1916.

Lim, Jimmy, 'Interview with Geoffrey Bawa', *Majalah Arkitek*, January–February, 1990.

Lim, William, and Tan Hock Beng, *Contemporary Vernacular*, Singapore: Select Books, 1998.

Ludowyk, E. F. C., *The Modern History of Ceylon*, London: Weidenfeld & Nicolson, 1966.

Lutfy, Carol, 'Ethereal Landscapes in Sri Lanka', *Architectural Digest*, USA, January 1998.

Macaulay, Rose, and Roloff Beny, *The Pleasure of Ruins*, London: Thames & Hudson, 1964.

MacCormac, Richard, 'Housing and the Dilemma of Style', *Architectural Review*, vol. 180, no. 1077, London, April 1978.

Mehotra, Rahul, *World Architecture: A Critical Mosaic*, vol. 8 *South Asia*, New York: Springer, 2001.

Midant, Jean Paul et al., *Dictionnaire de l'Architecture du XXe Siècle*, Paris: Hazan, 1996.

Morris, J., *Stones of an Empire*, Oxford: OUP, 1984.

Mostaedi, Ariam, *Design Hotels*, Barcelona: Broto & Minguet, 1999.

Nagel, Per, 'Lunuganga', *Living Architecture*, no. 16, Copenhagen, 1998.

Naik, Ramola, 'Profile: Geoffrey Bawa', *Indian Institute of Architects Journal*, vol. 62, no. 11, India, November 1997.

Nakamura, Toshio, 'The Architecture of Geoffrey Bawa', *Architecture & Urbanism (A+U)*, no. 141, Japan, June 1982.

Neng, Woon Chung, 'The Way of Geoffrey Bawa', *Majalah Arkitek*, no. 4, Kuala Lumpur, 1984.

Ondaatje, Michael, *Running in the Family*, London: Victor Gollancz, 1982.

Ondaatje, Michael, *Handwriting*, London: Bloomsbury, 1998.

Oppenheimer-Dean, Andrea, 'Seventh Annual Review of Recent World Architecture', *Architecture (AIA)*, vol. 77, no. 9. Washington, September 1988.

Palladio, Andrea, *The Four Books of Architecture*, trans. Isaac Ware, London: Ware, 1738.

Paranavitana, Senerat, *Sinhalayo*, Colombo: Lake House, 1967.

Pearce, Barry, *Donald Friend, 1915–1989 Retrospective*, Sydney: Art Gallery of New South Wales, 1990.

Plesner, Ulrik, 'Towards a Regional Architecture for Ceylon', *Sankha, Journal of Arts & Letters*, Colombo, September 1958.

Plesner, Ulrik, 'Woven Architecture', *Arkitektur (DK)*, no. 4., Denmark, 1959a.

Plesner, Ulrik, 'En 10 Ar Gammel Have Pa Ceylon', (A Ten-Year-Old Garden in Ceylon), *Arkitekten (DK)*, Denmark, 1959b.

Plesner, Ulrik, 'An Old Building Tradition in Ceylon', *Journal of the Ceylon Institute of Architects*, Sri Lanka, 1965–66.

Plesner, Ulrik, 'Polontalawa House', *Arkitektur (DK)*, no. 3, Denmark, 1969.

Plesner, Ulrik, 'Buildings are for People', *Arkitektur (DK)*, no. 3, Denmark, 1971.

Plesner, Ulrik, 'Ulrich Plesner', *Living Architecture*, no. 5, 1986.

Pope, Alexander, 'Of the Use of Riches', in Douglas Grant, *Pope*, London: Penguin, 1985.

Powell, Robert, 'Geoffrey Bawa: Seminal Works in Tropical Architecture', *Singapore Institute of Architects Journal*, no. 143, Singapore, July–August 1987.

Powell, Robert, *The Tropical Asian House*, Singapore: Select Books, 1996.

Powell, Robert, 'Beyond Bawa', *Singapore Architect*, no. 194, Singapore, 1997.

Powell, Robert, *The Urban Asian House*, Singapore: Select Books, 1998.

Powell, Robert, 'Bawa Revisited', *Monument*, no. 29, Sydney, 1999.

Powell, Robert, and Marcel Meili, 'Special Edition: The House', *Architecture & Urbanism (A+U)*, no. 314, November 1996.

Raheem, Ismeth, and Percy Colin-Thomé, *Images of British Ceylon*, Singapore: Times Editions, 2000.

Ratnavibushana, Anura, 'Ratnavibushana House', *Mimar*, no. 26. London, December 1987.

Raven-Hart, Roland, *Ceylon – History in Stone*, Colombo: Lake House, 1964.

Reid, H. H., 'Some Aspects of Bungalow Design', *Colombo House and Garden*, vol. 1, no. 1, Colombo, October 1938.

Reid, H. H., 'How Alterations Can Improve an Old Bungalow Design', *Colombo House and Garden*, vol. 3, no. 1, Colombo, April 1940.

Richards, J. M., 'Ceylon Pavilion at Expo 70', *Architectural Review*, London, August 1970.

Richards, Sir James, 'Geoffrey Bawa', *Mimar*, no. 19, London, January–March 1986.

Roberts, Karel, 'Re-creation of the old Sri Jayawardenepura', *Sunday Observer*, Colombo, 10 February 1990.

Roberts, Michael, Ismeth Raheem and Percy Colin-Thomé, *People In-between*, Colombo: Sarvodaya, 1989.

Robson, David, *Aided-Self-Help Housing in Sri Lanka*, London: HMSO, 1984.

Robson, David, 'Lunuganga – The Story of a Garden', *Mimar*, no. 40, September 1991.

Robson, David, 'Three Villages in Sri Lanka', *Mimar*, no. 43, June 1992.

Robson, David, 'Lunuganga – The Story of a Garden', ed. Pieris, Sita and P. L. Prematilleke, *Historic Gardens and Sites*, Colombo: ICOMOS, 1993.

Robson, David, 'An Island Parliament', *Caravan 4*, Brighton: University of Brighton, 2000.

Robson, David, 'Genius of the Place' in Kenneth Frampton, Charles Correa and David Robson, *Modernity and Community: Architecture in the Islamic World*, London: Thames & Hudson, 2001a.

Robson, David, 'Sage of Sri Lanka', *Architectural Review*, November 2001b.

Robson, David, 'Geoffrey Bawa presented world's top architecture honour', *Sunday Observer*, Sri Lanka, 23 December 2001c.

Robson, David, and Channa Daswatte, 'Serendib Serendipity: The Architecture of Geoffrey Bawa', *AA Files*, no. 35, London, May 1998.

Rollo, Joe, 'Super Bawa', *Wallpaper*, May–June 1999.

Sansoni, Barbara, *Viharas and Verandahs*, Colombo: Barefoot, 1978.

Scott, Rupert, 'Two Bawa', *Architectural Review*, May 1983.

Selvanathan, Puvan, 'Basically Bawa', *ID*, vol. 15, no. 4, Singapore, August–September 1997.

Sindicato Nacional dos Arquitectos, *Arquitectura Popular em Portugal*, 2 vols., Lisboa: Edicao do Sindicato Nacional dos Arquitectos, 1961.

Sippy, Sonia, 'Elemental Appeal', *Interiors and Lifestyles*, vol. 5, no. 2, India, 1997.

Skeen, George J. A., *A Guide to Colombo*, Colombo, 1906.

Smithers, J. G., *Architectural Remains, Anuradhapura, Ceylon*, Colombo: Ceylon Government Press, 1894, reprinted 1992.

Somasekeram, T. et al., *Arjuna's Atlas of Sri Lanka*, Dehiwala: Arjuna Consulting Co., 1997.

Southeast Asia Building, 'Sri Lanka: Expressions of Indigenous Architecture', *Southeast Asia Building*, vol. 17, no. 6, Singapore, June 1990.

Sri Lanka Institute of Architects, 'Gold Medal Citation – Geoffrey Manning Bawa', in *SLIA Silver Jubilee Souvenir*, Colombo: SLIA, 1983.

Surveyor General, *Ceylon: One Inch Maps* (72 sheets), Colombo: Survey Department, various dates.

Szenasy, Susan S., *Light*, London: Colombus, 1986.

Tadgell, Christopher, *The History of Architecture in India*, London: Phaidon, 1990.

Tan, Hock Beng, *Tropical Retreats*, Singapore: Page One, 1996.

Taylor, Brian B., *Geoffrey Bawa*, Singapore: Concept Media, 1986.

Taylor, Brian B., *Mimar Houses*, Singapore: Concept Media, 1987.

Taylor, Brian B., 'Club Villa, Bentota', *Mimar*, no. 24, London, June 1987.

Taylor, Brian B., *Geoffrey Bawa*, London: Thames & Hudson, 1995.

Tennent, Sir J. E., *Ceylon*, 2 vols (with illustrations by Andrew Nicholl), London: Longman, 1859; facsimile ed. Colombo: Prakasakayo Ltd., 1977.

Urban Development Authority, *Sri Lanka's New Capital*, Colombo: UDA, 1982.

Vale, Lawrence J., *Architecture Power and National Identity*, New Haven: Yale University Press, 1992.

Viladas, Pilar, 'This Side of Paradise', *Architectural Digest*, USA, September, 1994.

Walker-Smith, Melissa, 'Peace Plan', *Belle*, Australia, February–March 1992.

Weereratne, Neville, *43 Group*, Melbourne: Lantana, 1993.

Wendt, Lionel, *Lionel Wendt's Ceylon*, Colombo: Navrang/Lake House, 1995.

Wijesuriya, G., *Plans and Facades – Roadside Buildings from Negombo to Matara*, Colombo: ICOMOS Sri Lanka, 1996.

Woolf, Leonard, *Growing*, London: Hogarth Press, 1967.

Woolf, Leonard, *The Village in the Jungle*, London: Edward Arnold, 1913.

Wright, Arnold, 'Twentieth Century Impressions of Ceylon', London: Lloyd's G.B. Pub. Co., 1907.

Wynne-Jones, T. N., 'A Review of Fifty Years of Building, 1905–1956', *Institute of Engineers Transactions*, Colombo, 1956.

Wynne-Jones, T. N., 'The Changing Face of Colombo', *Ceylon Today*, Colombo, March 1953.

Yoos, Jennifer et al., 'Special Edition: The House', *Architecture & Urbanism (A+U)*, no. 338, Japan, November 1998.

Sinhalese words such as 'walaawe' (manor house) and 'wareechchi' (wattle and daub) are represented by commonly accepted transliterations. Family names often have a variety of spellings: thus Bandaranayake, Bandaranaike; Jayawardena, Jayewardene; de Soysa, de Zoysa.

ambalama	a shelter for travellers
arrack	a spirit distilled from coconut toddy
ayah	a nurse
baas	a craftsman
bodhisattva	a Buddhist saint who has reached final stage before nirvana
bo tree	*ficus religiosa* – the tree under which the Gautama Buddha received enlightenment
bund	the retaining structure of a reservoir
Burgher	the descendant of a European employee of the Dutch East India Company
cadjan	woven palm leaves used in making roofs and walls
Chola	an ancient South Indian kingdom
Culavamsa	a Sinhalese historical epic, sequel to the Mahavamsa
dagoba	a Buddhist relic mound
devale	a Buddhist temple dedicated to Hindu gods
ganga	river
gedige	an image house
goyagama	the farmers' caste in Sri Lanka
gurunansa	a village soothsayer
istopuwa	Sinhalese word derived from the Dutch 'stoep' – a raised verandah in front of a house
kachcheri	a provincial administrative office
korale	an ancient administrative district, similar to a county
kovil	a Hindu temple
Mahavamsa	the first of the great Sinhalese historical epics
mal laali	literally 'flowered planks' – floral fretwork
mashrabiya	a type of projecting timber window found throughout the Arab world
meda midula	courtyard
Moor	a person of mixed Arab descent – now often referred to as a Muslim
nirvana	in Buddhism, a state of enlightenment
oya	a mall river
Pallava	an ancient south Indian Kingdom
pancavasa	a monastic cell consisting of five pavilions arranged as a quincunx
pandol	a ceremonial gateway made traditionally of bamboo and palm leaf
Pandya	an ancient South Indian Kingdom
perahera	a Buddhist procession held on the night of a full moon
pila	raised plinth forming base of a traditional house
pilgame	a Buddhist image house
poya day	a day of Buddhist prayer corresponding to a quarter of the moon
Rajarata	the main Sinhalese Kingdom which covered the central part of the island during the Anuradhapura period
reeper	tile batten
Ruhunu	the southern Sinhalese Kingdom
tank	reservoir
samara	a yellow ochre coloured paint applied to plastered walls
sikhara	the carved dome above a Hindu shrine
temple cart	a chariot used in Hindu temples to carry a god – known also as a juggernaut
thaappa	rammed earth construction
thambi	Sinhalese slang for a Moslem
toddy	an alcoholic sap which is tapped from the coconut palm
ulu	half round tile
vatadage	a dagoba contained within a circular roofed enclosure
vihara	Buddhist temple
walaawe	manor house
wareechchi	wattle and daub
zemindar	an Indian landlord

Text

The two quotations from *The Cosmic Turtle* by Donald Friend appear with the permission of the trustees of Donald Friend. The poem 'House on a Red Cliff' is reproduced in full with the permission of Michael Ondaatje.

Illustrations

b = bottom
t = top
l = left
r = right
m = middle (vertical)
c = centre (horizontal)

David Adams
30tl, 31bc , 34br, 35tl , 35ml , 37br, 148tl, 274, 275

Bawa Archive
14, 16tl, 16ml, 17tr, 18tl, 18ml, 18bl, 19, 20tl, 20tr, 20ml, 21, 22tc, p22tr, 23tr, 24ml, 24bl, 25mr, 25br, 26, 39bl, 39br, 40tr, 41ml, 41br, 42, 44ml, 50tl, 51tc, 51tr, 52tl, 52tc, 52tr, 53tl, 53ml, 54br, 58t, 58ml, 59bl , 65t, 62b, 66b, 68br, 69tc, 70tr, 71tl, 71tr, 71br, 72tr, 72mr 73tr, 73br, 74b, 75t, 84b, 85m, 85b, 88bl, 89tr, 89ml, 89mr, 89b, 90br, 92t, 94tr, 95t, 96b, 97tl, 97tr, 97br, 102bl, 102tr, 107tr, 107bl, 107br, 114bl, 114br, 116br, 117tr, 117mt, 117mb, 117b, 118tl, 118b, 119t, 120tr, 121bl, 123tr, 123br, 124m, 124b, 125t, 125b, 126tl, 126bl, 126tr, 127ml, 127bl, 127mr, 127br, 129b, 132t, 134bl, 134br, 136mr, 140ml, 142br, 146br, 147bl , 147br, 148tr, 149t, 149m, 150tl, 151bl, 156t, 157b, 158–59b, 159br, 164b, 166br, 169tr, 169b, 172b, 173b, 174t, 178b, 183tr, 183mr, 183br, pp 187–198, 200mr, 200br, 201br, 206l, 210t, 210b, 212–13t, 213mr, 213bl, 216bc, 221bl, 221bc, 221br, 223tr, 227tr, 232b, 233b, 236, 237, 239, 240–41, 253b

Christopher Beaver
149b, 150tr

Hélène Binet, courtesy of the Aga Khan Trust for Culture
46, 47, 48, 61, 76l, 76r, 77, 78, 79, 80–81, 81r, 82, 83tl, 83bl, 83tr, 83br, 242–43, 244, 245, 246, 247, 248, 249, 250tl, 250bl, 250tr, 250br, 251, 252, 253tl, 253tr, 254l, 254r, 255l, 255r, 256, 257l, 257r, 258, 259, 264

Christoph Bon
1, 2–3, 6, 7, 8–9, 10, 11, 55r, 56ml, 90bl, 90mr, 98mr, 108, 110bl, 110br, 112bl, 112br, 113, 121tr, 121br, 122, 133tc, 141t, 143tl, 143tr, 144tl, 144bl, 172tr, 184bl, 184br, 228, 229, 230, 260

Channa Daswatte
135bl, 178t , 179t, 179bl, 179bc, 179br, 213ml, 214tl

Nihal Fernando
30tr, 32bl

Milroy Perera
162t, 162br

Ulrik Plesner
51tl, 54ml, 57bl, 67t, 67bl, 67br, 73mr, 93mr, 93b

Christian Richters, courtesy of the Aga Khan Trust for Culture
138, 141br, 158–59b, 160, 161tl, 161tr, 161b, 168r, 169tl, 170, 171, 176, 177t, 177bl, 177br, 180, 199, 200tr, 202–3, 204, 205, 206–7, 208, 209t, 209b, 216mc, 216–17, 218–19, 219tr, 220t, 220br, 222t, 222b, 224–25, 226tl, 226bl, 226tr, 226br

David Robson
17mr, 17br, 22bl, 29tl, 29br, 32bc, 32br, 33tc, 33tr, 33br, 35bl, 35mc, 35bc, 35br, 36ml, 37ml, 37bl, 38bl, 38bc, 38br, 39tr, 39mr, 40tl, 40ml, 41tl, 41tc, 44tl, 44br, 45bl, 45tr, 45mr, 45br,50ml, 50bl, 54bl, 56tr, 59tl, 62tr, 63tr, 63bl, 63br, 64tl, 64ml, 64bl, 64mc, 68tr, 69tl, 69tr, 69br, 70bl, 70br, 72bl, 72br, 84mr, 88br, 91, 94bl, 94br, 95mr, 96tr, 96mr, 98bl, 98br, 100, 101, 102br, 103t, 103br, 104l, 104tr, 104br, 105t, 105br, 106tc, 106tr, 106b, 111tl, 111tc, 111tr, 111bl, 111bc, 111br, 115, 116tr, 116mr, 118tr, 124tl, 124tr, 129tr, 130tl, 130tr, 130b, 131t, 131b, 132m, 132b, 133tl, 133tr, 135tl, 136b, 137tl, 137tr, 137br, 140tl, 140bl, 141mr, 145, 155tl, 155b, 156bl, 156br, 157tl, 162bl, 163tl, 163tr, 163bl, 163br, 165t, 165b, 166tl, 167t, 172mr, 173tl, 173tr, 173ml, 173mr, 174bl, 174br, 175tl, 175tr, 175bl, 175br, 182tl, 185bc, 185tr, 185mr, 186tl, 186ml, 211t, 211bl, 211br, 212bl, 212mr, 214bl, 214tr, 214br, 215t, 215bl, 215br, 216bl, 219br, 221tc, 221mr, 223mr, 223br, 223bl, 227br, 233tr, 234bl, 234br, 235tr, 235br

Isabel Robson
92ml, 92bl, 92br, 119b, 120tl, 120ml, 120bl

Dominic Sansoni
3br, 56tl, 56tc, 151tr, 151bl, 184ml, 185bl, 263br

Jürgen Schreiber
31bl, 31br, 33tl, 41tr, 128, 146bl, 164tr, 201tr, 212br

Harry Sowden
4–5, 40mr, 62tc, 84tr, 85t, 86, 87, 88mr, 99, 106tl, 110bc, 116tl, 133b, 135r, 137bl, 142bl, 152–53, 154, 155tr, 157tc, 157tr, 157mr, 167b, 182ml, 232tr, 234tl, 234tr, 235tl, 235bl

maps

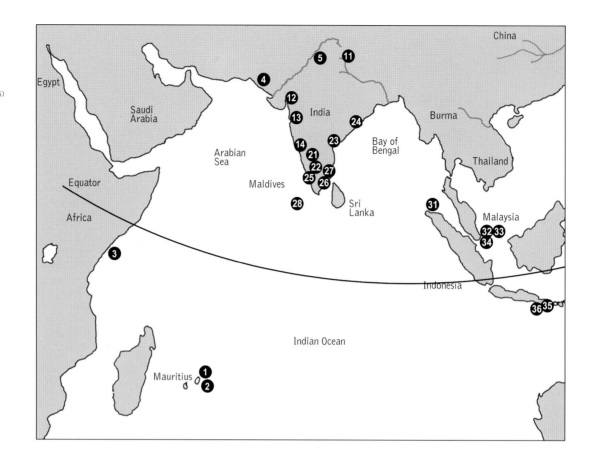

Bawa's Projects outside of Sri Lanka

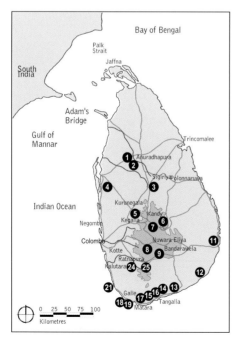

Bawa's Projects inside Sri Lanka

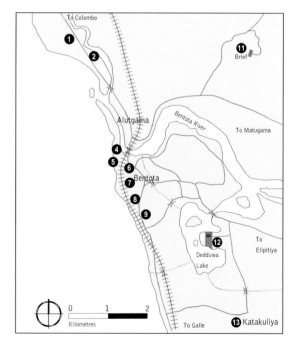

**Bawa's Projects in and around
Benota on the West coast**

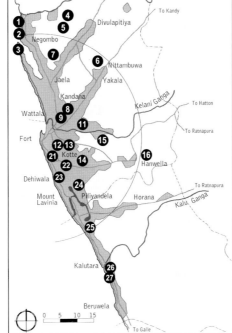

Bawa's Projects in the Colombo Region

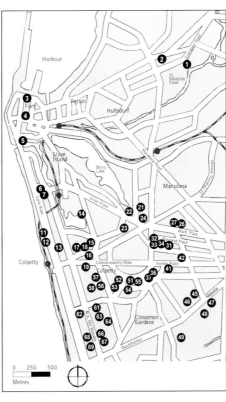

Bawa's Projects in Central Colombo

Rohmer